The Mandaeans

AMERICAN ACADEMY OF RELIGION
THE RELIGIONS SERIES

SERIES EDITOR
Paul B. Courtright, Emory University

A Publication Series of
The American Academy of Religion and
Oxford University Press

Religions of Atlanta
Religious Diversity in the Centennial Olympic City
Edited by Gary Laderman

Exegesis of Polemical Discourse
Ibn Hazm on Jewish and Christian Scriptures
Theodore Pulcini

Religion and the War in Bosnia
Edited by Paul Mojzes

The Apostolic Conciliarism of Jean Gerson
John J. Ryan

One Lifetime, Many Lives
The Experience of Modern Hindu Hagiography
Robin Rinehart

Sacrificing the Self
Perspectives on Martyrdom and Religion
Edited by Margaret Cormack

The Mandaeans
Ancient Texts and Modern People
Jorunn Jacobsen Buckley

AAR
AMERICAN ACADEMY OF RELIGION

The Mandaeans

Ancient Texts and Modern People

JORUNN JACOBSEN BUCKLEY

OXFORD
UNIVERSITY PRESS
2002

OXFORD
UNIVERSITY PRESS

Oxford New York
Auckland Bangkok Buenos Aires Cape Town Chennai
Dar es Salaam Delhi Hong Kong Istanbul Karachi Kolkata
Kuala Lumpur Madrid Melbourne Mexico City Mumbai Nairobi
São Paulo Shanghai Singapore Taipei Tokyo Toronto

and an associated company in Berlin

Published by Oxford University Press, Inc.,
198 Madison Avenue, New York, New York 10016

www.oup.com

Library of Congress Cataloging-in-Publication Data
Buckley, Jorunn Jacobsen.
The Mandaeans : ancient texts and modern people / Jorunn Jacobsen Buckley.
p. cm. – (AAR the religions)
Includes bibliographical references and index.
ISBN 0-19-515385-5
1. Mandaeans. I. Title. II. AAR the religions (Unnumbered)
BT1405 .B83 2002
299'.932–dc21 2001052364

The author gratefully acknowledges permission to reprint the following:

"The Mandaean Appropriation of Jesus' Mother, Mirai." *Novum Testamentum* 35, no. 2 (1993): 181-96.

"A Rehabilitation of Spirit Ruha in Mandaean Religion." *History of Religions* 22, no. 1 (1982): 60-84.

"The Salvation of the Spirit Ruha in Mandaean Religion." In *Female Fault and Fulfilment in Gnosticism* by Jorunn Jacobsen Buckley. Copyright © 1986 by the University of North Carolina Press. Used by permission of the publisher.

"Why Once Is Not Enough: Mandaean Baptism (Maṣbuta) as an Example of a Repeated Ritual." *History of Religions* 29, no. 1 (1989): 23-34.

"The Mandaean Šitil as an Example of 'the Image Above and Below.'" *Numen* 26, no. 2 (1979): 185-191. Used by permission of Brill Academic Publishers.

"The Mandaean Ṭabahata Masiqta." *Numen* 28, no. 2 (1981): 138-163. Used by permission of Brill Academic Publishers.

"The Making of a Mandaean Priest: The Tarmida Initiation." *Numen* 32, no. 2 (1985): 194-217. Used by permission of Brill Academic Publishers.

"Frouzanda Mahrad," a poem by Lamea Abbas Amara. Reprinted by permission of Lamea Abbas Amara.

1 3 5 7 9 8 6 4 2

Printed in the United States of America
on acid-free paper

For Tim and Jesse

Preface

I wrote a postcard to my professor, Gilles Quispel in Utrecht, to say that I would be unable to keep my appointment with him because I was going to Iran the next morning, over land, on eight hours' notice. Mark, my boyfriend, had come back to our apartment and asked whether I wanted to go to Iran the next day. We had an offer to drive a car from Amsterdam to Tehran for an Iranian businessman. Istanbul would be just midway. After a late evening meeting with the businessman and his family—they would drive their other car the same route—I agreed to go. I was on a Norwegian-Dutch fellowship in the Netherlands, and I grasped the chance to go to Iran because I wanted to meet Mandaeans in the Persian Gulf area. Since the late 1960s, I had studied Mandaeism. Now, it was late September 1973.

A fourteen-day-long, strange, and wonderful journey began. While we were in Yugoslavia, the war started between Israel and Egypt. For a day and a half, on the Turkish Anatolian high plains, continuously overtaken by Bulgarian cheese trucks spewing high-lead gasoline fumes, we contemplated Mount Ararat, in and out of thunderstorms, a serene 17,000-foot pyramid at the end of a long mountain range. At Dogubayazit, we entered Iran. The landscape of Iranian Azerbajan is impressed in my mind: dramatic brown mountains with green, steep slopes dotted by tiny sheep and shepherds; then came flatter deserts and haughty-looking camels.

In Tehran we stayed six days, spending much time trying to find information about the Mandaeans in the Gulf. No one seemed to know much. Finally, one official said, "Why don't you just go?" Indeed. The political situation down there had eased; because of the war, Iran and Iraq had established diplomatic relations so that the Iraqi soldiers could be ready on the western frontier in case Egypt needed help.

We took as our guide and translator a contact, Hawa, an Iranian professor of English in Tehran. The three of us boarded an evening plane to Abadan, Khuzistan. In the air, I briefed Hawa on Mandaeism, of which she knew nothing. In Abadan, an oil center, a couple of tall Texans in large hats were among the few guests in the hotel's lavish dining room, where a huge fish, carved out of yellow butter, swung its tail above a frozen, green waterfall. We ate excellent food and chatted with the cook, who told us he had been a chef in Copenhagen and would soon be headed for Tokyo.

The next day I watched a man struggle with his goat in the place where taxi rides could be negotiated. Hawa fixed us up with a driver who said he would take us to the church of the Subbi, the Mandaeans. I became suspicious, for the Mandaeans do not have "churches." It was a sad sight, a small, white painted Roman Catholic chapel, but boarded-up and abandoned. Try again.

At first, I did not think that the silversmith, Shaker Feyzi, was a Mandaean, for he had no beard. His little shop was not much more than a cavity in a wall. A group of black-clad women carried handfuls of heavy silver ankle bangles to Mr. Feyzi. They haggled, he bought, and later I purchased a bracelet from him. He was about fifty and very friendly, and we conversed and met his family. Mr. Feyzi stressed that he was an Iranian, and the requisite picture of the Shah and his family, Shah Reza Mohammad, the last of the Pahlavis, hung on the wall. "He is my Shah," said Mr. Feyzi, inviting no further inquiries on that point. We had already learned that any business that did not sport such a picture would be closed. We had also learned to approach anything resembling a political question with extreme care. The Savak, the Shah's secret police, could be anywhere.

"Come back in four months, at Panja," said Mr. Feyzi, "then we go in the river." He was referring to the intercalary feast at New Year's, when many Mandaeans are baptized. Now, only two families were left in Abadan, he told us, but there were many more earlier. Where had he learned English? From English-speaking soldiers during the Second World War, and later from Americans in the oil trade, who came to buy silver from him.

In neighboring Khorramshahr, the old Muhammerah, we met another, older smith, a goldsmith who gave his name as Aran. Other goldsmiths advised us to go to Ahwaz, the capital of the province. Soon we moved swiftly through the flat desert, leaving behind the junklike sailboats that seemed to float in the shimmering air above the waterway, the Shatt al-Arab. Patches of blooming roses and rows of tall date palms flew by, while the human-sized dust devils, the miniature dust storms, whirled like dancers in the distance. A mythological landscape.

In a large, prosperous-looking goldsmith shop in Ahwaz, we were first greeted with reasonable suspicion because we used the "inside" term, Mandaean, not Subbi. This showed that we knew something; the question was what? and why? I explained, via Hawa, and they soon relaxed and showed us a Mandaean calendar, and we admired the jewelry. We should visit their priest, they suggested. Could we do that? Sure, why not?

We entered the enclosed courtyard of the house of Sheikh Abdullah Khaffagi, the head of Mandaeans of Iran. I spotted cows tethered off to one side. A strikingly beautiful woman, veil-less, with high cheekbones, blue eyes, and dark blonde hair, came across the courtyard and smiled at us. Enchanted by her, Hawa paid her a compliment, laughed and clapped her hands. We were led up the stairs by a young man, one of the priest's grandsons, as I recall. He warned us not to touch the old man, who must remain pure. Glasses of Coca-Cola were brought, and we sat down to wait in the upstairs room. Sheikh Abdullah appeared in the doorway, with a slight smile and twinkling keen blue eyes. He was about ninety-five, bent over approximately the same number of degrees, white bearded, clad entirely in white, with white cloth slippers (no animal hide must touch him). Living separately from his family, he cooked his own food. Now we smiled and bowed, but we did not stretch out our hands to him.

The sheikh sat down on a cushion on the floor, his covered knees almost up to his ears. We conversed for an hour, he showed us letters from European scholars (in Mandaic) and told us that he had met Lady Drower many times and had visited Professor Rudolf Macuch in Tehran.[1] I let him know that I had met Lady Drower once, a few years earlier, when she was ninety-one, less than a year before she passed away.

The priest fetched several Mandaean books and scrolls to show us, all in their individual white cloth bags. He also gave me a paper copy of the imprint on the Mandaean *skandola*, the ritual iron ring with an iron chain. This is used to seal newborn babies on their navels, and it also seals graves. Sheikh Abdullah showed us his ring and explained that the four animals depicted on the seal—the lion, the wasp, the scorpion, and the encircling snake—were "the elements of life."

Then he began to tug at something under his cushion. We helped him pull out a large cloth bag, like the others, but this one was heavy as a rock. It was an archetypal book, *The Book of John*, made entirely of lead, inscribed with stylus on lead pages bound together like a regular book. No wonder it was heavy. Its edges were frayed and worn. We leafed through it reverently. C. G. Jung might have fantasized about a tome like this. There is probably not its like in the world. Sheikh Abdullah told us that the book was 2,053 years old and written by John the Baptist himself. There and then, it seemed a likely view.

Cosmological and mythological topics came up. What will happen to us at the end of the world? we asked. There we sat—Hawa, a secular Iranian with a Sufi father; Mark, an American Jew; me, a Norwegian apostate Lutheran—all somehow representing traditional neighbors and enemies of the Mandaeans. Perhaps it had been frivolous to ask. Sheikh Abdullah avoided answering us directly, saying he did not know. But, showing better diplomacy and taste than we did, he might just as well have been being polite. In any case, the Mandaeans will go to the Lightworld, the heavenly world. Paradise lies beyond the gate at the North Pole, ours is just one of 365 universes, and the earth is flat and stands still. And it will soon end. Such were the sheikh's words.

We thanked him, took farewell, and, with heads reeling, descended the stairs to the world still there.

Acknowledgments

It is more than thirty years since I began studying the Mandaean religion, and for the past decade my contacts with Mandaeans worldwide have increased dramatically. Though originally a "desk scholar," I have in recent years been able to use my knowledge of the religion in a more immediately practical context: as an expert witness for Iraqi and Iranian Mandaeans seeking asylum on political and religious grounds. Therefore, my study of Mandaeism and my close relationship with its people cannot be separated. A recent, illustrative example is the conference on Mandaeism, the first of its kind, that took place under the sponsorship of the ARAM Society for Syro-Mesopotamian Studies, at Harvard University in June 1999. At this event, Mandaeans by far outnumbered scholars, and thanks to the presence of Mandaean priests, the traditional Mandaean baptism (*maṣbuta*), was performed in the Charles River in Allston, Massachusetts. The story of this event does not form a part of this book, however; neither does my ongoing legal work on behalf of Mandaeans or the numerous post-1996 interactions, visits, and celebrations with them.

Instead, the contents of the book reflect large segments of my research efforts from the beginnings of my doctoral studies in the United States in 1975 to my (second) trip to Iran in 1996. Having concluded my studies in the history of religions in Norway in 1973, I wanted to pursue a Ph.D. degree in the United States on the topic of the Mandaean female mythological figure Ruha. It is therefore with pleasure that I thank the University of Chicago Divinity School's History of Religions program for admitting me into its doctoral program in 1975, despite the school's lack of a specialist in Mandaic studies. Risking a chance on an unknown European with a firm idea of her dissertation topic, my Ph.D. committee, consisting of Jonathan Z. Smith, Robert M. Grant, and the late Arthur Vööbus, supported my esoteric project. I wish to express my special indebtedness to Jonathan Z. Smith for his courageous open-mindedness and his continued interest in my work.

Countless others have been helpful along the way, not the least scholarly organizations and other forums under whose auspices I have been able to present my research, chiefly among them the American Academy of Religion, the Society of Biblical Literature, and the American Oriental Society. My variegated, nonlinear career has landed me, during more than two decades, in unemployment, in part- and full-time positions, and, luckily, supported by the odd grant. To all present and former colleagues who have shown interest in my studies, thank you for your enthusiasm! In the past, Kurt Rudolph and the late Rudolf Macuch have shown steady support. In 1971, I was able to briefly meet with Lady E. S. Drower—the tireless worker in the Mandaean field—and in 1988 her daughter, Mrs. Margaret ("Peggy") Hackforth-Jones, graciously placed into my hands a large carton containing her late mother's scholarly papers and correspondence. Peggy remains a treasured friend. To Elaine Pagels, Gilles Quispel, and Franz Rosenthal I also wish to express my appreciation. The late Cyrus H. Gordon, my benefactor when I first came to the United States in 1971, deserves special mention, for he remained a warm supporter throughout the years. I also wish to thank Marcia Hermansen, who "found" the U.S. resident Mandaeans for me.

Among the many Mandaeans, I can single out only a few for my deeply felt respect and gratitude. In San Diego, California: Lamea Abbas Amara and Shafia Amara; in New York: Nasser and Shukrieh Sobbi, Mamoon and Shafia Aldulaimi; in Sweden: Issam Hermiz; in Ahwaz, Iran: the priests Sheikh Jabbar, Sheikh Salah, Sheikh Najah, and Sheikh Talib. Also in Ahwaz: Sheikh Salem Choheili and his family, the Mandaean Association, J. Kataneh and his family, and Said Berengi and his family. In Tehran: Asad Askari and his family. Among non-Mandaeans in Tehran, I wish to thank these persons and organizations: Masood Frouzandeh, Professor Fathullah Mujtabai, the History Department at the Shahid Behesthi University, Dr. Mohammed S. Mahfouzi, and the Ibn Sina Society.

Organizations that supported parts of research for this book are the University of Greensboro, North Carolina's Excellence Foundation Research Grants, 1983 and 1984; the National Endowment for the Humanities Travel Grant to Collections,1989; the American Philosophical Society's Grant, 1993; and the American Academy of Religion Individual Research Grant, 1994. I hereby express my thanks to all of them.

Accolades go also to Paul Courtright, a friend who, having also been my chairman in two departments of religion, found a home for this book. I thank Scholars Press and Oxford University Press for taking on this project and seeing it through to reality.

There is no denying that this book has occupied much of my world for years, and that almost everyone I know has orbited into the project's sphere to some degree. Those who have lived with me through all phases of it are my stepson, Jesse Buckley, and my husband, Tim Buckley. In love and gratitude, I dedicate this book to them.

February 2002 J. J. B.
Brunswick, Maine

Contents

Abbreviations xv

I BEGINNINGS

1 Introduction: The Mandaean World 3

2 From Iraq to California: Grains of Musk 21

3 Šitil: An Example of "the Image Above and Below" 35

4 Ruha 40

5 Miriai 49

II RITUALS

6 To the River: In Iran, April 1996 59

7 Baptism (Maṣbuta) 80

8 The Ṭabahata Masiqta 87

9 The Initiation of the Tarmida 98

III NATIVE HERMENEUTICS

10 The Ducks That Came to the Marshes: New York 113

11 An Inscribed Mandaean Body 130

12 Interpretive Strategies in *The Scroll of Exalted Kingship* 134

13 Mandaean Language Games and Obstacles 144

14 Thousands of Names, Hundreds of Lineages 153

Frouzanda Mahrad 161

Glossary 165

Notes 171

Bibliography 191

Index 197

Abbreviations

DC	Drower Collection of Mandaean texts, Bodleian Library, Oxford University
Coronation	*The Coronation of the Great Šišlam*
Exalted Kingship	*The Scroll of Exalted Kingship. Diwan Malkuta ʿLaita*
GL	*Left Ginza*
GR	*Right Ginza*
John	The Book of John
Mandaeans	The Mandaeans of Iraq and Iran
Prayerbook	The Canonical Prayerbook of the Mandaeans
1012	The Thousand and Twelve Questions (*Alf Trisar Šuialia*)

PART I

BEGINNINGS

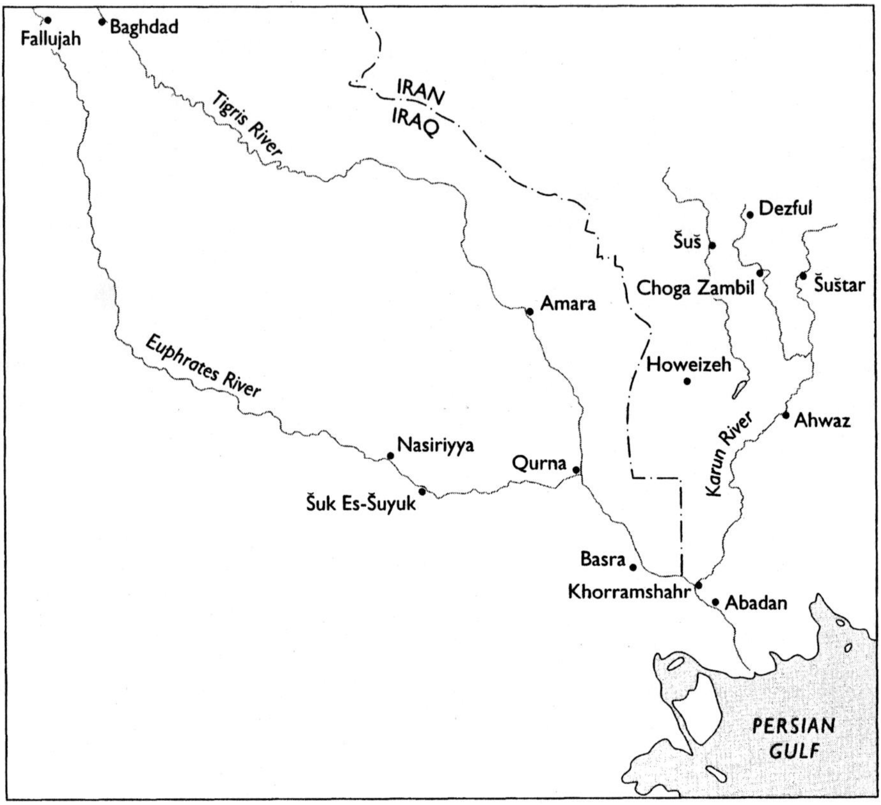

Mandaean territories.

1

Introduction

The Mandaean World

Mandaeism: Origins and Glimpses of History

The Mandaean religion is commonly classified with Gnosticism, and the origin of the Mandaeans can be traced to the Jordan/Palestine area. Central religious terms such as *yardna*[1] (running water), *kušṭa* (truth), and *manda* (knowledge) point decidedly toward the religion's western origins there. Exactly when the Mandaeans emigrate from the Jordan valley to the rivers and marshes of present-day southern Iraq and southwest Iran (Khuzistan) is still subject to debate. Discernible from the second century C.E. on, the Mandaeans perhaps leave their western habitat in the first-century migration, as Rudolf Macuch argues,[2] though others, such as Kurt Rudolph, still considers the third century to be more likely.[3] Three (of four) Parthian kings named Artaban, who span three centuries, appear as candidates for the role of protector of the Mandaeans eager to leave the Jordan/Palestine area. Whatever the case may be, the Mandaeans arrive during early Christian times into Iraq and Iran, probably incrementally and via the Harran area.

Early on, the religion clearly experiences more or less hostile contacts with various forms of Christianity and becomes acquainted with Babylonian remnants, Zoroastrianism, Manichaeism, and other religions. Parts of Manichaean hymnic literature are borrowed and translated from Mandaean poetry.[4] From the seventh century onward, Mandaeism persists under Islamic rulers. A complete portrait of Mandaean history through the centuries is impossible to acquire, but glimpses appear here and there.

Mythological traditions contain grains of history, as in the emigration legend *Haran Gawaita*, which mentions an Arsacid king Artabanus—but does not specify *which* Artabanus—as the protector of the persecuted Mandaeans leaving their western habitat for the east. If the emigration takes place in the first half of the first century, as Macuch holds, one must assume that Mandaeism already existed in some original form. Alone among scholars, Rudolph has drawn attention to a number of links between features found in Mandaeism and in the Coptic Gnostic Nag Hammadi documents.[5] This area of scholarship urgently awaits further investigation. Given Mandaeism's affinities with other forms of Gnosticism, one might be able to combine research in the earliest data and strata of Mandaeism with those of other Gnostic sources. This would be crucial for the aim of obtaining a clearer historical picture of Gnosticism's beginnings.

According to *Haran Gawaita*, the Mandaeans know of the destruction of Jerusalem and its Temple in 69–70 C.E. However, according to the text, they do not emigrate as a result of this calamity. In Mandaean eyes, the punishment of the Jews is deserved, but the Mandaeans have another consideration: they abandon Adonai after Mary (Miriai) becomes pregnant by witchcraft, or by someone other than her husband.[6] Miriai, the Jewess turned Mandaean, is a heroine—as I will explore in chapter 5—though her son Jesus swerves from his true, Mandaean heritage. Historically and mythologically, it is significant that, according to *Haran Gawaita*, Mandaeans consider themselves former Jews. In this context it is worth mentioning that the language of the Babylonian Talmud is quite close to classical Mandaic.

Macuch insists that the Mandaeans must have arrived via northern Babylonia and Media into Khuzistan already in the second century, and that the religion was fully developed with texts and rituals at this time. As noted, technical terms, including major cultic ones, point westward to the Jordan area, though strong secondary Babylonian and Persian influences on Mandaeism soon become notable. But the idea that Mandaeism is of Babylonian origin, as Edwin Yamauchi holds, is vociferously opposed by Macuch.[7]

Since 1987, I have been researching parts of Mandaean history by studying and comparing accessible Mandaean colophons, which are lists of scribes appended to nearly all Mandaean documents. At present, my findings show that the earliest attested, named historical person in Mandaeism is the woman Šlama, daughter of Qidra (cooking pot). This woman, named in relation to her mother and/or initiator into priesthood, is the earliest recorded Mandaean copyist of the text called the *Left Ginza*. The Mandaean holy book, *Ginza* (treasure), is separated into a right (*GR*) and a left (*GL*) part.[8] *GL*, much of it in poetic form, deals largely with the soul's ascent to the Lightworld, and this section of the *Ginza* belongs among the religion's most ancient textual material. Šlama may be dated to approximately 200, for she appears several generations before the famous early copyist Zazai of Gawazta, who flourished in the 270s. One may note that Zazai belongs to the decade of Mani's death.[9]

Whether the Aramaic-speaking people in Elymais, near Susa, may have been Mandaeans is impossible to know, but the Aramaic inscriptions from Tang-i-Sarwak, Khuzistan, stem from the second century and resemble Mandaean letters. Macuch thinks that the Mandaean letters precede the Elymaic ones.[10]

Under Persian rule, during the time of the later Arsacids, the Mandaeans evidently enjoy royal protection. This situation changes as the Sasanid ruler Bahram I comes to power in 273. Mani is executed at the beginning of his reign, as the influential and zealous Zoroastrian high priest Karter continues to suppress adherents of non-Zoroastrian religions, such as Mandaeans, Manichaeans, Jews, Christians, Hindus, and Buddhists. During these dangerous years, one might surmise a consolidation of Mandaean literature in an attempt to rescue and codify the religion. Zazai's extensive copyist activities testify to this.

The persecutions instigated by Karter do not quench Mandaeism, however. Except for a few copyists' names in the Mandaean colophons, the religion seems to fade from recorded history for centuries. But a particular form of literature emerges, perhaps as early as the third to seventh centuries: the inscribed, so-called magical bowls, and also lead strips. Firm historical evidence comes from scribal information in the Mandaean liturgies, which state that in 639–40, at the beginning of the Muslim expansion, the Mandaean "head of the people" and "head of the age," Anuš, son of Danqa, appears with a delegation of Mandaeans before Muslim authorities.[11] Showing the Muslims the holy Ginza and proclaiming the chief Mandaean prophet to be John the Baptist—who was well regarded by Muslims—the Mandaeans ask for protection. They know that the two criteria of a holy book and a prophet are essential for acknowledgment as a "People of the Book" (*ahl al-kitab*), that is, a legal minority religion, and they appeal to this.

The Mandaeans appear to succeed, for the religion flourishes, with intense scribal activity. Mandaean texts are collected, compared, and consolidated as conscientious leaders among the priestly copyists exert themselves to weed out local variations in ritual texts. This is a time of creating canons. Famous copyists such as Ramuia, son of ʿQaimat, are active in the mid-seventh century and the woman priest Haiuna, daughter of Yahia, somewhat later. The town Ṭib, in Wasiṭ, Iraq, emerges as one of the great Mandaean scribal centers.

In 831, the Calif al-Mamun, on his way to wage war in Turkey, comes across the planet-worshiping Harranian Sabeans and presents them with the choice of becoming Muslims or facing death. Much has been written about the possible connections between the Harranian Sabeans—Neoplatonist "pagan" astrologers and scientists in the town of Harran (now in far southern Turkey)—and the Mandaeans.[12] Still known today as "Sabeans" ("dippers," "dyers," "baptizers," "converts") by their Muslim neighbors, the Mandaeans carry a double name, one used externally, the other internally. Certain exchanges between the two kinds of Sabeism did occur, though the religions are, at best, only distant relatives. But the incidence in Harran shows that in the ninth century, minority religions remained under scrutiny and that *Sabeism* was a fluid term. Far south of Harranian territory, Mandaeism remains active in that century, with the luminary copyist ʿQaiam, son of Zindana.

During 932–934, the status of the Mandaeans becomes an issue for the Abbasid Calif al-Qahir Billah. He asks the Shafiʿi scholar al-Istakari about the Sabeans (i.e., Mandaeans) of Wasiṭ, in southeast Iraq. This suggests that their protected minority (*dhimmi*) position has become uncertain. To avoid further investigation by the authorities, the Mandaeans pay a bribe of 50,000 dinars and are left alone. Even in the time of the scholar Ibn-Fuwati, who lives approximately 1300 and who records this story, the Mandaeans do not pay the poll tax. So, they successfully bypass the laws pertaining to officially recognized minority religions.[13] This feat testifies to the Mandaeans' talent for shrewd political adjustment. Of course, had times been different, they might have been persecuted, not tolerated.

Around the year 1200, the geographer Yaqut states that Ṭib, the Mandaean scribal center of centuries past, is inhabited by Nabateans, who speak Nabatean and are Sabeans. They consider themselves to be descendants of Seth, son of Adam.[14] There can be little doubt that these are Mandaeans, for we do not know of others settled there at that time who considered themselves Seth descendants.

In the mid-sixteenth century, Portuguese missionaries begin to encounter Mandaeans, whom they mistakenly designate as "Christians of St. John," and during the next few centuries European religious officials, travelers, adventurers, and representatives of enterprises such as the East India Company become acquainted with Mandaeans as well.

An interesting report, based on archival work on this time period, can be found in Edmondo Lupieri's book.[15]

Tacked onto the *tarik* (postscript to a colophon) of a Mandaean exorcism written in 1782 is a much older tarik, from approximately 1480.[16] In it, the Mandaean copyist Yuhana Šitlan tells of sufferings and persecutions. At the time of the writing of the exorcism, the Mandaeans under Qajar rule in the 1780s in Iran also are experiencing great hardships.[17] About fifty years later, the Mandaeans are threatened by complete extinction by the great cholera epidemic of 1831—the so-called Plague of Šuštar—in which half of the inhabitants of that city die. Mandaeism is rescued solely because of the great, heroic restoring efforts of a few learned laymen (*yalufas*). The entire priesthood has perished. One of the surviving sons of a priest tells heartrending stories of the cholera's aftermath. His name is Yahia Bihram, and he is one of the yalufas who becomes a priest in 1831.[18]

Having survived the epidemic, Mandaeans such as Yahia Bihram may again have seen concerted attacks against the religion in the 1870s.[19] According to oral information (some of which is attested in colophon postscripts I have not yet researched sufficiently), one of Nasruddin Shah's local representatives in Šuštar, Khuzistan, is responsible for a massacre on the Mandaeans. This happens against the will of the Shah, who asks his representative to desist, and the Shah remains a good ruler in Mandaean eyes, even today. Nevertheless, many Mandaeans die, and those who are able to flee know that their fellow religionists have been thrown into wells and drowned. A calculated, cruel death for baptists! In April 1996, I stood with several Mandaeans on the traditional spot of the Šuštar massacre as Sheikh Jabbar, the leader of the Mandaeans in Ahwaz, prayed for their dead.[20]

Like others, Mandaeans suffered during two recent wars and their aftermath: the Iran-Iraq war of 1980–88 and the Gulf War of 1991. Partly as a result of these conflicts, the majority of Mandaeans now living in emigration left their homelands only very recently. Their numbers are debated. Scholarly estimates have long hovered around 14,000 to 15,000, which is clearly too low. Many Mandaeans calculate the population at anywhere from 3,000 to about 100,000, the majority living in Iraq. Others insist that the numbers are much higher than 100,000. For a variety of reasons, exact figures are impossible to ascertain. Iranian and Iraqi authorities may have their own demographic data on the Mandaeans. Mandaeans themselves may harbor conflicting views on how to categorize those married outside the religion, those forced to convert to Islam, and the secularized. Whether in "the old countries" or in emigration, current Mandaean communities face urgent, difficult identity questions. Many tend to determine their heritage in terms of ethnicity or culture, giving less emphasis to the religion.

At the moment of this writing, Iranian Mandaeans are hoping that their protected status as "People of the Book," in force during the Shah's reign but removed when Ayatollah Khomeini came to power, will be reinstated. There are hopeful signs. In Iraq, the Mandaeans have at least pro forma protection, but in the ruined economy and the current political climate, their lives are regularly endangered, and various forms of victimization occur. Because Mandaeans traditionally are goldsmiths, many are accused of hoarding gold and other precious metals. Also, confiscations of shops and goods have become increasingly common. It is no wonder, then, that many Mandaeans seek to move elsewhere. Today, an increasing number of Web sites keep Mandaeans connected.

Characteristics of the Religion

Scholars have long debated the term *Gnosticism* and have noted that the word *Gnostic* is barely recorded as a term of self-designation in the ancient world putatively harboring Gnosticism. However, as self-designated "knowers," the Mandaeans (from Aramaic *manda*: knowledge) do constitute the only still surviving group of Gnostics. Other late antiquity Gnostics died out or were overrun long ago, largely due to the growth of orthodox forms of Christianity. But the Mandaeans alone have persisted.

They defy easy categorization. Neither Jewish, Christian, nor recognizably "pagan," they possess an extensive literature containing multifarious mythological traditions, and they continue to practice intricate rituals whose precise origins and antecedents are difficult to determine. A modern variant of their own ancient Mandaic language (an East Aramaic dialect) is still kept alive, mainly in Iran.[21] Various Mandaean communities, such as the one in and near Northbridge, New South Wales, Australia, are making efforts to rescue their linguistic heritage, including the spoken language, called *raṭna*. This is distinct from the classical, written language of Mandaean literature and traditional ritual use.[22]

Many aspects of the religion, particularly on the mythological level, resemble those found in other Gnostic systems. But it has a distinct identity, not attributable merely to language and geography. Mandaeism's own enormous literature spans a number of genres and is barely studied these days, let alone fully known. And the religion's lengthy and detailed rituals resist easy interpretations.

Anyone starting to study the religion's multifarious, complex mythological, ritual, and esoteric exegetical traditions gradually becomes attuned to its plural, encompassing worldviews, its cosmologies. One must ask: What is the many-faceted universe within which Mandaeism breathes and makes sense? Can a common ground be found, one on which the religionists themselves might nod and say, yes, such and such a scholarly interpretation seems reasonable? Alone among the ancient Gnostic religions, Mandaeism is alive, and its constituents must be reckoned with as interlocutors with scholars. It is not possible to cling to outdated models of "objective" scholarship in which the scrutinized subject remains mute and unable to interact with scholars who might adhere to stereotypical ideas about Gnosticism.

"Meaning" does not remain static but is regularly subject to discussion, whether internally in Mandaeism or in scholarly work on it. Like most living religions, Mandaeism has its battles, competing views, clashes of symbols, and a welter of apparently incompatible mythological structures. But such dynamics demonstrate that the religion remains in conversation with itself, and these debates should not be interpreted as glaring contradictions, hopeless fragmentation, or loss of identity.

To begin, one might reasonably state that in Mandaeism the world is basically three-tiered: an upper, heavenly Lightworld (*alma d̲-nhura*: "world of light"); a middle, earthly, human world, named Tibil; and a somewhat gloomy underworld, an area that receives less attention than the two others. Much energy is focused on the Lightworld, which in some texts is envisioned and/or mapped out in detailed descriptions. Mandaeism has this interest in common with other Gnostic systems, which see human beings living in fundamental alienation on earth while the true home lies up above, in the light. There resides the supreme First Life, who also carries names such as the King of Greatness or the King of Light, depending on the literary tradition or stratum. In downward or outwardly expanding order come the subservient beings of light: Second Life, Third Life, and numerous others.

The religion offers both an emanation model of creation and one that posits two oppositional worlds, the Lightworld and the world of darkness, existing at the beginning of time. But the emanation model is by far the most common, and the sheer mass of variations in the creation mythology makes it impossible to appoint one, specific version as "the original."[23] Evidently, Mandaeans have enjoyed and accommodated variety in this respect, a characteristic that might frustrate scholars yearning to pinpoint a singular, original myth.

Most of the Lightworld beings, called *ʿutras* (sing.: *ʿutra* "wealth," but meaning "angel" or "guardian"), were involved in the creation of the world(s) at the beginning of ime. In varying ways, they continue to uphold and look after the Lightworld and earth, and especially to keep contact with the Mandaeans of earth. *Laufa* (connection) is a central Mandaeaen concept, and it expresses this contact between the worlds. The term carries a practical—and not merely an abstract—significance. At the first creation, the Lightworld beings established the laufa, which is constantly reestablished and reconfirmed by Mandaeans on earth as they perform rituals. Prayers, along with all other rituals, were sent down to earth by the forces of light in order to be conveyed back up by humans. So there is an unceasing give-and-take between the two realms as earthly activity spins the life thread between the human world and ensures the connection to the Light.

The Lightworld contains different kinds of ʿutras. Some of those who became too caught up in the world creation are now incarcerated in the *maṭartas*, (toll stations) in the vast spaces between earth and the Lightworld proper. Here they are stuck in sorrow and punishment until the end of time. It is commonly understood that when no Mandaeans are left on earth, it will simply cease to exist. Then the last of the four world ages will have been completed, and the jailed ʿutras will ascend, liberated, to their rightful Lightworld home. This time of imprisonment reflects the Mandaean ambivalence regarding creation and concrete life in the earthly world. For, just as soul and spirit are trapped within human bodies, ʿutras are stuck in their own prisons in the long interim between creation and end time.

Other ʿutras are more positively envisioned, predominantly as saviors and messengers. These movable figures regularly trek to earth to reveal Lightworld teachings and to assist Mandaeans. Manda ḏ-Hiia (Knowledge of Life) occupies the preeminent position among ʿutras. Another one, Anuš, performs miracles in the style of Jesus and destroys Jerusalem. (Such traditions are clearly polemical toward Christianity and Judaism.) Šitil—a brother of Anuš and usually less prominent than Anuš and the third brother, Hibil—inhabits curiously interstitial roles. Partly because of his middle role, I have chosen Šitil as the subject for one of this book's chapters.

Presiding at the pinnacle of the Lightworld is the First Life, majestically enthroned, the royal chief of the saving ambassador ʿutras, of those imprisoned in the maṭartas, and of all Mandaeans. Unlike the ʿutras, the First Life does not travel about but rests serenely above, overseer of everything below. Female Lightbeings, usually envisioned as wives of the male ones, are commonly acknowledged. Such evidence for gender balance in the Lightworld is striking, for many other forms of Gnosticism harbor overt forms of misogyny.[24] Prominent among female figures in the Lightworld is Simat Hiia (Treasure of Life), who appears in the recurrent Mandaean formula "In the name of Yawar Ziwa [i.e., Yawar Radiance] and Simat Hiia." Several Lightworld females appear in chapter 4, which focuses on Ruha.

At first glance, she seems to be the only undisputedly evil being in Mandaeism. The traditionally demonic beings in Mandaeism are the zodiac spirits, the planets, and their mother Ruha, the personified evil spirit, a parody of the Christian "Holy Spirit" (Ruha ḏ-Qudša). According to a few traditions, she originally belonged in the Lightworld, but Ruha mainly epitomizes lust, music, and the emotions. Many myths pair her with her tragically undeveloped dragon son ʿUr. Envious of human beings, Ruha tries to trap them by allying herself with her counterpart in the human beings, the spirit (*ruha*), who, as the middle component in a person, wobbles between the elevated soul and the fleshly body. On the level of Mandaean anthropology, as a native science of the human being, this tripartition is of central importance, especially as envisioned in ritual life. As a counterpart to the Lightworld, the underworld plays a major role mainly in a few large, dramatic creation myths featuring a Lightworld envoy, usually Hibil, who travels downward to subdue the underworld prior to the creation of Tibil, the earth.[25] Krun, the great flesh-mountain, rules on the bottom of the seven-leveled underworld but is defeated by Hibil. As in Manichaeism, the Mandaean underworld is a primordial given, arisen from itself, and when it catches a glimpse of the Lightworld, it attacks. After Hibil's exploits have sapped the underworld's strength, that realm seems to play only a minor part in the further affairs of the universe. This might be so because, as the earth comes into being, it and the maṭartas appear hellish enough. Souls of wicked Mandaeans go not to the underworld but upward to be purified in suitable maṭartas until they are fit for further ascent. Unbaptized dead infants spend time in a special limbo world where they are suckled by a tree with breastlike fruits.[26]

The chief concern for Mandaeans is, then, how to live in the middle realm, that is, in Tibil. Another overarching interest is how to die, to obtain a proper ascent to the Lightworld. The chief Mandaean rituals are time-consuming. But one could also put matters in the opposite perspective and say that the rituals are time-creating. Highly complex, the rituals of life and death—with their patterns, rhythms, and symbolic worlds—are difficult to interpret in their full depth. Some are undertaken by priests only, shielded from the eyes of the laypeople.

Priests, of whom there are two main classes, *ganzibras* (treasurers) and *tarmidas* (original meaning: "disciples"), essentially hold the position of ʿutras on earth. Similar to the ʿutras, they may move—ritually rather than literally—between the realms. Keeping up the laufa, the priests act as "ʿutras-from-below," and because priests are humans, their starting point is of course the earth, not the Lightworld. Preparing themselves for rituals, the priests are able to harness Lightworld energies and thereby in a sense effect their propulsion upward. Suitably, at the end of ceremonials, the priests deconsecrate their insignia and again assume "human" status.

The sixty-eight-day-long priest initiation for the tarmida is the subject of chapter 9. Rituals such as the death mass (*masiqta*), treated in chapter 8, and the priest initiation are both built from clustered, separate ritual elements, which are arranged like building blocks. For instance, a tarmida initiation contains several baptisms and a number of meals. At death, the souls and spirits of all Mandaeans (priests and laypeople alike) go to the Lightworld, provided the death has been pure and the death rituals have been performed properly.[27]

As baptist Gnostics, the Mandaeans possess as their most central ritual the baptism (*mašbuta*). On Sundays and on special holidays baptism takes place, and it must be performed by a priest (any Mandaean may do a kind of self-baptism, but these constitute other, minor Mandaean washing rituals). The maṣbuta is not an initiation ritual but a repeated baptism in flowing, fresh water, the primary form in which the Lightworld manifests itself on earth.

Daunting remedies—in terms of sheer time and details—await priests who commit errors in death rituals or other ceremonials. Mistakes in rituals affect both the performer and the one for whose benefit the ritual is conducted.[28] After bodily death, a successful masiqta merges soul and spirit into *one* ascending entity that will reside in the world of ideal counterparts (*Mšunia Kušṭa*). In this particular area of the Lightworld, the risen entity joins its departed relatives and ancestors. Here lives the nonincarnate portion, the *dmuta* (image) of each person. A soul, safely arrived in this upper world, has traversed vast cosmic distances and endured many tests presented by the toll house watchers, the jailed creator ʿutras and other, less tragic but more demonic, beings.

As noted, all the major Mandaean rituals aim to reinforce the laufa, to reconnect the people with the Lightworld. While the maṣbuta temporarily puts living Mandaeans in direct contact with the Lightworld, the death rituals convey the dead to the upper world. Funerary meals strengthen the living and the dead. And the community must produce priests whose task it is to create the laufa from below. This uppermost class of leaders hold the Mandaean communities together, act as go-betweens with secular authorities, instruct the people, and are experts in astrology and in writing talismans. Also, in terms of the ongoing production of transcribing the vast corpus of religious texts, the priests (and, more rarely, learned laymen) are still the carriers of this task.[29]

Overview of Mandaean Literature

The Ginza

In the spring of 1998, I received in the mail a copy of the first-ever printed Mandaean holy book, the *Ginza*. The Mandaean Research Centre of Northbridge, New South Wales, Australia, has produced this hefty tome,[30] in Mandaic fonts developed in their community. For nearly two millennia, the *Ginza* has been transcribed by Mandaean priests, always in the same format. As noted earlier, the work is separated into a right and a left part, *GR* and *GL*, and the two parts are organized in such a way that on reaching the end of *GR*, a reader must turn the volume upside down to read *GL*. The two parts face one another in the manner of two inscribed bowls enclosing the text within. I think that this may very well be the *Ginza*'s model, for traditional Mandaean inscribed clay bowls are often found buried in this same fashion.

The most revered among Mandaean texts, the *Ginza* is a conglomerate. The codex may have reached its final, collected form in the mid–seventh century. As noted, at that time Mandaean authorities presented the book to Muslim leaders as proof that the Mandaeans had a holy book and therefore merited exemption from forced conversion to Islam. But it is quite likely that the various parts of the *Ginza* already had been collected for internal Mandaean purposes,[31] and not solely to present a holy text to the authorities. The first useful *Ginza* to be published in the West was Heinrich Petermann's *Sidra Rabba*,[32] which remains the only critical edition, containing a Latin translation and Petermann's transcribed Mandaic. Mark Lidzbarski's introduction to his edited German translation of the *Ginza* gives valuable information, and so do his individual introductions to each *Ginza* tractate.

Of the eighteeen tractates making up *GR*, the first and second ones contain very old traditions, though no part of *GR* appears to be as ancient as *GL*.[33] *GR* 1–13 comprise, first, *GR* 1 and 2, which are basically two versions of the same work.[34] *GR* 1 has only one tractate, containing a series of moral teachings and a Mandaic "world history," while *GR* 2 consists of four sections. Creation stories, moral exhortations, a confession of sins, revelations about history, end-of-the-world speculations and polemics—especially anti-Christian materials—are all present. So, *GR* 1 and 2 offer a representative selection of Mandaean religious concerns.

By far the largest of the *Ginza* tractates, *GR* 3 is a vast, poetic creation myth of persuasive narrative power. The next two tractates deal with underworld journeys, heroic ʿutras, the soul's travels through the maṭartas, and with the baptism of the Mandaean savior and messenger Manda ḏ-Hiia (Knowledge of Life) by John the Baptist—the latter story is found in *GR* 5, 4. *GR* 6 contains the marvelous story of the Noah/Utnapishtim-like Dinanukht (the one who speaks according to the religion),[35] the half man, half book who goes on a journey to the upper worlds.[36] Words of wisdom from John the Baptist make up *GR* 7, while in *GR* 8 Manda ḏ-Hiia warns believers against Ruha. Polemics dominate the first part of *GR* 9, and the young boy created from the heavenly Jordan in *GR* 9, 2 may be of Orphic origin.[37]

Creation stories dominate the next couple of tractates. *GR* 12 has seven sections composed of varied contents, while *GR* 13 is a priestly, exhortatory prayer for the community. The first (of seven) *Ginza* colophons occurs after *GR* 13, which indicates that this part of the Ginza was considered to be a unit. There is no doubt that *GR* 1–13 alone testify to a fully developed Mandaean Gnosticism. Many of the religion's chief literary genres are present, in prose and poetry: moral teachings, creation myths, polemics, liturgy, sapiential traditions, and so forth.

Each of the next five tractates carries a colophon, which demonstrates that they once were separate documents. Most of these contain poetry. The right part of the *Ginza* ends with *GR* 18, an apocalyptic world history in which the Old Testament Egyptian Exodus is given a Mandaean twist. According to *GR* 18, the world is 480,000 years old, but my current Mandaic calendar—printed in New York[38]—states that it is now 445,368 years since Adam's birth.

Turning the *Ginza* upside down, one finds that *GL*, the part of the *Ginza* that concentrates on the fate of the soul after the body's death, consists of three tractates. *GL* 1 has four sections, and the prose piece *GL* 1, 2 tells the wondrous story about the first man to die, Adam's son Šitil. *GL* 2's twenty-eight sections of poetry begin with the formulaic "I am a Mana[39] of the Great Life." Sixty-two poems dealing with the destiny of the soul constitute *GL* 3. A few of these pieces belong to the prayer category *ʿnianas* (responses) found in the Mandaean liturgical collections.

The Liturgies

The heart of Mandaean religious life is found in its rituals, hence the importance of prayers and liturgies. First translated by Lidzbarski, a sizable portion of the prayers became available in 1920, while Drower in 1959 published her larger, English translation of what is termed *Qulasta* (collection), the corpus of Mandaean liturgies.[40] In the back of Drower's *Prayerbook* one finds all the prayers in Mandaic, in facsimile. Over 400 numbered prayers are included, but some, especially toward the end of the collection, are duplicates. Among the Mandaeans themselves, smaller, well-thumbed volumes of prayers for specific liturgical purposes are commonly used.

Originally, what became the *Prayerbook* consisted of eight different units, for the collection contains eight colophons. The prayers are of varying length; some are only a few lines long, others take up several pages in Drower's translation. At the beginning, we find the baptism liturgy, the masiqta prayers, and two *ʿngirta* (letter) prayers. This is an ancient section, going back to the third century, according to colophon information. At specific segments in the ritual sequences, the text offers directions and other forms of explanations to the priestly officiant. For instance, after prayer 19 the text states, "This is the set prayer for the baptism wreath. Recite it over the myrtle wreath and place it on the heads of the souls that thou baptisest."[41] Three very long hymns of praise,[42] 75–77, make up the next unit, and then comes a ʿniana series used for baptism, masiqta, and other rituals. The next segment, which includes the daily prayers, is composed of specific groupings of prayers for the different days of the week. Priests pray such sets three times a day, and prayer 104 is also uttered by Mandaean laypeople. In contrast to the *Prayerbook*'s second and third units, the fourth segment carries a colophon stretching back to Zazai of Gawazta, as did the text's first segment.

The very important prayer 170, called "Our Ancestors," appears in the next section. Used at specific times of the year, this prayer asks for forgiveness of sins for the reciter and for a long list of Mandaean ancestors, mainly priests.[43] A peculiar feature of Mandaean liturgy is the occasional alphabet hymn, a prayer featuring clue words in alphabetic sequence at the beginning of each stanza, running from A to T.[44] Prayer 179 is such a prayer, praising central Lightworld entities. Hymns for priest initiation ceremonials and for marriage are also included in this part of the *Prayerbook*.

Priest initiation liturgies occur also in the next part of the text, for here begins the antiphonal series "When the Proven, the Pure One, Went," recited at marriage and at the creation of a new tarmida.[45] The next segment covers prayers already included in other parts of the text, and the last part includes the priest coronation hymn series, 305–29, which are recited alternately by the chief officiant and by the other priests present at the initiation of a new tarmida. The last of the *Prayerbook*'s colophon appears after prayer 329, and the end of the book contains a number of prayers without a colophon. This looks like a certain looseness in the "canon." Some very long hymns occur toward the end.

All in all, one may say that the contents of the *Prayerbook* reflect a variety of facets of Mandaean religion. Mythological references, cosmological teachings, and moral precepts are presupposed in almost all of the liturgies, so that a reader familiar with the foundations of Mandaean teachings may perceive clear or veiled associations to—and even revealing ideological uses of—these materials in the prayers.[46] Especially with respect to the major rituals, one may detect how Mandaean baptism and masiqta ritual segments are carefully anchored in mythological materials. But, as in any liturgical tradition, it would be difficult to reconstruct the overarching mythological structures on the basis of prayers alone. Liturgies take for granted an already established worldview, and they work to reinforce it.

The Book of John

Much cherished by Mandaeans but hardly studied at all by scholars, this conglomerate document, named for the chief Mandaean prophet, occupies an important place in the religion. A leaden copy of this book was shown to me in Ahwaz in 1973, as noted in my preface. The only translation remains Lidzbarski's from 1915,[47] which, in the latter half of the book includes his own Mandaic transcription in stunningly beautiful calligraphy. Like the *Ginza* and the liturgies—though unlike many other Mandaean texts—*John* is always in book, that is, codex, form.

Its age, in terms of colophonic information, can be assigned to early Islamic times, though *John* undoubtedly retains much material that is considerably older. Lidzbarski divides the text into thirty-seven tractates and bestows on them titles according to content. Here we find, despite the title of the book, a focus on John the Baptist mainly confined to the lengthy sixth tractate of the book. This deals with John's miraculous birth and preaching and includes the prophet's polemical conversations with a defensive Jesus. Most of the sections in this tractate begin with the mysterious formula "Yahia preached in the nights; Yohana in the evenings of the night," which retains both the Aramaic and the Arabic forms of John's name.[48]

Tractates are devoted to specific ʿutras. Some of the Lightbeings are shown in degrees of distress, for instance, Hibil in tractate 21, which Lidzbarski names "Hibil's Lament."[49] Other featured Lightworld beings include the personified Truth (Kušṭa) in tractates 1 and 5 and the ʿutra Anuš mimicking Jesus' deeds in Jerusalem (tractates 20 and 37). Very intriguing material on Miriai, Jesus' mother, appears in tractate 7.[50] Several tractates take a striking interest in female entities connected with the Lightworld.

Mythological themes and moral exhortations dominate in *John*; some of these are found elsewhere in Mandaean texts, while others are unique to the text. Several tractates focus on polemics. There is a conspicuous emphasis on suffering Lightworld beings—Hibil is only one example. In fact, *John* carries a strong emotional force, its moving descriptions of pain, longing, and alienation perhaps reflecting—and projecting upward to the Lightworld—the tribulations of Gnostics under persecution.

Ritual Commentaries: Esoteric Exegetical Literature

The largest and most complex among the ritual commentaries is *The Thousand and Twelve Questions*, edited and translated by Drower. This not a coherent book in itself but a compendium of texts. Drower's transliterated texts take up the first 108 pages of her edition, and a booklet containing the facsimile text is tucked into a pocket on the inside back cover. Separated into two books, the first containing two sections and the second having seven sections (with subsections), *1012* at first gives an unwieldy impression. Certainly, this is not a text for novices in Mandaean studies. Depths of mysteries are explored, usually through utterances by a Lightworld being, such as the Lord of Greatness, (*mara ḏ-rabuta*), at the request of a prototypical priest. *1012* offers detailed commentaries on different kinds of death masses, on meals for the dead, and on the marriage ceremony. The original, Lightworld celebration of such rituals is held up as exemplary for earthly officiants, who are admonished to avoid mistakes in rituals. How to rectify such errors if they do occur is one of the text's most conspicuous features. Detailed instructions show how officials must deal with errors committed at any given step, and/or in any given formula, of the ceremonials.

A secret treatise on the original creation of the body appears in Book I, ii of *1012*. Physiological-metaphysical and alphabetical speculations are interspersed everywhere,[51] and esoteric creation mythologies abound throughout the text. The Lightworld speaker repeatedly emphasizes how secret this text is, and that it must not be made available to anyone except, according to the recurring Mandaean formula, only "to one among thousand, two among two thousand." *1012* is perhaps the quintessential Mandaean text demonstrating the priestly craft. A fruitful way to use it, for scholars, is as a guide to the step-by-step sequence of certain rituals. It can be profitably consulted in conjunction with other texts, whether liturgies, other ritual commentaries related to *1012*, or mythologies.

As he concludes his copying task of *1012* in or after the middle of the seventh century, the well-known Mandaean copyist Ramuia, son of ʿQaimat, states, "When I wrote this Diwan it was in separate treatises. I wrote them down and collected these reliable mysteries one by one, and combined them into fourteen writings, (making) two or three discourses into one.[52]

Addressing himself to fellow priests and scribes, Ramuia adds that in order to keep these separate texts united, he has made them into a single scroll, "so that its beauty, fame and honor may be yours, and forgiveness of sins."[53]

Other, smaller texts belonging to the same category as *1012* are *The Coronation of the Great Šišlam*, *The Great "First World"* and *The Lesser "First World," The Scroll of Exalted Kingship*, and *The Baptism of Hibil Ziwa*. All of these are scrolls and, except for *Coronation*, have illustrations in the classical Mandaean stylized manner.[54] Apart from *Exalted Kingship*, Drower edited and translated all the others, publishing them during the decade 1953 to 1963. *Coronation* and *Exalted Kingship* are commentaries on the tarmida initiation, the first text being much shorter, almost like a catalog when compared with the exuberantly esoteric and expansive mind-set of *Exalted Kingship*.[55]

The Great "First World" and the *Lesser "First World"* belong together, for the first one deals, ostensibly, with the creation of the Lightworld, and the second with its lower image: the earthly world. But both are esoteric ritual commentaries, in the style of *1012* and *Exalted Kingship*. Macro- and microcosmic speculations abound as metaphysics and anatomy hover side by side in dizzying priestly mental constructions. Facsimiles of both texts are rolled up in a carton container that accompanies the translation in regular book format.

The Baptism of Hibil Ziwa deals with the first baptism, that of Hibil Ziwa. It is set in the context of Hibil's return from the underworld (a myth elaborately expounded in GR 5, 1), marking the end of a trip necessitating the ʿutra's baptism in order to restore his purity. *Hibil Ziwa*, then, becomes a commentary on the maṣbuta, the baptism ritual. The scroll is lavishly illustrated, and its facsimile is folded up in the back of the book and can be unrolled across a room as a long, narrow runner, showing Lightworld beings and trees.

Despite scholarly skepticism, most of these ritual commentaries are ancient, as their colophons demonstrate. Further investigations of the age of these texts belong to my seemingly endless historical research on Mandaean colophons.

Other Works

Hibil Ziwa is bound together with *Haran Gawaita* (Inner Haran). As noted already, the later is the intriguing "history" of the Mandaeans leaving Jerusalem for the east. Broken off at the beginning, *Haran Gawaita* starts with a diatribe against Jesus, whose mother became pregnant by witchcraft. The real historical value of this tale is much debated,[56] but the work contains information about Mandaean settlements in Babylonia and names historical persons.

Oddly enough, another historical source is the Mandaean book of astrology, *Sfar Malwašia: The Book of the Zodiac*, published by Drower in 1949, her first translated edition of a Mandaean text. The document offers numerous place-names, many of which are difficult to ascertain geographically.[57] Clearly indebted to Babylonian traditions, this work has received almost no scholarly attention.[58] Astrology is the province of priests, and traditionally, every Mandaean has his or her horoscope read. Unlike the Mandaean texts mentioned in the previous section, this text is in loose-leaved, *kurasa* form. It has no illustrations. A facsimile of the text is given in the back of Drower's translation.

Šarh d-Qabin d-Šišlam Rba: The Scroll of the Marriage of the Great Šišlam,[59] contains instructions for the Mandaean marriage ceremony and gives the hymns belonging to the ritual. Unlike the majority of ritual scrolls, this one is not illustrated, and the text plumbs no symbolic depths. It has, therefore, a quite straightforward character. At every marriage, the officiating priest reads through the entire book. The hymn cycle "When the proven, the Pure One Went" occurs here, as well as in the *Prayerbook*, as noted earlier.

One of the most lavishly illustrated texts is *Diwan Abatur*, which gives detailed information on the maṭartas and on Lightworld geography. "Purgatory" inhabitants are identified, the question-and-answer format known from other commentary literature appears, and a version of the world creation is included. Folded up in a pocket in the back of the book is the facsimile of the scroll itself. Twenty feet long, the ream[60] is an impressive piece of art. It is all here: priestly prototypes, heavenly ships, threatening animals, demons with clanging cymbals, the Lightworld tree nourishing unbaptized infants, and the scales at the entrance to the Lightworld proper.

Another illustrated scroll is *Diwan Nahrawata* (The scroll of the rivers), translated into German and published by K. Rudolph in 1982.[61] It shows mountains, rivers and canals, plants and trees of decidedly earthly geography. But the pictures are entirely stylized. Some place-names can be identified, others not. Photographs of the scroll are included at the back of the volume.

Many of the texts in the Drower Collection (DC) in the Bodleian Library in Oxford remain unpublished. Drower let some of the smaller texts, mainly exorcisms, appear in scholarly journals and other such forums, as they are not large enough for book formats. Mandaean texts unknown in the West are surely preserved in private Mandaean libraries in the Orient. One-third of the forty Mandaean manuscripts that K. Rudolph saw in 1977 in one such private collection in Dora, near Baghdad, carried titles unknown to him.[62]

More than fifty Mandaean clay bowls and about eight lead strips have been published.[63] These objects reflect what one may call Mandaean "folk culture," and many scholars habitually refer to the bowls as "magical." From the late nineteenth century on, a number of scholars have worked on the bowls, and Macuch, as usual the defender of early datings, has been involved in disputes with others on this issue.[64] The bowls are often inscribed with the words spiraling out from the center, though some carry the text in triangular segments. One unpublished bowl has its lines (which appear mainly to be names) fanning in petal fashion from the bottom of the bowl.[65] The paint on the bowls may be black or reddish. As noted, bowls are frequently buried in pairs, one enclosed upon the other, evidently to secure the formulas protected inside. One scholar currently researching bowls is Erica C. D. Hunter.[66]

Surprises occur in the search for Mandaean literature, and not just in the Orient. Books or scrolls that hardly anyone ever sees or that attain no mention in scholarly works still lie tucked away in research libraries. In 1996, I made a few such finds in the Bodleian Library at Oxford. First, an impressively illustrated scroll called *The Scroll of Exorcism (of) the Great Name of the Lord of Greatness and the Image of Truth* is indicated as having been bought through Drower in 1954.[67] The text's contents are unknown to me. Second, the oldest manuscript in Europe is also the smallest book volume of any Mandaean text that I know. It measures four by five inches and is a leatherbound collection of prayers, transcribed in 1529.[68] In contrast, a third work, *Hunt. 6*, a collection of texts transcribed in 1615, is an enormous volume at sixteen inches high and twelve inches wide and containing 536 pages. Some of its thick, yellowed pages, which are edged like a washboard, bear ancient water stains. I have determined that this is a *Ginza*, but it has not been studied by scholars.

Brief Note on Scholarship

As noted, Europeans became aware of the Mandaeans mainly during the sixteenth century, when Portuguese Jesuit missionaries tried to convert them. Young Mandaean men were induced—or outrightly kidnapped—to serve in at least one of Portugal's colonial wars, in present-day Sri Lanka. The missionaries and other officials were the first to bring Mandaean texts to Europe.[69] Libraries such as the Vatican Library, the Bibliothèque Nationale in Paris, the British Museum in London, and the Bodleian Library at Oxford University hold Mandaean texts, and inscribed clay bowls and lead strips are housed in various collections. The Bodleian Library has the largest collection, the Drower Collection, given by Lady E. S. Drower toward the end of her long career.[70]

When Theodor Nöldeke published his Mandaean grammar in 1875, he rightly judged that the time was ripe for such a work. Still, he had little regard for Mandaean texts as religious literature, as he found them confusing and downright insane. True to his time's theories of climate-dependent intelligence, Nöldeke held the marshes in southern Iraq to be unsuitable for the development of mental faculties.[71]

In the early 1800s, the Swedish scholar M. Norberg published a flawed Latin translation of the *Ginza*.[72] Later in that century, H. Petermann transcribed the *Ginza* in Mandaic letters and translated it into Latin.[73] Petermann also gave valuable accounts of Mandaean life as he saw it during his travels in the mid-nineteenth century.[74] Scholars such as Wilhelm Brandt and Richard Reitzenstein became interested in Mandaeism. [75] This was due in part to the notion that Mandaeism might belong to a hypothetical, pervasive Iranian-based Gnostic "system." The early part of the next century saw the activities of M. Lidzbarski (d. 1928), a Polish Jew who hated his own tradition, ran away from home at a young age,[76] and became the first great scholar of Mandaeism. Any scholar working in the religion today still uses Lidzbarski's translations of *John*, the liturgies, and the *Ginza*.

Spurred partly by the works of Lidzbarski, Rudolf Bultmann entered the increasingly lively scholarly arena of Mandaean studies by publishing his famous article on the Mandaean and Manichaean connections to the Gospel of John.[77] At this time scholars had swung around to entertain early Christianity as a serious arena for Gnosticism and as a competing parallel to the idea of Gnosticism's Iranian origins. Hans Jonas's magisterial work can still be consulted for its thorough overview of scholarship at that time, and his choice of Mandaean sources as Gnostic textual examples served to make known the religion's mythologies.[78] A host of scholars were engaged in what was dubbed the "Mandaean fever" of those decades; however, it must be conceded that some of the scholars harbored ideological concerns, having more or less overt religious-political axes to grind, faiths to defend, and origins to prove.[79]

Lady Ethel S. Drower (1879–1972) broke the traditional scholarly molds. A successful author and an experienced Near Eastern traveler, she was an autodidact who dwelled intermittently in Iraq and befriended Mandaeans there during four decades after the First World War. Lady Drower remains unchallenged as the primary fieldworker on Mandaeism and as the chief collector of the Mandaeans' manuscripts.[80] She remained active into her eighties. Franz Rosenthal has said that she has done more for Mandaean studies than even Lidzbarski.[81] Today, older Mandaeans still remember her fondly.

Drower's coworker in the decades-long work of producing a Mandaic dictionary was R. Macuch,[82] the primary linguist of ancient and modern Mandaic, and a tireless worker with Iranian Mandaeans on their spoken language. In 1953, he discovered, to his own and Lady Drower's delight, that spoken Mandaic, long assumed to be extinct, was still alive in parts of Khuzistan, Iran.

Another scholar dedicated chiefly to Mandaeism is the historian of religions Kurt Rudolph, whose extensive works on the religion, the tradition of its history, and its phenomenology remain authoritative. Taking his clues from the predominance of dualistic versus emanation patterns of Mandaean creation mythology and from the various terms for the Lightworld and its denizens, Rudolph has carefully sifted the different strata of the Mandaean literature, including the *Ginza*.[83] His early two-volume work on Mandaean religion remains the most thorough to date.[84] Moving competently between the Gnosticism in Nag Hammadi texts, Manichaeism, and Mandaeism, Rudolph's work has a breadth uncharacteristic of most scholars of Gnosticism. His essays on Gnosticism and late antiquity are conveniently collected in a recent volume.[85]

Any new scholar entering the field of Mandaeism will be indebted to Drower, Macuch, and Rudolph. It should also be said that the Mandaeans themselves, increasingly sophisticated about scholarly studies in their religion, take a vital interest in what outsiders say about it. Further work on the religion may therefore be expected also from the Mandaeans' own ranks.

My own study of the religion began in Norway in the middle to late 1960s, as a result of reading Hermann Hesse, Jorge Luis Borges, and Hans Jonas's massive two-volume *Gnosis*.[86] I am often asked why I study Mandaeism, and my answer is threefold: because the Mandaeans are still alive, because they have an enormous literature, and because almost nobody else studies them. From the very beginning, my concentration on Mandaeism became an exercise in the history of religions, that is, for my purposes Mandaeism serves as an example of *a* religion. Viewing any religion as a systematic ordering of experiences and knowledge of human interactions with otherworldly entities, I try to make sense of the specifically *Mandaean* way of ordering experiences and forms of knowledge.

Parameters and Purposes of the Present Work

Because the Mandaeans, unlike other Gnostics, are still alive and active in their tradition, it seems improper to write about them in the past tense. The religion's continued life demands that scholars avoid relegating them to a distant past, one in which the Mandaeans themselves have no voice. We have a scholarly, moral responsibility to duly respect these last surviving Gnostics, who can teach us much, not only about themselves but also, in a comparative perspective, about Gnostics long ago.

I do not aim to present a complete portrait of the Mandaean religion. Rather, through chosen frameworks, this book tries to show how and why Mandaeism works the way it does, in thoughtful action and practical thought. It is with an eye to Mandaeism's wider, more general usefulness as an example of how a religion creates itself that I offer what follows.

This book takes rituals seriously, for even more than in the study of mythologies, a particular danger lurks in the interpretation of rituals. It may be easy enough to trace ritual steps and segments and to undertake an immediate comparison of, say, the Mandaean repeated baptism, the maṣbuta, with Christian forms of baptism. But it is a different task to interpret the Mandaean baptism in accordance with its own cosmology and soteriology. Especially with respect to Gnostic religions—allegedly so "brainy" and intellectual—scholars have too often tended to exclude the study of rituals, as if practices were somehow scandalous.[87] In more recent years, however, scholars seem to be taking Gnostic rituals more seriously.

If rituals aim to concentrate the attention and imagination in order to create other realities and other worlds, interpreters need to grasp the Mandaean understanding of the difference between its "here," the earthly world, and its "there," the Lightworld, without leaping to automatic conclusions based on other Gnostic examples. In Mandaeism one encounters, for instance, a horror of asceticism and celibacy, characteristics commonly associated with other forms of Gnosticism. (Both features need to be rethought in Gnostic studies.) The rather muted Mandaean dualism appears less stark than one might expect in a Gnostic religion.

I view rituals as work. To explain what I mean, I will refer in the next few paragraphs to a particular focus in Martin Heidegger's analysis of the structures of understanding in *Being and Time*.[88] (Many years ago, I was a philosopher before I became a historian of religions.) People already live in a world they have understood in a preliminary sense, according to Heidegger. Understanding is, for Heidegger, a given, an "existential," a fundamental, a priori category of human existence. Understanding leads to practice, and abstract thinking constitutes a third step. Practice becomes the basis for explicit interpretation, such as conceptual thinking. But this step is not of any particular interest to religious insiders, except, perhaps, for levels of esoteric exegesis.

Not surprisingly, it is the second step, practice, that I find useful for an interpretation of rituals in Mandaeism. Rituals occur in a world that is already informed by mythology, and the ritual implements fit the religious work space. The intention of the work is circumscribed in what Heidegger calls the care structure (Sorge), which shows what the work is intended to accomplish. In the dynamics of the work, both tool and worker recede and become non-ostentatious. Theoretical contemplation of the work does not lead to completion of the work; instead, the proper, practical relation between worker and tool is essential. As supposed aliens in this world, that is, "stereotypical" Gnostics, Mandaeans seem strikingly interested in concrete tools deriving from the material world.

How is the Mandaean soteriology discernible in the ritual work? As long as the ritual proceeds according to its work rhythm, the Lightworld is accessible, made present. The tools are "ready-to-hand," as Heidegger would say. While an outsider—let's say a student—might ask why a priest is wielding a certain item or performing a particular action, the officiant does not, normally, stop in midaction to contemplate his ritual staff, for instance. He is not likely to gaze at it in a distancing manner and ask abstract questions about what it "means" or about the meaning of life. Rather, it is in the work that the existential called understanding (Verstehen) realizes itself most authentically, Heidegger would say. Ritual practice brings the already understood life-world into clear view. But students must first find out what that Mandaean world is.

Mandaean rituals are precise and complicated, rely utterly on words and deeds in tandem, and seem to demonstrate confidence about the very possibility and efficacy of ritual work. The rituals challenge any facile prejudgments about world-weary Gnostics. The priestly craft aims at overcoming distances, making the laufa (the connection between earth and Lightworld) explicit, and reconfirming it. Freeing soul and spirit takes time, and the river needs to be made ready for baptism in just the right way. Hard work requires complex work structures. These are pragmatic issues.

Familiarity and alienation exist together. In this book, I emphasize the tensions within the religion, for it is precisely the issues a religion never manages to solve fully that merit our special attention. To my mind, rituals reveal the creative tensions within Mandaeism. Polemics offer another illustration, for when Mandaeism spends much effort on restating that it does not, never did, and never will resemble certain other religions, it obviously has considerable experience with those religions. Identity is won at a cost. When Mandaeism rails against, say, Judaism and Christianity, its own contours become clearer.

Internally, a religion can tolerate paradoxes where outsiders may see only contradictions. Mandaeism never quite solves the problem of where a figure such as the creator Ptahil belongs in an ideal categorizing system of "good" and "evil," but lets him roam. Thus, Ptahil invites thought, puzzlement, and ultimately, no final answer. Where and when he appears determines how a given text evaluates him. Double-sided ʿutras are portrayed in some contexts as sinful, imperfect figures involved in the deplorable activity of world creation, and in others as lofty Lightworld beings above reproach.

Setting the stage for chosen mythological figures, the next chapter introduces a Mandaean poet. Chapters focusing on Šitil, Ruha, and Miriai follow next. Part II—on the rituals of baptism, death mass, and priest initiation—begins with a description of my visit with the Mandaeans of Iran. Interpretation issues are introduced by a chapter on the New York Mandaeans. Part III contains a chapter on solving a puzzle in *The Great "Lesser World,"* one on issues in *Exalted Kingship*, and one on Mandaean language games, and ends with a brief look at my ongoing colophon research. This, latter area is the topic of another, future book.

Because of the difficult political situations in the traditional Mandaean homelands, the chapters involving living Mandaeans have been thoroughly censored and edited, with invaluable help by Mandaean friends in many countries. I am grateful for their care in these matters, for any scholar writing about present-day Mandaeans must take current political realities very seriously. I can only hope that no Mandaean will be adversely affected by what has emerged as the final versions of the "fieldwork" chapters.

2

From Iraq to California

Grains of Musk

During a hectic lunch break at the annual meeting of the American Academy of Religion in 1991, I saw a former classmate hurrying toward me. Many years earlier, at the University of Chicago, Marcia and I had taken a course together at the Oriental Institute. Visibly excited, she said, "Jorunn, I have to talk to you; I have found the Mandaeans for you!"

"You must be kidding! Tell me! Do you have a minute?"

She did. Marcia Hermansen, then a professor at San Diego State University, told me that about forty Iraqi Mandaeans lived in San Diego and its environs. She had become a friend of the Amara family and suggested that I come to meet the Mandaeans and to give a talk in her department the next fall.

And so I did. This was the first time I met with Mandaeans in the United States. The Amara family, headed by Lamea Abbas Amara—a well-known poet in the Arab world and a former political and cultural activist—gathered together about seven Mandaean families for a potluck dinner. Every time I turned to talk to someone, more delicious food mysteriously appeared on my plate. It was a very convivial evening, with much to talk about, much to learn and enjoy. But my time was short then, and it became clear that I must return for a longer visit: That happened a year later, in December 1993.

I am sitting at the dining table in Lamea's apartment, transcribing priest lineages from her grandfather's Mandaean books—handwritten, priceless documents. The radio hums, the TV is on, other people talk, and rainwater drips from the ceiling into a bucket because the landlord has not managed to repair the roof. Lamea is on the phone, talking animatedly in Arabic with someone in Washington, D.C., about her upcoming poetry reading there.

Lamea, who is in her sixties, dark and intense, with the personality of an archaic queen, lives with her sons and her sister in San Diego.[1] They produce a magazine, *Mandaee*, mainly in Arabic, a little bit in English, which seeks to link Mandaeans all over the world and to instruct its readers about Mandaeism. The Amara family members left Iraq in increments, and they have been monitoring the events in their homeland since the Iran-Iraq war of 1980–88 and the war in the Gulf in 1991.

Lamea Abbas Amara, the poet. Photo by Jesse Buckley.

Shafia Abbas Amara, the author, and Lamea Abbas Amara. Photo by Jesse Buckley.

"I am not against anybody," explains Lamea, "but I was a leader; we were the revolution generation." She is referring to the turbulent time of 1963 in Iraq. I learn that Lamea was the only woman in the 1959 Iraqi delegation to China, where she met Mao Tse-tung and the Dalai Lama when the latter was a young man. For several years she was a UNESCO delegate to Paris, and she has known high-ranking politicians and come and gone in many embassies. She writes fiery love poems—and political ones.

"I was killed in 1963," she remarks to me one day, matter-of-factly.

"What do you mean?" I am startled. She is referring to the heady, revolutionary days of 1963, when the authorities thought they had caught Lamea but actually tortured and killed another young woman. Lamea spent the years 1979–85 in Lebanon during the war there: hiding, writing, sometimes being hungry.

I ask about the Mandaeans in Iraq, about her own and her sister Shafia's experiences, and those of her sons. Throughout the centuries—if not millennia—Mandaeans have known that political upheavals usually spell trouble for them. If a coup overturns the present system, they may become victims again. Surely, the Mandaeans suffer along with other Iraqis, as the economy during the continuing embargo is among the weakest in the world. Money is basically worthless, but a sizable number of Mandaeans in Iraq (now chiefly in Baghdad) are in the gold and diamond trade. Such assets, at least temporarily, give them something durable in a ruined economy. But many go hungry, and even those who have and deal in precious metals are often targets for robberies and killings.

Religious Origins, Neighbors, and Fences

Three suras in the Qur'an state that specified religions apart from Islam possess part of the divine truth and therefore, according to legal tradition, need not be forced to convert to Islam. Judaism and Christianity are among the specified religions, but a third group, the so-called Sabeans, has caused dispute throughout Muslim history.[2] What does the term mean? Through the centuries, Mandaeans have fallen under the umbrella "Sabeans." But the issue remains unsettled, and the relationships between the four religions are complex and subject to variations.

In the 1960s, Lamea had a Jewish couple as neighbors and friends in Baghdad. The husband, who had a high position in the Jewish community, told Lamea that after the Six Day War with Egypt and the Arab countries, when Israel had gained more territory, he was approached by some families posing as Jews. They said they had merely been pretending to be Muslims, but now they could reveal their true identity. Lameas asked, "Did you accept them as Jews?"

"Of course not. They were known to have been Muslims for many generations."

What about me, here in San Diego, among Mandaeans? Though a lapsed Lutheran, and by culture a Christian, I ponder my status. Can the family let me eat with them in their house? Yes, of course. Lamea and Shafia admit me to the kitchen, even to cook dinner. Shafia hovers around me, pencil in hand, and writes down my actions as I prepare to serve poached salmon in the Norwegian manner. They make jokes about my jar of Postum (I don't drink coffee): "Fake coffee for the fake Mandaean!" Shafia shows me how to eat Mandaean style—delicately and elegantly. I fail miserably, creating a mess trying to deal with a small quantity of rice and vegetables in my right palm while trying to push some of it with my thumb towars the tips of my index finger and middle finger. From there, I must not stick my fingers in my mouth, but use the thumb to push the food into my mouth without spilling. I give up and resort to the fork.

Morga, a tasty meat and vegetable stew, is often simmering on the stove. Rice and bread are staples, chicken with a strong, sour broth appear regularly, and sometimes spaghetti with a sauce no Italian would quite recognize. When I first met the family in 1992, Lamea gave me big packets of dates cured with sesame. The family had bought the dates in the desert and filled the back of a pickup truck lined with a sheet. The driveway at Marcia's former house may still be spotted with dates that slid off the truck bed when the fruit was hosed down after the desert expedition.

Under the sink hides a large bucket of curing olives, picked from the trees around the apartment complex. Green vegetables, salads, and fruits are always present in the apartment. I see no alcohol in the house, and nobody smokes. Lamea once wrote a thesis on the Mandaean diet, which she holds to be extremely beneficial. She attributes the long life of the priests to their healthy food. Mandaean priests keep their teeth until they die in old age, she tells me, and they do not die of cancer or heart attacks, but "from lungs," pneumonia—an understandable effect of dipping in water during the cold season.

When it is just the three of us—Lamea, Shafia, and I—Lamea sometimes hands out candy, which she hides from "the children," the boys. Gifts of sweets and cookies disappear into a cupboard, sheltered from them. Zaki, still recovering from a heart attack he had while in Jordan, is careful with his diet and brings home bags of fruits and vegetables. Zaidoun returns from a Christmas reception at the university with lots of pomegranates. *Ruman!* Gleeful, we dig in. The Americans at the party considered the fruit to be only decoration, not food.

"I never used to cook," says Lamea with a sigh, "but now I cook all the time." In Iraq, the family lived a different life, with cooks and nice cars and houses. Everything is gone; nothing can be taken for granted. At least, in America there is food. But they worry about the conditions of relatives and friends back home, the lack of food and necessities, the dizzying rate of inflation.

Zaidoun explains to me the three classes: the priest families, the regular people, and those who are considered "Gentiles." This structure still struggles with the more modern notion of treating everyone as equals. Within Mandaean priestly families, special rules obtain. Lamea tells me that when her grandmother had her period or if she had just had a child, Lamea's grandfather, the priest, would cook his own food and bake his own bread. I suddenly see the wisdom of having several wives.

Rules were not Jesus' strong suit. He made the Mandaean religion easier by relaxing the regulations, according to the prevalent Mandaean view. Originally a Mandaean, Jesus created a religion of his own. A leader, he was "an intellectual," explains Lamea, and he wanted to strengthen his position. In order to become a priest, he sought baptism from John the Baptist. Jesus knew full well that being initiated into priesthood by a prophet would have certain advantages. While not being the first prophet, John inhabits a special position as religious renewer in Mandaeism.

Neither John nor Jesus is Jewish, but Mandaean. Many Mandaeans I have met wish to discuss these two figures with me. "You wrote in your book that John was Jewish," says Lamea, disapprovingly. I admit that I did, and I explain that this is a common notion among scholars. Of course, we might be wrong—who knows! I throw up my hands, trying to balance things out, and I comment that Jesus, branching out on his own, did not do too well in Mandaean terms. But Lamea emphasizes the main point: that Jesus wanted power, and that he knew he could obtain it only through John.[3]

Issam Hermiz, my Mandaean friend in Sweden, told me years ago that Jesus wanted to be baptized by John because Jesus was already planning to start his own religion, to become an apostate from Mandaeism. But Jesus wished first to secure the salvation of his soul. The two men were cousins, and their mothers were on good terms with one another, with Mary (Miriai) helping her kinswoman. "If Mary was not a Mandaean, she could not assist her aunt," Lamea declares, and nails down her proof: "I never saw a girl from another religion come to my grandfather's house to help my grandmother. This is forbidden. She could not even come into the house."[4] So it must be right that Mary and Elizabeth came from the same religion.

The Christian Gospel tradition is criticized, for John the Baptist, given his character, could not possibly have said to Jesus, "I am not worthy of opening your shoes," Lamea claims. This is ridiculous and out of character—for John is not a humble man, but strong-minded, I am told. In fact, he even went against the power of the king (Herod) and the government. Moreover, John initially did not want to baptize Jesus, for he knew that Jesus would make the religion easy.

These days, Mandaeans may run into situations that demand ingenious responses to the question of their identity. I tell Lamea about Issam's story. Several years ago, I sat in his living room outside of Stockholm, and we talked about the eternal question of Mandaean identity: Are the Mandaeans Jewish, or what? He says he will tell me what happened to him recently because he wants to know whether I think he reacted correctly. He begins, "You know that I work for a large bank, designing computer software. At lunch time, we line up for our food trays. One day in line, the guy behind me notices my tray, and he comments, 'Why do you always get such good-looking food?' I answer, 'I don't eat meat, especially not pork.'"

Here Issam pauses briefly, making a face at the very thought of Swedish sausage, with its unspecified, unsavory contents. I cannot restrain myself but barge in, "So, he probably asks you, 'Are you Muslim?'"

Issam nods, "Exactly." And he continues, "I reply, 'No.' So the man looks at me and wants to know, 'What are you, then?' I hesitate a second, and answer, 'There are those other than Jews who do not eat pork.'" Issam implies that, in a sense, he is "half Jewish." After that occurrence, one of the bank's leaders, who is Jewish and who had heard what happened, would greet Issam with special respect when he passed him in the corridors.

In May 1994, Majid ʿArabi, a young goldsmith in the San Diego suburb of El Cajon, shows me a video of his own baptism in January of that year, when he went back to Baghdad for the first time in about fifteen years. We sit in Lamea's living room—Majid with his wife, Abir, and his little daughter, Nura, along with Lamea, Shafia, my stepson, Jesse, and myself. Majid tells me that he left Iraq, alone, in 1980 because he could see a war coming. He went first to Morocco, then to Europe, and finally to New York. Having already learned the goldsmith trade from his grandfather, Majid apprenticed himself to Jewish Hasidic gold and diamond specialists in Brooklyn. He stayed for five years before he took the bus across the country to San Diego.

Majid ʿArabi Al-Khamisi,
the goldsmith, San Diego.
Photo by Jesse Buckley.

Shafia Abbas Amara,
Majid ʿArabi Al-Khamisi,
and Lamea Abbas Amara.
Photo by Jesse Buckley.

He loved being with the Hasidim. "We are so similar! The same clothes, the same habits, the same humor—everything! I was amazed!" Majid beams.

I ask him whether the Hasidim knew he was a Mandaean, whether they knew what that meant. No, they didn't , and they didn't care, but they knew he was not a Muslim. To the Hasidim, Majid was some kind of Christian. Then Majid asks me the question he seems to have pondered for years, "Are they Mandaeans? Are we Jews?"

I shrug my shoulders and say, as so often, "Well, that's the question, isn't it? Who knows!"

Judaism, Christianity, and Islam all have a special place in their hearts for Ibrahim (Abraham). Some Mandaeans, too, see him as the first monotheist. And Lamea stresses that Mandaeism was once, long ago, an extremely widespread religion. Socrates was a Mandaean, as were many Egyptian pharaohs, and even some Roman emperors. In the middle of the excitement about the Dead Sea Scrolls, Lamea went to hear a presentation on the scrolls at San Diego State University. After the lecture, which was given by a museum director from Israel, Lamea went up to him and declared, "I am from those people who wrote the Scrolls."

Immediately, he replied, "You are from Iraq; you are a Sabean."

On the subject of identity, I ask one day, "Can you tell, in Iraq, who is Mandaean and who is not?"

Not necessarily. During the 1970s, in Sweden, Issam explained to me how Mandaeans may find out whether they are dealing with a coreligionist. A Mandaean would say something innocent, like "Do you want a cup of coffee?" to the other person but would add the word *Mandai* at the end of the sentence. If the guest would catch the word, it would mean that he is one of yours—if not, he would have concluded that you just garbled your words a bit.

Lamea tells me that her children were registered as Muslims, for protection. "We did not want them to go through the discrimination that we experienced," she says. Before 1958, Iraq had a strict quota system regarding access to higher education for minorities. The Mandaeans, being perhaps 2 percent of the population, suffered under these conditions. But after the revolution in 1958, these rules were relaxed, and many Mandaeans excelled in education. In fact, years ago I had heard that Mandaeans were considered especially intelligent, with a high percentage being doctors, engineers, intellectuals, scientists, teachers, and so on.

Zaki, Lamea's eldest son, is one of several Mandaean air pilots. Mazin, her middle son, was in the army for sixteen years, sent to a very dangerous position in the 1980–88 Iran-Iraq war because one of Mazin's superiors hated Lamea and wanted her son killed. But another superior acted in the opposite direction, for he admired Lamea and saw to it that Mazin got a desk job, safer than being at the front.

One day as I am sitting with my transcription work, Zaidoun comes in with two serious-looking weapons. "Who have you been shooting?" I inquire. "Who? Who?" he echoes, jokingly, his eyes dancing. Two dry rattlesnake skins hang on the wall above the sofa, and Lamea has told me that Zaidoun killed the snakes in the mountains. A former Iraqi champion in marksmanship, Zaidoun has been practicing target shooting. Had not Iraq been excluded (due to the war) from the 1988 Olympics, Zaidoun would have represented his country. Years before, he was sent to Yugoslavia to an international marksmanship competition and beat everyone.

Mandaeans distinguish themselves in various ways. One day a tape comes in the mail from Baghdad. Lamea and Shafia are excited and insert the tape into the little yellow boom box. The slow, sonorous voice belongs to their cousin, now the "state poet" of Iraq, directly protected by the state and living "in a palace by the river," Lamea specifies. The cousin is reading one of the *Ginza* myths about Adam's creation, in Arabic. He proclaims it solemnly, with dramatic pauses, and the echo makes it sound like he is speaking in an immense hall. The two sisters sit and listen, moved, awed. "Beautiful." After a while, they turn the tape off.

Earlier, Lamea has told me that translation of Mandaean texts into Arabic is forbidden, but that it ought to be done, and preferably by three or four people together. The secrets of the Mandaeans are in the language, says Lamea. This sounds like an exhortation to let them remain secrets. What of all the translations of Mandaean texts into European languages (I myself am guilty of one)? "Never mind!" Lamea does not care to discuss it. There seems to be some ambivalence on this point, but in the interest of cultural and religious survival and promulgation of knowledge, translations should be done, or so Lamea implies.

The conversation returns to the state poet. Lamea tells me that *she* could have been in that position, but she refused. "I don't want to owe them anything." I understand. I also learn that this cousin's privileged position presents certain problems for the Mandaeans. On the one hand, it is good to have one of their own in such a position, for it may protect the rest of the community in some sense; however, some see the man as being bought by the government.

In 1973, ten years after Lamea was "killed," she was called in to the president of Iraq, Ahmad Hassan al-Bakr. He was sitting with several of his ministers. "Do you know why we wanted you to come?"

"I don't know."

"The people love you; we need you."

"I wish you had asked about me ten years ago," Lamea replied softly.

Past and Present

Lamea recalls the house of her maternal grandfather, Sheikh Jawdat of Amara, before the Second World War. It was Sheikh Jawdat who gave her the texts that are now in her apartment. She makes a drawing for me. Around a central rectangular courtyard are arranged a *diwaniyya* (a sitting room for men); the shed for the cows and chickens; the outhouse; the *tannur* (the oven for bread baking); the kitchen, with high shelves out of reach of the children, hanging clay containers for water, and an eating area for the wintertime; and bedrooms. At the back, at one of the short ends, are a door and steps to the outside. There is also a covered terrace. In the summer, the people eat outside in the courtyard, near the garden with fruit trees and its central palm tree. As I listen and look, I think back to the fall of 1973 and the house of Sheihk Abdullah Khaffagi, in Ahwaz.

"For thirty-six hours, at *Dehwa Rabba*, New Year's, every Mandaean family locks the house and does not leave it," Lamea tells me. In advance, they have surrounded the garden with a kind of temporary fence and have sent their cows to their Muslim neighbors. The cowshed is empty, for a specific reason: if any of the family women menstruate during those thirty-six hours, they are put there. Lamea remembers her sister sitting in the cowshed, being fed by her family.[5]

Why the shut-up during the thirty-six hours? There are two explanations, says Lamea: one, it is a commemoration of a disaster; two, at New Year's, for that day and a half, all the *natri* (watchers) go up to the Lightworld. Therefore, the earth is left without protection, without guardians, and it is dangerous to venture outside.[6] People must not touch anything that grows during this time. Because the natri are off duty, only food that is already secured and protected can be prepared and eaten within the household limits. The information about menstruous women is new to me, and I see it as an understandable strategy in a challenging situation. Blood is, after all, usually impure. But because no Mandaean may go outside during this feast, the girl must be sequestered within a specific area.

The palm tree in the middle of the garden is of special importance at any time, not just during the feast. Shamash, the sun, shows the time by the palm tree's shadow, Lamea informs me. "Oh, it is time to milk the cow! It's time to bake the bread!" She adds, "Without Shamash, there is no life. A house into which Shamash does not enter is a poor house. When he leaves at sunset, there is no ceremony, for without the sun, they cannot do any prayer." Priests have long beards and hair in order to resemble Shamash, says Lamea.

What is up there; who is up there, of and among the heavenly bodies? After a while, I learn not to ask too many questions about the dead. It is a difficult problem for Mandaeans in U.S. exile who, then still without priests, cannot have proper death rituals. In fact, my first question to Lamea was: How do you die in this country? Before I came to San Diego, an elderly couple had returned to Iraq to die, despite the situation there. No Mandaean had yet died in the San Diego community as of December 1993. But what will happen when someone does? Lamea says that she has a *rasta* (ritual garment), and "the men will be *hallal*is [laymen who assist with the dead] and take care of the person." Lamea points to a vase on the table and says, "I have myrtle for the *klila* [wreath]." In New York City, I hear, the Mandaeans rely on the Roman Catholic Church and on the rental of grave plots. In San Diego, the local Chaldean priest has so far refused to marry Mandaeans. This is a painful situation, as the Mandaeans feel close to Christianity.

Early on in my relationship with Lamea, she still had her dream of a Mandaean ceremonial center in Florida. It was to be on a river, with a *mandi* (community center) and a priest: she envisioned baptisms, marriages, and ceremonies for the dead taking place there. So far, there are no such centralized solutions.[7] I express my worry about the fate of Mandaean souls, where they might be now. But Lamea prefers not to talk about it, not because she does not worry but probably because the problem is so immense.

In a related conversation, Lamea lays out her views on the soul and of afterlife. "The soul is never destroyed," she begins, then describes paradise, the Lightworld, as a peaceful place of abundant food, music, fresh breezes, and no need to communicate by talking, for everybody knows what the others want. "There is a person like me waiting for me. She is waiting, very happy to embrace me when I come—I have a poem about it.

Here, on earth, we live only temporarily, as in a prison; it is a suffering place. But we are going to a beautiful place. Everything and everybody have a heavenly counterpart; trees, too."

"Trees?" I interrupt. "How about this chair?"

"Yes."

"Really?"

"Yes, because you carry it in your imagination. You will carry it with you." She continues, "When you die, your soul goes back to its origin. The soul is given to the child by God. And at the end of life, the beginning becomes the end—like a big pot of water. The water always moves; it is a never-ending cycle."

The various names of God—El, Adonai, and the rest—are just names, but God is one, Lamea explains. I ask, "Are there women also?" "Yes, Simat Hiia!" She protects children and their mothers, like Astart (Astarte/Ishtar). As we discuss Ishtar, Lamea informs me that the gate of Babel was really the gate of Ishtar, and before that it was the gate of El. The gate is still there, and the temples of Hammurabi and Nebuchadnezzar, too. Both have been restored.

Some years ago, I am told, the Iraqi government announced an award for the best answers to the question of how the famous hanging gardens of Babylon were watered. "Everybody started to think," says Lamea. "Of course, in those days in Babylon, there were no machines." We ponder the engineering problem, and I suggest a line of a thousand people with buckets. "Perhaps," Lamea replies, without much conviction. She points out that you need water only at certain times of the year. The government picked out 200 answers as the best, but I forgot to ask whether they all got rewards.

As I sit at the dining table for eight days transcribing priest lineages from Lamea's books, I am doing my own kind of dipping into that vast Mandaean wellspring: the lists of names. Filling page after page, muttering names and comparing lineages, I sometimes recognize a name and its lineage and exclaim, "Aha! I know him!" The family members come and go, peering at my work. Lamea writes up a report for her magazine on what I am doing. After I explain my work to Zaidoun, he says quietly, "May Manda d̲-Hiia help you!" I ask Shafia what these hundreds of priests in past generations would think if they knew what I was doing. She has just been wondering about this, and she has decided that they would be very pleased and bless me.

Bowls of olives and cups of Postum break the work, and I try to keep a safe distance between any food or liquid and the sacred books. Guests wander by and throw a glance at the text, asking, "You read *that*?" I feel a tinge of sacrilege handling the books, taking them out of and wrapping them back into their cotton cloth bags, sifting the grains of musk that have been put into the bags to keep the books enveloped in the ruha d̲-Hiia, the breath of Life.

I notice that Majid, on the evening when we watch his baptism video, reverently inhales the aroma of and kisses one of the *Ginzas* as it passes through his hands. He says he must be clean to handle it. I wonder about myself, and about my stepson, Jesse, who is with me on this occasion to meet the family and to take photographs. With a freshly hatched bachelor's degree from the University of California at Berkeley's anthropology department, Jesse is allowed to see and handle the books. He marvels at the clash of cultures: while the rocker Cindy Lauper prances and sings on TV, he carefully leaves through sacred scripture of an awesome kind.

Priests and Goldsmiths

Lamea's ancestor Sheikh Mohi is considered a saint by both Muslims and Mandaeans. He worked miracles, even after his death. Once he stopped a flood in the river al-Aqiqa, near Nasoriyah. The flood rose, people piled up sandbags, and the Muslims called on their holy men, but to no avail. Then they called on the name of Sheikh Mohi, and the flood stopped immediately. In gratitude, the Muslims built a saint's memorial for him.

Right after Sheikh Mohi died, his grieving sister tried to take the dust from his grave. Throwing herself on the grave, she became practically glued to it, and people tried in vain to pull her away. When she finally got loose, she apologized to Sheikh Mohi for her excessive display of grief and promised to mourn for the dead in a more respectful manner. Lamea assures me that there were reliable eyewitnesses to this scene.

I hear a story about a family quarrel, a priest lineage fight, many years ago. Lamea begins:

> When the ganzibra died, several men in the family wanted to take his place. One side of the family said, "It is our turn." So, one of theirs became the ganzibra. But this was contested. It is forbidden for the Mandai to kill somebody, so the slighted side of the family gave money to an outsider to kill the new priest. But the stranger does not know who the priest is, he only knows that his house is on the river. So, he waits for him nearby. And the sheikh appears, with a family member. As he is about to jump into a small boat, his wife calls on her husband by name, "You forgot something!" Then the stranger knew who he was, and he shot him with a big shotgun.

Lamea pauses, looking at me intently. "Now you know that the man who was shot is a ganzibra. And he must not die with his blood. They change his white clothes, the rasta, seven times. He is still bleeding. It is forbidden to die like this. And the rasta must be pure and white. With the eighth rasta, there is no blood, and he dies."

She continues. "The dead man's brother swears and decides to kill somebody from that side of the family. He wears wool—very rough, instead of cotton—and he will wear it and not change it until he has avenged the murder. The people complain to the local sheikh of the Muslims, and the brother is put in jail. The heavy chains on hands and feet, the big ball of iron, in a room without a window.

"Because the prisoner is a priest, he is allowed to get food from his family. One of his cousins comes with food. The priest asks the boy to bring him a knife hidden in the food, in the bread, a small knife. He gets it, digs through the night with the knife, through the wall, one meter thick. He puts his wool dress, his *abaya*, on his head, with the iron chain. It is winter. He crosses the river, the Euphrates, swimming. He comes to the sheikh of the other Muslim tribe, on the other side of the river, and he says to him, '*Dahilek*! I am in your protection!'

"The sheikh looks at him, sees the ball and chain, and notices that the abaya is not wet. It is early dawn, very cold—so, so cold. 'The man who crossed the Euphrates without wetting his abaya, carrying the heavy chain and comes to me—nobody shall touch him! I send all my men, no one shall kill such a man,' says the sheikh. He asks, 'What do you want?' 'I want to go home.'

Lamea explains to me that he had been in jail in another town. "They opened the chain on him. He had not eaten. They sent some men and a horse with him to take him home.

"Back there, he saw a dream. He saw his brother, the dead man, who said to him, 'Brother! Go to your normal life. Don't avenge the murder. The sheikh (on the slighted side of the family) will never have sons who can become priests.'"

Lamea stops for dramatic impact, then adds, "Till now, it's true. Someone was blind, handicapped, and nobody could become sheikh." She continues, "'I will do it for you,' explained the dead man to his brother." Finally, Lamea adds, "When the sheikh was killed, the women cut their long, long hair—their curls—and put them on long strings at home, like Ishtar did when Tammuz died and Ishtar asked the women to cut their hair."

Mostly, it is outsiders, not insiders, who may present dangers to the Mandaeans. When Lady Drower tried to make contact with Lamea's grandfather, Sheikh Jawdat, and his family, he warned them, "Don't tell your secrets to the stranger!" Drower, somewhat naively, felt that the Mandaeans should claim their own territory, as did the Assyrians, who in the 1930s rebelled in the north of Iraq, wanting their own state. "Very dangerous," says Lamea.

In the seventeenth century, the Portuguese military forced Mandaean men to do military service in the colonial wars. Coming to the Mandaean silversmith shops, the Portuguese asked who they were. They replied that they were followers of John the Baptist. A good number of Mandaeans were sent to Sri Lanka (then Ceylon). Now we—Lamea, Shafia, and I—wonder what happened to the Mandaeans there. No one ever heard from these men again. We ponder whether they were absorbed into the Ceylonese population, converted, or whether any remained separate, all alone?

"And why have you become a Mandai?" a Palestinian Christian friend of the family asks me, inclining his head with a sincere expression. He is an elderly man, and we have been invited to his house for a lavish dinner. He asks politely, with curiosity. "I am not," I reply. "It is not possible to convert, not permitted." This is surprising news to him. Lamea does not explain the matter; she just smiles. As we are about to eat, Lamea makes the sign of the cross. I ponder this. The next day I ask her about it. "Oh, I often do that. It cannot hurt. For example, on an airplane, I do it."

One evening we go to Majid's to see a video of a very popular Baghdadi singer who recently came to San Diego to entertain the Arabic community. Majid was one of the sponsors. Lamea and Shafia are riveted to the screen, while Zaki and Zaidoun watch with expressions of interest mixed with critical distance. The slightly effeminate singer wears a yellow suit and, confident in his popularity, an expression half bashful, half defiant. Men in the audience come up to him while he is singing to shower him with money. He stands in a rain of green. In the car, on the way home, the singer's merits are hotly debated. I ask about music and dance, behaviors repudiated in traditional Mandaeism. No, Mandaeans are not entertainers.

Still, Mandaeans dance. Majid has another video, this one of the party thrown for him when he came back to Baghdad after fifteen years. Women are by themselves, talking and smiling. The men dance, and Majid, looking happy, moves in the middle of a group of them. The atmosphere is festive, Majid being treated as a long-lost son. "These are my relatives," he lets me know as he points to the screen. "All of them?" I ask, incredulously. "Oh, these are just two hundred or so!" The dancing? "They have to behave like Arabs when they party. Otherwise, it will be seen as a possible political club—not good," Lamea explains.

Lamea, Shafia, and I form our own club of sorts. Lamea dubs the three of us "the golden girls," after the trio on TV. On a snack break while visiting Mandaean goldsmiths in the suburbs of San Diego, we are sitting in a shop that sells frozen yogurt. We compare our ages; I am the youngest. Lamea assures me, "When you are fifty, you'll be pure; no more period."

I think of purity, food, and marriage. The young men we meet, the goldsmiths, are married to Mandaean women. The first time I met Lamea and her family, at the potluck dinner, a couple of strikingly pretty young mothers came with their babies. Baby girls wear tiny gold armlets and earrings. Gold is the metal of the soul, says *Exalted Kingship*. The danger of extinction does not seem imminent for the artisans of the young generation, although many think that the Mandaean identity will soon dissolve, mainly through intermarriage.

The young goldsmiths seem to thrive. One, Zahir Ghanim, used to be a jewelry and gem buyer for the department store Marshall Fields in Chicago before he set up his own business outside San Diego. On my first evening in San Diego, his wife presents me with a fine pair of silver earrings. In Khalid's newly opened shop, we wait by the mirror-covered wall until the meaty, rich-looking Nestorian is finished with his Christmas purchases. He is in no hurry, sipping coffee from a styrofoam cup. After passing a fan of green money across the counter, he leaves with a plastic shopping bag full of gold. People from the Orient tend to support each other in business. While we wait, I survey the selection of religious merchandise. There is something for us all: curvy, elaborate gold pendants with Allah's name for the Muslims, stars of David for the Jews, gold crosses and demure Madonnas for the Christians, and Babylonian lions and gates of Ishtar for everybody.

But in the small shop of an older man, Amjed Bahur, a real *'ustad*, a craftsman, I feel transported back to Iran. Here is the kind of jewelry seldom seen—handmade, with striking designs. Later, I learn that he is among the few here in America who knows the old, secret recipe for the Mandaean trademark in jewelry, which is the black dye, *mina*, used on silver to make miniature landscapes, marsh scenes with boats and palm trees, or abstract, geometric patterns. I admire a tiny, beautifully made gold dagger in its scabbard and pull out the miniature weapon, not quite the length of my thumbnail. I recall a piece of jewelry I saw in a Mandaean shop in Ahwaz in 1973, a gold ring holding a perfect, tiny bull's head, with horns, nostrils, eyes and all. Mr. Bahur gives me a blue fajence bead, just arrived from Baghdad. I wear it on a gold chain, alternating it with a drabša (Mandaean banner), a present from Majid. Later, when I meet Mr. Nasser Sobbi in New York, he gives me a silver drabša to keep on my key chain. Protective charms are piling up.

In October 1994, Lamea came to give a poetry reading at the Islamic Center in Sharon, Massachusetts. We dressed up and went, my husband and I, being among the few Westerners at the event. Lamea looked regal, in a black chiffon gown with gold embroidery, and our gaze was drawn to her sparkling gold choker with a large ruby gem set at the center of her throat. We sat at round tables, ate glorious Middle Eastern food, listened to live music—tabla, oud, and qanoon—and engaged in conversations.

Lamea's performance was videotaped. She sat at a table on the stage with a young woman who read some of Lamea's poetry in English translation, while other poems were given in Arabic only. Looking intently at the audience and leaning toward the microphone, Lamea cast a spell on all, and people clapped, laughed, sighed, or drew in their breath sharply as if they had been stabbed—all according to the content of the poems. An Iraqi woman at our table was overcome and had to run outside to cry. During breaks, a gentleman looking like a retired Harvard professor walked around the room happily snapping his fingers. At the end, an elderly woman stood up and thanked Lamea, saying that the event had brought back her childhood memories of the Arab immigrants to the United States. They used to spend evenings in each other's homes reciting Arabic poems. "Why don't we do that anymore?" she asked wistfully.

Still breathing the atmosphere of poetry, people seemed reluctant to face the night air outside.

3

Šitil

An Example of "the Image Above and Below"

It was in Lamea's house that I first became familiar with the coexistence of Mandaean mythology, history, and the present day. We moved relatively effortlessly between horizons of time and space. The dynamics somehow resembled that of many Mandaean mythological figures, those who travel between realms, hard to pin down, resistant to stasis.

Scholars of Gnosticism have paid scant attention to the Mandaean Šitil. In his book on Seth, A. F. J. Klijn offers only a one-page mention of him,[1] and other investigators interested in the scholarly construct called "Sethian Gnosticism" devote little space to Šitil.[2] To me, it seems odd that an attempt to create a tradition history of Seth in his Gnostic permutations would bypass the Mandaean Šitil. As an emblem of the movable image, he appears to cross divine-demiurgic-human boundaries.

"In the name of Hibil, Šitil, and Anuš" is a recurring formula in Mandaean prayers and other texts. All three brothers are ʿutras, sometimes seen as belonging in three different generations. Less flashy than his two brothers, Šitil engages in no glorious battles or grand salvific schemes, such as Hibil does, nor does he become involved in healing and preaching competitions with Jesus (one of Anuš's specialties).

And yet, Šitil is the purest of all souls. The souls of departed Mandaeans enter the scales of Abatur on their way to the Lightworld. Weighed against Šitil's soul, which sits on the right side of the scales, an ascending soul is tested. If it is found to be as light and as sinless as Šitil, the soul may continue unimpeded to the Lightworld on a ship of light across the river that surrounds the world.[3] If the soul is found wanting, it enters into a suitable maṭarta for further purification.

How did Šitil obtain this role as the purest of all souls? *GL* 1, 1, tells the story.[4] The section starts with a poem emphasizing the utter stability of the Lightworld and its denizens. Next, Hibil, Šitil, and Anus are held up as illustrious examples of such stability. They are Mandaeans—the text calls them "our brothers"—and at the same time their ʿutra status is unmistakable. They give alms generously, and they remain unshaken in the face of the trials and tribulations of the earthly world, Tibil, which is lit up by their presence.

The Great Life, the primary entity on the pinnacle of the Lightworld, dwelling in its own splendor, ponders and decides that it is time for the death penalty, for the first earthly man to ascend to his origins. Adam, the first man, is a thousand years old and ought to return home before he becomes senile. Firm in its determination, the Great Life summons the angel of death, Ṣauriel Qmamir Ziwa, "'Death' he is called in the world, but 'Kušṭa' ('Truth') by the knowledgable ones, those who know of him," reads the text.[5] Ṣauriel, who cannot be bribed and who accepts no substitutes, descends to Adam with the Great Life's message. Adam becomes enraged, spits bitterness on the earth, and refuses to go. He screams, beats his breast, and insists that it is customary to eat the younger, tastier, green parts of a plant first, so why should he die now?

The angel returns to the Great Life with the embarrassing report—which the Great Life, in its omniscience, already knows. The Great Life further strengthens its request to Adam, and Ṣauriel again descends with the message. Adam wants to live for another thousand years and suggests a substitute: his youngest son, Šitil, who is only eighty, has never slept with a woman, consequently has no offspring, and is innocent of bloodshed. Ṣauriel travels back up with this report, and the Great Life agrees to take Šitil instead. The angel of death calls to him, "O Šitil, son of Adam! Up with you! Die, as if you never existed, and depart, as if you were never created! For your soul is wanted for the *kana*,[6] by the great first parental house, and by the place where she [i.e., the soul] formerly dwelled."[7]

Ṣauriel explains the matter of substitution to Šitil, who, though somewhat taken aback, dares not oppose the will of the Great Life and agrees to die instead of his father.

In preparation for his ascent, Šitil prays and sheds his body of blood and flesh before he puts on a garment of radiance and a turban of light. Gleaming more brilliantly than the sun and the moon Šitil soars upward, taken by winds and storms up to a cloud of light, where he prays, entreating the Lightworld beings to let his father, Adam, see the glories that he, Šitil, now beholds. He asks them to remove the blinders from Adam's eyes, the plugs from his ears, and the fleshy nature of his heart so that Adam may gaze at the upper world. Šitil's wish is granted. Adam sees, is amazed, calls out to his son, and wishes to die immediately.

But he may not. Now Šitil takes a stern, rebuking role toward his father, declaring that no one may decide on the hour of death. Šitil uses eloquent rhetoric. Nobody swallows spittle already spat, he declares, and a fetus does not reenter the womb. In fact, Šitil claims to be such an untimely abortion, because he had to leave the earth prematurely, like an infant with its mouth full of milk, like a bride taken away during the wedding. Then, Šitil ascends further upward and at the end declares that the perfect people will imitate him by going on the same path that he has broken to the light.

Thus, Adam's young son becomes the first man to die and the first one to ascend to the Lightworld from Tibil. One notes how the story changes the relationship between Adam and Šitil, for while the son is still on earth, he plays the role of obedient son, but when he has risen to the light, he scolds his father. The reversals upset the expected pattern, for the first man, Adam, should be the first one to depart from the world. Despite the assurances that Ṣauriel accepts no bribes or substitutes, just the opposite has taken place, and the first death became the first vicarious death. Šitil's purity above all other humans is ensured because he died instead of his father.

It is also because of his death that the Mandaean tradition elevates him from human to ʿutra status. In this way, the *GL* story shows the conjunction of two different traditions, one in which Šitil is human, and one in which he is an ʿutra. However, we might just as well say that Mandaean texts assume a characteristic doubleness in Šitil. This doubleness is the mark of the Mandaean idea of the dmuta, the image. Far from being a merely abstract idea, the term *dmuta* conveys a dynamic relationship between the earthly image and its Lightworld counterpart. More precisely, the Lightworld image dwells in Mšunia Kušṭa, the world of ideal counterparts, which is a specific section of the Lightworld. The earthly image can only function insofar as it is energized by its dmuta in the upper world.

Everything, every human being and all ʿutras, seems to have such an image. What one might expect of a given mythological figure characterized by great mobility depends on where that figure happens to be at any moment. Due to the dmuta, the figure's identity is constant, but the figure may show itself as positive or negative depending on location and on the company it keeps. There is an underlying Mandaean psychological idea at work here, for personality traits may vary, but the fundamental, dmuta-given identity remains constant. Therefore, one should proceed cautiously in assigning any Mandaean ʿutras definite designations like "positive" or "negative." It is all a matter of circumstances. Plots thicken if an ʿutra usually encountered in unblemished Lightworld environments suddenly becomes entangled in world creation.

Only rarely does Šitil turn up in cosmogonic settings. But one of the tractates in *John* gives a world creation myth featuring Hibil, Šitil, Ptahil, and Ayar (personified Ether) as creators.[8] Ptahil is the only figure one would expect to find in such a work crew, for the three others are usually cast in roles of revealers and saviors, not as creators. But here things are different. As Hibil builds up a moat, measures out the water, and divides it into channels, a fifth figure, Šihlaun, enters the work stage. He addresses Hibil and Ayar, calling them "his brothers," but he mocks their plans, listing all the things they will be unable to perform correctly. After Šihlaun's long harangue, Ptahil (usually the prototypical world creator) steps up and says to him:

> I will form the solidification, and Ayar shall hover over it. I will shovel away the black waters, and Hibil shall make a hollow for it.
>
> I will create the earth, and we shall bring the garment from ʿUr.[9] Hibil and Šitil shall spread out the roof of the tent.[10]

Šihlaun becomes enraged, strikes Ptahil, and curses him, literally saying, "Who do you think you are?"

Nevertheless, all the ʿutras (except for Šihlaun) take their part in the creation, as Ptahil proposed, and more. Šitil and Hibil create the hollow for the waters, and Šitil makes the heavenly spheres. There are further details about the division of the construction, which is completed to satisfaction. Then arises the question of overseers, and the sons of Yušamin[11] are installed to watch over and light up the world. Somewhat surprisingly, his sons are said to be the planets (at least in part), but they are not demonized. Only after eighty years, when Yušamin's sons tire of their job, are the *real* planets brought in to take over their function.

Several elements deserve comment in this story. One notes, first, that the ʿutras are quarreling among themselves, that they are not battling against demonic forces. The creation itself is seen as a positive event. Only Šihlaun criticizes it, and he is silenced. The story looks like a spoof of the usual Gnostic pattern, according to which the creation of the world is deplored. Even when the planets arrive to replace Yušamin's sons, there is no hint of any negative comment. The story illustrates the flexibility of the dmuta idea, for while ʿutras are involved on earth—or in the realm of the-earth-to-be—they may seem almost human, subject to emotions, hard at work with matter, and significantly untainted by it. Had they been portrayed within the geography of the Lightworld as lofty revealers, their personalities would have been displayed in a different manner.

In descending order, the three main Mandaean creator ʿutras usually are Yušamin, Abatur, and Ptahil. All three have complex double personalities, which are negative or positive depending on where they show up, what they are doing, and how the given myth evaluates their actions. Because of the Mandaean ambivalence regarding creation, one can find creation myths where the act is positive, negative, or undecided in terms of worth. The exuberant wealth of different Mandaean creation myths demonstrates a particular point: that these are worth telling over and over, in manifold varieties. Consequently, the evaluation of the actors in these myths also varies.

Yušamin is both a Lightworld ʿutra beyond reproach and the prototype of a priest who has made mistakes in ritual. As such he is called Yušamin the Peacock, characterized by his excessive pride. Abatur is Abatur Rama, "the Lofty," and also ḏ-Muzania, "of the Scales," which refers to his detested job as guardian of the scales, where souls are weighed. Abatur was forced into this job as punishment for his involvement in the creation, and he will have to continue in this position, though complaining bitterly, until the end of the world. Ptahil, insufficiently instructed by his father, Abatur, in how to create the world (according to one myth), suffers for his mistakes. All three are jailed in separate maṭartas for the duration of the earth.

Usually the triumvirate Hibil, Šitil, and Anuš are portrayed as saviors less than as creators. But the story in *John* serves to warn readers not to draw fast, facile conclusions based on expectations of creator versus savior ʿutras. If the creation, as in this rather unusual myth, is not a problem, the creators in it may escape unscathed. However, Šitil always seems to be above reproach, for in no story, that I know, does he become tainted. His purity and vicarious death in the *GL* story show a rare human being, virtually sinless. Unlike some other ʿutras, for instance, his older brother Hibil,[12] Šitil never complains like a lost Gnostic soul on earth.

It is interesting to contemplate Abatur, as the personified scales, whose position as judge might otherwise seem a powerful one. But in the Mandaean view, Abatur's position is a form of punishment, a thankless, contemptible task. One is invited to imagine Abatur tortured by his job of weighing souls, constantly forced to behold the spotless Šitil in the right scale, constantly reminded of his own lost purity. Šitil is, of course, superior to everyone, including his own father. *1012* stresses Šitil's unique position, stating that Šitil represents the soul, vision, and the yardna, while Adam is body and blood, darkness of the eyes, and earth.[13] Further exalting Šitil, the text calls him "father of mysteries and of all kings, and father of souls, (and) of constructed things."[14]

According to Mandaean teaching, there are four world ages, and each one has a Lightworld guardian and a human couple as caretakers. Each world epoch ends in destruction, by epidemics, fire, and water. We are now living in the last, evil age, supervised by the ʿutra Anuš and by Noah with his wife. When this age has spent itself, the world will finally be annihilated. Šitil guarded the second age, and it was under his leadership that the true *Naṣoraeism* (*naṣiruta*, i.e., the priestly-level knowledge in

Mandaeism) established itself.[15] From what we have seen of Adam's career in the *GL* story, it is no wonder that *his* guardianship over the first world age was seen as less than perfect. The son, rather than the father, is the measure of perfection.[16]

Still, Adam possesses two sides, for Mandaean texts testify both to an Adam Kasia, "the hidden Adam," who is a Lightworld being, and to the earthly one, Adam Pagra, the bodily Adam. Šitil, son of Adam—despite this appellation—is the same as Šitil, the ʿutra.[17] The striking difference in the portrayal of the two figures, Adam and Šitil, is that no hint of negativity appears regarding the latter.

Adam and Šitil both have masiqtas (death-masses) named after them. Mandaeism has many kinds of masiqtas.[18] A masiqta of Šitil is required at specific unclean deaths. These include: for a priest who dies without his tiny myrtle wreath (klila); for a woman who dies on or after the seventh day after childbirth; or for anyone dying during the thirty-six hours of seclusion on New Year's Eve.[19] In the case of someone dying in one place and being buried in another, both the masiqta of Adam and the one of Šitil are required.[20] There is also a specific baptism of Šitil, obligatory for a defiled priest, for one who has unwittingly officiated at a marriage in which the woman was not a virgin, and at a baptism of an infant who died during the proceedings.[21] One notes that in the baptism examples, the specified pollution concerns the priest, not the person for whom the ritual is performed.

The references to Šitil in the particular instances of the two major Mandaean rituals, masiqta and baptism, may be quite incidental to the topic of Šitil himself. Or it may be that the impurities requiring his masiqta are considered to be particularly severe. In any case, Šitil's main role is that of ʿutra, and he marks the ideal of purity because of his death, as told in the *GL* story. I have presented him here as an example of the dynamic workings of the idea of the dmuta (the image above and below). Being undeniably "good," Šitil, whether in his human or in his Lightworld aspect, possesses traits associated with both realms, and his duality does not run along a predictable "good-evil" axis. As a contrast to Šitil, I will in the next chapter present another double-sided figure, Ruha. Much more dramatic than Šitil—and, unlike him, much maligned—Ruha plays a decisive role in the creation of the world. In a marked departure from most traditional treatments of Ruha, I concentrate on her ambiguous aspects, even leaning toward her positive traits.

4

Ruha

Mandaeism presents Ruha (Spirit) largely as a leader of the forces of darkness opposing those of the Lightworld. Traditionally, most scholars have labeled her as evil, and it is true that she possesses abundant negative traits. One of her epithets is Ruha d̲-Qudša (Holy Spirit), a devalued Christian Holy Spirit, it seems. A mistress of the detested Jewish god Adonai, Ruha is also the mother of the malignant zodiac spirits and of the planets.

Still, there are good reasons to see Ruha as a fallen wisdom figure, resembling Sophia (Wisdom) in other Gnostic traditions. Mandaean materials testifying to such a view of Ruha include passages in which she speaks and behaves in ways one would not expect of a force hostile to the Lightworld. She displays dramatic mood swings, suffers, and utters revelatory speeches uncharacteristic of a figure of darkness. Instead of seeing these passages as atypical occurrences thwarting a scholarly, imposed negative pattern, I think it is useful to take them as clues to Ruha's own ambivalence and to her ambiguous personality. This chapter, therefore, offers a sustained examination of the stories in which Ruha appears as ambiguous or in a downright positive light. Four sets of mythological traditions, taken from a variety of texts, will serve to illustrate my point.

Hibil Ziwa's Descent into the Underworld

GR 5, 1, tells a long, dramatic story of the ʿutra Hibil Ziwa (Radiance) traveling to the underworld.[1] Before the creation of the earthly world, Tibil, disturbing rumors reach the Lightworld, for underworld forces plan to wage war against the Light. Hibil is sent out on a mission to find out whose plan it is and to prevent the attack. Descending from the Lightworld, the well-equipped Hibil begins a long and dangerous journey down through the lofty spheres and the spaces of what is not yet Tibil, to the seven underworlds. In the first of those seven worlds, he encounters Ruha. The text gives no information as to why she is there or whether this is indeed her home. Hibil stays with Ruha for a thousand myriad years, though hidden from her view. Then he continues downward through the worlds, accomplishing his task of subjecting the dark forces in each of those regions. At the bottom, he vanquishes the great flesh mountain, Krun, whose digestive system is destroyed as Hibil, clad in a suit of armor full of knives, sabers and sharp points, hurls himself into his mouth.[2]

After Hibil has forced Krun to give him a kind of passport containing mystical powers, Hibil turns his way upward. Just before he reaches Ruha's world again, he steals two objects that contain the strength of the darkness: *mrara ugimra*, (bitterness and jewel). Invisible, he arrives in Ruha's world as she is about to be married to her brother, the demon Gaf. Disguised as a demon, Hibil impresses Qin, Ruha's mother, who gives him her other daughter, Zahriel, in marriage. But the ʿutra does not consummate the marriage nor touch the demons' food. He tricks Qin into revealing certain darkness secrets to him, secrets hidden in a mirror. Stealing the mirror, Hibil disguises himself as Ruha's husband, Gaf, faces her, and proclaims, "Up! We will travel to your parents!" She is surprised and asks where the parents are. Hibil says that they live in the world just above.[3]

This is a remarkable exchange, for it implies that Ruha's real parents are not those she imagined. Of course, Hibil may be lying. He forsakes Zahriel and takes Ruha upward, and a kafkaesque journey ensues. Ruha is anxious, for the journey seems endless, and Hibil's answers to her questions remain unenlightening. Furthering Ruha's desperation, Hibil does not bring her to her parents but, having locked the doors of the underworld behind him, imprisons Ruha in a world of her own. Here she spends myriads of years, pregnant by Gaf with ʿUr, the dragon monster. On and off, Hibil visits her, only to confuse her even more. Now it seems that Hibil's parents are hers, too, and Hibil says that they do not want to see him, their own son. Utterly bewildered, Ruha curses the parents but yearns for them, too.

In another text, Hibil explains why Ruha, at this stage, is unfit to see her parents, "How can we rise up towards my Parents, when these creatures that I brought are not like Us, nor is their appearance radiant like that of the uthras, the children of light? My Parents will not now desire to have them in Their presence!"[4] To continue with *GR* 5,1: Ruha hopes that her dragon son will be able to free her from her misery, but she has to wait. Hibil pays her another tactical visit, and before she gives birth to ʿUr, Hibil's father in the Lightworld commends the actions of the Light forces, declaring, "Had we not done this and had you not organized things, we would have been unable to cope with ʿUr and his mother."[5] It is clear that Ruha and her son must be kept under strict control.

Haran Gawaita speaks of four creations, two male and two female, that Hibil carried away from the underworld,[6] and *1012* identifies the "egg" (*hilbuna*), Ruha, with "bitterness and jewel," stating that the power of the darkness was lacking from the day that Hibil carried away the hilbuna.[7] Ruha, then, is the entity incorporating the powers of darkness, which the Lightworld had to conquer. Her world of imprisonment is called "the world of Lacking,"[8] and here she must dwell until the creation of the earthly world begins to unfold.

ʿUr wonders why Ruha's parents seem to close the door in the face of their own daughter, and Ruha herself is stricken by doubt, "Am I such a one?—I am searching and pondering everything."[9] Mother and son desperately try to escape, but to no avail. Finally, Ruha shows her son a magic mirror in which he beholds the upper and lower worlds. Now he feels a great yearning to fight the Light that he has seen in the mirror.

But Ruha has drawn different conclusions from the vision in the mirror, and she urges him to wage war against the darkness instead.[10]

Hibil now appears and wrests the mirror from Ruha, who bewails her loss, feeling her powers of sorcery and magic waning. Hibil then defeats ʿUr and chains him. Mother and son lament his fate, but Hibil consoles Ruha, emphasizing that ʿUr, not Ruha, is his enemy. He tells Ruha to remain where she is. It is interesting that Hibil does not intend to destroy Ruha. He obviously has other plans for her; otherwise it would seem strange that he brought her up from the underworld. So, still stuck in her limbolike world, Ruha stays put, awaiting further notice of possible liberation.

The Creation of Tibil and of the Human Beings

Drower observes that "the visit of Hibil Ziwa to the world of darkness resulted eventually in the creation of the material world and of humanity."[11] Hibil's removal of Ruha from the underworld indicates that this is not her proper place and that she incorporates certain powers necessary for the next stage of development, the creation of the world and of people, both of which will possess some of her essence, the spirit. This is why she is such a crucial figure in what follows.

In *GR* 3, a large creation account, we find a description of the interactions between Ptahil and Ruha, the two main agents in the world's creation. Uneasy as collaborators, each strives to remain in charge, and when Ptahil feels his strength subside, Ruha swells in hers. Ptahil has come down from the Lightworld to play his role as creator, but already on leaving his lofty home, he anxiously senses how the "living fire" in him abates. Unsettled, he asks, "As I am a son of the Great One, why has the living fire in me changed?"[12]

Ruha and ʿUr are still jailed,[13] but now mother sleeps with son in order to liberate him. After seven days she bears the seven planets, whose aspect displeases her: "I requested, but it was not given to me; what I wanted did not come about; none of them resembles the others."[14]

Meanwhile, Ptahil is doing his best to create the earth, but he fails, for it will not solidify.[15] Ruha observes his failure, sleeps with ʿUr again, and produces the twelve zodiac spirits. But they are not what she hoped for, and again she laments, wishing that they would have looked like Ptahil. Events roughly repeat themselves for a third time, Ruha now giving birth to the five planets (sun and moon not included). She dislikes them and complains that she has lost her sorcery powers. Furthermore, the sexual activity has failed to liberate ʿUr, too. So far, then, *GR* 3 has emphasized both Ptahil and Ruha as unsuccessful creators.

The next project is the creation of the first human being. The planets and Ptahil manage to create Adam, but he cannot stand up on his two feet, for the powers of his creators are insufficient. The lacking element is the soul, which Ptahil and the planets are unable to supply. Only after the soul has come from the Lightworld does Adam stand up. But according to *1012*, the soul came accompanied by the evil spirit into man from the Lighworld, and this spirit introduced deceit, falsehood, and excitability into the body. The text states that this was permitted, "so that the Soul should not dominate her (*the earthly spirit*)."[16] We see here an example of the ambiguity in the view of soul versus spirit and also note the Mandaean tripartite anthropological model. It is interesting to observe that, according to *1012*, Ruha's elemental correlate, the spirit, arrives from above. Indeed, another tradition in *1012* says, "For when the Body was formed, **a Soul (*nishimta*) was formed, and when the Spirit took shape in the Body, the Body formed the Vital Spirit (*ruha*).**"[17]

In one *GR* myth Ptahil says to Ruha and her angels that he will create his image as man, Adam, and Ruha's image as woman, Hawa (Eve).[18] Ruha is found worthy to be the pattern for the female. But when Adam dies, Ruha tempts Hawa into noisy mourning for him[19]—behavior strongly repudiated in Mandaeism, even today, for ascent into the Lightworld is cause for happiness, not sorrow. Far from rejoicing, Ruha complains at Adam's death, because he, as soul carrier, is now lost to her. She says, "Woe unto me! For I did not know about their treasures, which I yearned for."[20] The "treasures" indicate the soul and its capacity to return to the Lightworld, an ability that Ruha lacks.

When it is time for Hawa to die, Ruha shows her attachment to the first woman: "Why are you leaving life, you noble one, and leave the house without masters? Where shall we go and in what shall we trust?"[21] Hibil comes to lead Hawa out of earthly life, and Ruha wails, "You take away from us everything desirable, and what is worthless, you leave behind for us."[22] Ruha clearly has knowledge of what is valuable, and she sounds like a Gnostic with a troubled conscience.

In *GR* 3 Ruha seduces the young Adam, son of Adam, disguised as his wife. Surprisingly, she teaches him about the origin of the separate sexes, saying that if there was no imbalance, they would have been created as one *mana* (vessel), but because there is imbalance, "they have made you a man and me a woman."[23] The unavoidable imbalance is due to the involvement of the planets and the fallen ʿutra (Ptahil) in the creation of mankind. It is remarkable that Ruha here plays the revealer, while young Adam receives the epithet "lying prophet."

The tension between the two natures, male and female, is rendered in the dramatic imagery of rape in *1012*. The earth (elsewhere identified with Ruha) cries out to the male principle, the yardna, the living, running water coming from the Lightworld, "Do not penetrate me!"[24] At the same time, because of the positive emphasis on fertility, it is clear that this overpowering is legitimate, even desirable. The Lightworld water rushed down, spoke to the earth, and "clothed all of her [the earth's] mysteries, covering her aridities with green foliage. And her baser mysteries he drew upwards, he steadied her babbling tongues, cleared her vision and turned the spheres."[25] This myth seems to partake of ancient mythological traditions regarding the Mesopotamian flood seasons.

Elsewhere in *1012*, Ruha is explicitly identified with the earth, who upholds and keeps to herself all life:

> Behold this fair body that was nurtured by her! (*At death?*) she encloseth it and consumeth it and maketh it as if it had never existed. And all the kindly mysteries which she produces and tends—like oil for a lamp—eventually she turns on and devours them with teeth of wrath. This is the Earth of the Parents: She raised up physical life and she is the Great Mother, from whom all swarming creatures, burgeonings and increase proceeded and (by her) were maintained.[26]

The "Great Mother" takes up considerable space in some of the speculative portions of *1012*. In *Exalted Kingship*, she also appears, for here the candidates for priesthood admit that they have been nurtured in earth's, Ruha's, lap, but they stress that their father is the Pure Ether in the Lightworld. In their long and complex initiation ritual, these priest candidates symbolically pass from the Mother to the Father, that is, from earth to Lightworld, in their preparation for full priesthood.[27]

It is now clear why Hibil brought Ruha up from the underworld, for her presence was needed at the creation, which, though imperfect, still found no objection in the Lightworld. Externally, Ruha is earth, and within human beings, the middle element, the spirit wobbling between body and soul. Her nature is unavoidably ambiguous, and the varied portraits of her do not mean that the Mandaeans contradict themselves, but that they admit her problematic nature and never cease pondering it. Earth and human beings alike are unthinkable without her. Up above, the planets and the zodiac spirits have her as their origin. Her own home is originally in the Lightworld, and one question is whether she, like a good Gnostic, has any chance of salvation. But first let me look at her relationships with some of the ʿutras.

Ruha and the ʿUtras

In command of her seven planetary sons, Ruha sets out to build the city Jerusalem.[28] Anuš ʿUtra warns her that 360 Mandaean disciples (or priests) will arise in the city if she erects it. She tries to build her city in several places, but Anuš puts a curse on the plan each time. Finally, Ruha erects Jerusalem's seven pillars, and the Jews thrive. From a lofty vantage point Anuš first watches the events and then makes his way downward to the city, where he preaches and converts some of the people to Mandaeism. The enraged Jews kill the offensive believers, and Anuš intends to destroy the city in retaliation.

Through much of this tale, Ruha seems evil and hostile to the Mandaeans. But things become more complex, for the text asks repeatedly, in a lamenting tone, how Ruha could have obtained the information that Anuš would thwart her plans. There is obviously some ambivalence here, for the ʿutra *did* speak to her, while, at the same time, the story seems to deplore this. I take this wavering to indicate a recognizable problem in Gnostic texts: when an evil figure obtains information from saviors, one suspects either that the evil one is eligible for salvation or that there will be an attempt at collaboration between the dark and the light force.

In this case it is the latter, for when Anuš arrives in Jerusalem, Ruha knows that she will lose unless she can work out a compromise with him. As Anuš begins his demolition work, Ruha bows down to him, pleading, "By your life, Anuš-ʿutra! Do not destroy this place Jerusalem, which I have built!"[29] He does not listen, and the frightened Jews try to hide. Ruha suddenly switches sides, turns against her Jewish subjects, and offers to help Anuš: "Please! Give me permission! I will bring down the gates of the walls upon them [the Jews] so that they die on the spot. The Jews who sinned against your disciples [or: 'priests'] shall be killed."[30] Infuriated, Anuš refuses any collaboration, and he single-handedly puts an end to the city.

In another *Ginza* tradition, Ruha asks Hibil who his creator is and how he, Hibil, will ascend to the Lightworld.[31] He tells her, which amounts to giving her the gnosis! And Ruha launches into an admonishing speech that would better suit Hibil:

> The Naṣoraeans who wear a perverted garment shall not ascend. The Naṣoraeans who testify to money and possessions shall not ascend. . . . All souls that do evil will become thin like a hair on the head. Whoever denies the name of Life shall die a second death. He will die a second death, and his stature will become dark and will not shine.[32]

Not unlike Anuš in *GR* 15, Hibil reacts violently. He hits Ruha with a bolt of radiance and takes away her power. She is obviously not yet eligible for Lightworld collaboration.

Elsewhere, Ruha tries to bribe Hibil and asks him to sing and preach to her. He refuses brusquely, saying that he is no music-making gypsy: "I am a man from the other world! I am an iron shoe whose word and song are cudgels and clubs for evil spirits!"[33] Surprisingly, Ruha replies by blessing Hibil: "Well then! May the Truth preserve you, you good one, and preserve the word that you have spoken!"[34]

In one of the Mandaean prayers for a specific weekday, in this case Tuesday, Ruha recognizes an ʿutra as someone coming from above. Still, she wishes that he had never come into the corruption and falsity of this world and that her eyes had never seen him. He answers that her eyes are those of falsehood, but that if she wishes to see the truth, she must go to the house of those who know him.[35] Ruha's ambivalence is intriguing. She bewails the fate of the ʿutra while she remains in a state of error, but she obtains guidelines for his gnosis. So, in this prayer, every Tuesday for nearly 2,000 years now, the priests express the yearnings of the ambivalent human spirit.

No other allegedly "evil" being in Mandaeism speaks so consistently like a Gnostic. Ruha reveals knowledge properly belonging to pious believers or to ʿutras. Why does Ruha have the gnosis, and who instructed her? The question was raised repeatedly in a plaintive part of the long poem *GR* 15, 11, as seen earlier. There, Anuš clearly had warned Ruha in advance. In *John*, the elevated ʿutra Manda ḏ-Hiia (Knowledge of Life) and also an ʿutra named Gubran are said to have instructed Ruha in the gnosis, and this has caused consternation in the Lightworld.[36] Considering that it is dangerous to instruct reportedly evil figures in the secrets of the Lightworld, one wonders about the saviors' motives for doing so. As a preliminary answer, one may conclude that Ruha increasingly resembles a malfunctioning Gnostic, and that this is why she appears as a candidate, however reluctant, for salvation.

Ruha's Self-Revelations and Identifications with Lightbeings

GR 6 tells the wondrous story of Dinanukht, half man, half book, who sits between the waters, reading in himself.[37] Diṣai, another, smaller book, comes to him and speaks disturbing, prophetic words. Dinanukht tries to burn and drown the intruder, but to no avail. After Diṣai repeats his message, Dinanukht leaves him alone and falls asleep. Suddenly, he has a vision:

> Then came Ewat, the Holy Spirit, to me in my dwelling and said to me, "Why are you lying there, Dinanukht? Why do you like to sleep? I am the Life that was from the beginning. I am the Truth (kušṭa) which existed even earlier in the beginning. I am radiance; I am light. I am death; I am life. I am darkness; I am light. I am error; I am truth. I am destruction; I am construction. I am light; I am error. I am blow; I am healing. I am the elevated man who is older and who was there before the builder of heaven

and earth. I have no peers among kings, and there is as yet no crown in my kingdom. There is no human being who can give me a message in the foggy clouds of darkness."[38]

Ewat is Ruha, and, in part, her self-declaration has already been spoken by Diṣai. The little book started by saying, "There is a Life that was from the beginning, and there is Truth that was there even earlier in the beginning."[39] The speech that so disturbed Dinanukht is now confirmed by Ruha's revelatory proclamation. One notes that Ruha says that *she* is the oppositions (and more), while Diṣai merely testified to her existence. This is cosmic speech, a declaration of a figure inhabiting central oppositional Mandaean categories.[40] Ruha also defines herself as a preexistent male figure.

Immediately, Dinanukht begins an ascent to the upper worlds. He passes through the maṭartas, and in the third one he meets its ruler, who is Ruha herself, now appearing as a seductress. In the last tollhouse, the world of Abatur, Dinanukht beholds the oppositions proclaimed by Ruha. That world is the storage place for the dichotomies, and it also houses the pre-existent souls not yet sent to earth. Dinanukht would like to ascend beyond Abatur's realm to the Lightworld itself, but further access is denied him. He must return to earth to preach his vision, which distresses him, but he complies. Back home, Dinanukht acts so strangely that his wife, Nuraita, accuses him of insanity.[41]

The central message in *GR* 6 is the sets of dichotomous, yet complementary, elements that are Ruha. She is everywhere: on earth, in the preexistent world, and in the third maṭarta. The question remains whether she inhabits the Lightworld, too.

John contains a brief story in which Manda ḏ-Hiia visits the underworld (a theme recalling Hibil's visit there, in *GR* 5, 1).[42] A female figure approaches Manda ḏ-Hiia in the world of Gaf. She carries several names, but all are compounds of Niṭufta ("cloud" or "drop"), a frequent title or name for female Mandaean Lightworld entities. The story describes her emerging, "from the inner habitations . . . from the howling darkness . . . and the black water came out, too, and [she] arrived at the seven walls that enclose the earth Siniawis."[43] For sixty-two years she sits at the outer wall until the scent of the Life settles and a messenger appears, inviting her to rise upward to the Life who loves her. Because of her underworld associations, there are good reasons to identify Niṭufta with Ruha, and to see this story as a closure to that of *GR* 5, 1, where Hibil left Ruha in a limbo world. Ruha has now found mercy with the Lightworld.

Abatur gives several names for Ruha, and some of them are the same as in the *John* story.[44] In addition, she is identified with her underworld mother, Qin, an identification that also occurs in *1012*. Here, an instructor teaches that Hibil is light and Qin (Ruha) is darkness: "Between them I cast strife, (yet) their voice is one, degrading or uplifting, urging to good or to evil. . . . Good and Evil . . . I mingled together, for they are living waters and turbid water; they are life and death. Error and truth . . . wound and healing . . . they are spirit and soul."[45]

Ruha's sign is that of "the Left,"[46] of the spirit (as opposed to the soul). *1012* explains, "Behold, Light and Darkness are brothers. They proceeded from one Mystery. . . . Were it [the body] not marked with the mark of Darkness, it would not be established, nor come forward for baptism and be signed with the Sign of Life [the sign of 'the Right']."[47] This means that the deficient sign of the spirit is a prerequisite for liberation. To live the temporary life ruled by Ruha is a necessary step toward eligibility for the Lightworld.

In *Abatur*, Hibil tells Ptahil that Ruha and her creatures are completely subdued and that the seal of Life has been placed upon them.[48] This implies nothing less than salvation, and it seems more inclusive than the information in *GR* 5, 1, where Hibil assured Ruha that it was ʿUr, not Ruha, who evoked the Great Life's anger.

Part of a very long prayer in the *Prayerbook* compares the blessing given to those commemorating their dead with the blessing bestowed on Simat Hiia (Treasure of Life), who is usually the wife of the ʿutra Yawar Ziwa but at times is identified with Ruha. The prayer refers to Simat Hiia's rising out of the worlds of darkness. She is called the bride of her liberator, the ʿutra, who remains impure from his infernal travels and cannot be cleansed "until Simat Hiia arose."[49] So, the liberator needs his partner to rise up before *he* is eligible for the Lightworld again. The tables seem turned in comparison to *GR* 5, 1, for the female now, in *Prayerbook*, prayer 376, possesses much more strength.

A lengthy prayer of praise, prayer 75, includes Ruha's lament:

> My Father, my Father,
> Why didst Thou create me? My God, my God,
> My Allah, why hast thou set me afar off
> And cut me off and left me in the depths of the earth
> And in the nether glooms of darkness
> So that I have no strength to rise up thither?[50]

The last part of this echoes the end of Ruha's self-proclamation in *GR* 6. It is important to note that this lament does not occur in isolation but belongs in a section of the prayer where the evil powers are overcome by the Lightworld and offer praises to it.

Ruha covers a remarkable range of "geographic" as well as emotional territory. Hibil brought her up from the infernal world so that she would, in time, make life possible in and on the earth. "Ruha is the breath of life in the created world, and our breath is from her, " says one of Lady Drower's informants.[51] Then, at creation, Ruha displays highly ambivalent behavior toward her offspring and toward the ʿutras. Her alliances waver, but she clearly yearns for gnosis and does obtain it. Her self-revelation and identifications with Lightworld figures show that her real home is, indeed, in the Lightworld. Curiously, in comparison to other Gnostic myths, it is precisely the typical "fallen Sophia" story that is lacking in Mandaeism, for as far as I know the Mandaean texts at present, there is no myth that explains her appearance in the netherworld.

As "generic" spirit, Ruha reflects a Mandaean's own vacillation between ignorance and gnosis, and as an autonomous mythological figure, she engages in equally unbalanced behavior. Until the material world perishes for lack of believers, Ruha rules and impersonates the earthly world, caught between light and darkness. But at the end, she will be due for redemption, in accordance with Hibil's promise to her in *GR* 5, 1.

The notion of the dmuta, as presented in chapter 3, helps to explain the variations in Ruha's character. As a feature of Mandaean dualistic thought, the dmuta also implies an inherent dynamics, as opposed to a static dualistic schema. Such an active principle effectively undercuts any expectations one might have regarding "predictable" behavior in a figure deemed to be "good" or "evil." The Mandaean tripartite anthropological model of soul, spirit, and body also, in its particular way, breaks any stolidly dualistic interpretive mold. "What . . . the middle beings were to 'mediate' was precisely the realization of an otherwise merely abstract dualism," says Jonas about mediating figures in Gnosticism.[52] That is, without mediation a mythological dualism remains dead, inert.

In the next chapter, I shall present a female figure quite different from Ruha: Miriai, Jesus' mother. By using her, Mandaeans engage in polemics against Judaism and to a lesser extent against Christianity. To serve Mandaean, internal purposes, the religion elevates Miriai to a remarkable degree. If Ruha as "Holy Spirit" represents a sort of borrowing in which ambiguous and mainly negative traits predominate, Miriai exemplifies a loan for very different ideological reasons.

5

Miriai

Several Mandaean texts feature Miriai, a young Jewish woman who converts to Mandaeism. Whether there is any historical core linking Miriai to Jesus' mother remains an open question. In any case, her name indicates that, at least in some of the Mandaean traditions, she is the mother of Jesus. Only in a few places is the Muslim name Mariam used for her.[1] In most traditions she is portrayed as an altogether positive figure, and her associations with Jesus are absent. It is a puzzle why she appears in Mandaean texts at all, and her presence raises the issue of the possibility of a brief, Christian stage in early Mandaeism.[2] At the very least, one must assume that the Mandaeans early on knew some of the Christian traditions about Mary.

In this chapter, I show how the Mandaeans present Miriai in their mythologies. As noted in chapter 1, *Haran Gawaita* gives the Mandaean migration legend. Even though Miriai does not appear in this legend, she still has her own part in the Mandaean community's earliest "history." Mysteriously, *Haran Gawaita* says of her:

> And [the Mandaeans] loved the Lord, that is, Adonai, until in the House of Israel there was created something which was not placed [i.e., was placed by unnatural means] in the womb of Mary, a daughter of Moses [*miša*]. It was hidden in her womb for nine months and bewitched her until the nine months were fulfilled and she was in labor and brought forth a messiah [*mšiha*].[3]

This seems to mean that the Mandaeans were "good Jews" until the birth of Jesus. The pregnancy results from witchery, which exonerates the woman. The use of the name Miriai is instructive, for one might have expected the more negatively tinged Mariam. Punning on the similarity between Miša (which also means "oil") and mšiha, the text emphasizes the connection between Judaism and the emerging Christianity.[4] *Haran Gawaita* juxtaposes two pregnancies, for a bit further on in the text Elizabeth (ʿNisbai) is presented. In contrast to Miriai, ʿNisbai became pregnant by a pure seed, and she brings forth the Mandaean hero and prophet, John the Baptist.[5]

Even if the resulting infants are placed in opposition to one another, the two women are not. The Mandaeans must have known about the ties between the two women, perhaps from sources such as the "Gospel of Luke" and the Christian infancy gospels.

However, in *John* things take a decidedly Mandaean turn, with Miriai figuring prominently in a migration legend different from the one in *Haran Gawaita*. For in *John* she is associated with Mandaean female Lightworld beings and even becomes a priest. In yet another context, in a section of the weekly Mandaean liturgy, an anti-Jewish polemical story is told in which Miriai converts from Judaism to Mandaeism.

Miriai in *John*

First, let me turn to the two lengthy *John* traditions about Miriai. These sections appear in sequence,[6] and in the first one Miriai states that she is the daughter of kings in Babel.[7] (This city is often conflated with Jerusalem in Mandaean texts, and, in view of the substantial Jewish population in Babylon in the early Christian centuries, the confusion is understandable.) Carried at a tender age in the priests' robes into the temple, Miriai is then raised by these priests and compelled to perform harsh work for Adonai there.[8] After what seems like a break in the story, Miriai is suddenly at her parents' home, where her father prepares to go to the synagogue (*bit ama*) and her mother to the Jewish temple (*mqadšia*). Before they leave, both warn Miriai against stepping outside, lest the rays of the sun fall on her.

Of course, Miriai ventures out, the sun rays affect her, and despite her best intentions to follow her father to the synagogue, her feet take her to the Mandaean temple (*maškna*). She enters while the Mandaeans are in the middle of their service, with the brethren giving sermons (*drašas*) and the sisters offering responses (*ʿnianas*. Miriai falls into a swoonlike sleep, unaware that the service is soon over and that the celebrants have left her alone. While she sleeps, her "sister in truth (kušṭa)" warns Miriai to get up before the day breaks, for at that hour "the priests and sons of priests go out and sit in the shadows of the ruin Jerusalem."[9]

Miriai leaves the maškna, and her father finds her, brusquely demanding to know what his disobedient daughter has been doing. He accuses her of being a prostitute, which she denies. Still, the father calls on everyone to come and see Miriai, who has scandalized her family and kin by leaving Judaism for the Mandaean religion, "to love her Lord."[10] Miriai now prefers white, the Mandaean color, to the Jewish dyed ones. Moreover, she takes no interest in silver and gold (which the Jews love), and she favors the Mandaean priestly headgear, the *burzinqa*, over the Jewish *ṭuṭifta*. Possessed by the extraordinary courage of the fresh convert, Miriai curses the Jews and their priests, calling for dust and ashes into the mouths of her opponents and for horse manure on the heads of the Jewish leaders in Jerusalem.

Here, in *John*'s first story about Miriai, one notes the automatic association of conversion and adultery. I suspect that there is a pattern of equating women's conversion with adultery, with sexual sin, a parallel seldom found if the convert is male. One needs only to look to the Old Testament to see an entire people, the Israelites, collectively cast into a female, adulterous role over against Yahweh, the scorned husband raging about his unfaithful wife (cf. Hosea; Ezekiel 16). There seem also to be echoes of the type provided by Thecla in the Christian apocryphal story about Paul and Thecla, in which a young woman falls for an alien man, thus enraging her parents and committing a social sin.[11]

It is interesting to note the Mandaean emphasis on contrasts: the Mandaean temple versus the Jewish house(s) of worship; the opposed priestly headgears; white versus colors; her new religion as Miriai's rightful place versus Judaism. Underlying the dichotomy between the two religions is a pun much savored in Mandaeism (though not mentioned in this text): the Mandaean word for miscarriage or abortion is *iahṭa*,[12] based on the root *HṬA* (to sin). "Jews" are *iahudaiia*, and it only takes a change in one consonant, making the *ṭ* into a *d*, to bring out the wordplay showing that the Jewish religion is really one of those not yet full-born, still on in imperfect or badly developed fetus stage. But to be a Mandaean means to have a fully human status.

John 's second tale about Miriai takes the reader to the mouth of the river Euphrates, where Miriai stands transformed as a vine giving shelter to birds that wish to build their nests there. The vine's leaves and fruits are precious stones and pearls. A sweet scent emanates from the vine, which provides sacred food and drink for the birds.[13] Sudden hurricanes attack the vine, however, and some birds manage to hold on, while others are blown off.

The ʿutra Hibil Ziwa appears as a white eagle to converse with the birds still clinging to the vine. The survivors wish to know what has befallen their lost companions, but Hibil Ziwa tells them that it is better not to ask. He then reveals that the others have been torn to pieces. (This clearly reflects a story of violent persecution.) Hibil Ziwa has come for two reasons: first, to admonish the remnant true believers to remain steadfast and second, to furnish companionship (*ṣauta*) to Miriai, for he himself will be her healer.

But Hibil focuses on the believers; the attacked vine, Miriai, may have healed herself. Hibil carries water in his white bucket to the plants, which are no longer birds, for "plants" (*šitlia*) is a common eponym for faithful Mandaeans. They grow to twice their former size. Miriai is now outrightly identified with Simat Hiia (Treasure of Life), the primary female Lightworld principle,[14] and with Truth, Kušṭa. Hibil then flies off to wake up the sleeping Gnostics, and he curses the Jews who persecuted Miriai. One of these Jews is singled out. He is Zatan, one of the seven pillars of the Temple, and he has spread lies about Miriai.

The enraged Jews appear, having pursued Miriai to the mouth of the Euphrates. Wanting to kill her and to hang her seducer on a pole, the Jews accuse the alien man of having broken down Jerusalem's dove cotes and trapped its doves. But now, rising to the demanding occasion, Miriai has been transformed from a nurturing vine into a priest. This is quite extraordinary, for to my knowledge this is the only Mandaean myth that presents a female priest.[15] Sitting on her throne, book in lap, priestly staff (*margna*) in hand and the priestly belt (*himiana*) enclosing her waist, Miriai presides with a priestly banner (drabša) stuck into the earth beside her. As she reads, the worlds shake. She prays and preaches, while fishes and birds listen in rapt attention. Sweet *riha* (incense) envelops her entranced, wide-awake audience.

This spectacle makes the Jews even more angry. Among them, Miriai's mother cries and pleads, asking her daughter to remember her former, exalted position in Judaism. The mother mentions a significant contrast: the *ʿuraita* (Torah) used to lie in your lap, she says to Miriai–instead of the Mandaean scripture lying in your lap now. Jewish priests and their sons used to kiss Miriai's hand, and the Jews at home were desolate after Miriai left. Now they stand on the rooftops of Jerusalem looking for her, hoping for her return.[16] Since Miriai left, the Jews, who formerly loved gold, now regard it as worthless, and lamps are extinguished in mourning over her absence. Miriai's mother continues to plead with her daughter: "Come! Teach the little ones writing! And bring the Torah from the shelf! From the day when you laid down the *hala* (*hallah*), it has become a miscarriage (or: 'excrement'). And bring it to your lap (or: 'shelter') and let us hear your voice as it was before!"[17] With haughty laughter, Miriai dismisses her mother's entreaties, accuses the Jews of worshiping a vault (*azga*—perhaps a confusion with the Muslim Dome of the Rock), and insists that she has not been seduced in any sexual sense. Hibil Ziwa, still as eagle, now reappears, chains the Jews, and drops them to the bottom of the ocean. Next he destroys the Jews in Jerusalem, their city, and the Temple.[18] Hibil preaches to Miriai, and the two exchange kušṭa, the sacred hand clasp. Then, in heroic fashion, the ʿutra embraces Miriai and lays her down on her throne while calling himself her "good messenger."[19] But no seduction scene ensues. Instead, he asks *her* for the kušṭa, which only a priest can give. This seems to show who really is in charge at this point. Like a true savior, Miriai promises him, " I and you will wind our way upwards and victoriously ascend to the Place of Light."[20] Here end *John*'s stories about Miriai.

One notices several points in this material. First, Miriai's role is that of a "founding mother" who provides life-giving food and drink to the community. Second, the storm hurling off a portion of the birds shows a community in distress, subject to persecution. Third, Hibil Ziwa asks the remaining birds to be companions for Miriai. The word for "companion," *ṣauta*, has a number of meanings, but here I would like to stress that while the usual gender balance appears, the genders are reversed, upsetting the expected pattern. A superior male may need a female as a spiritual or sexual companion, but here the community is put in a male role vis-à-vis Miriai. She maintains her superior position, while the males are her faithful believers. Fourth, the expected rescuing hero figure Hibil Ziwa appears to subject himself to Miriai, despite his initial "macho" posturing. Gender balance comes through, however, in the parallel actions of Miriai as vine, feeding her birds with her own substance, and Hibil Ziwa, who waters his plants. Last, and not least, comes the stunning portrayal of Miriai as female priest, in full regalia. One must conclude that the story offers very daring messages regaring gender hierarchy and gender balance.

Because this is also a highly polemical tale, its treatment of the Jews is instructive. The Jews possess no power over the imposing female priestly figure, and Miriai's mother is defeated, unable to lure her daughter back into Judaism. Miriai's former, powerful position in that religion may, in fact, have prepared her quite well for her newfound role. Judaism's loss is Mandaeism's gain, and the Mandaeans emigrating from Jerusalem now have a new home on the Euphrates, under the tutelage of a female leader. (One may see this as a reflection of the mythical-historical scenario of the Mandaeans traveling eastward under King Ardban's protection). Hibil Ziwa's destruction of the Jews and their city may well recall what the Mandaeans knew of the events around the year 70 C.E. Similar to certain Christian interpretations, the Mandaean view emphasizes the just punishment of the Jews for their hostility against other, "quasi"-Jewish, religions in their midst.

John's story is subversive in many ways. It permits a female figure to turn into a priest, and it reverses the usual pattern of expected behavior for ʿutras such as Hibil Ziwa. Even though Hibil, manfully, appears to rescue a grammatically and mythologically female soul, he also, toward the end, asks Miriai for the handshake, and she promises him salvation. The initial hint of *hieros gamos* (holy marriage) is not played out, for it is the community, rather than Hibil Ziwa, who is Miriai's ṣauta. Even if one sees Miriai as the soul rescuing the spirit (Hibil), according to the common pattern of salvation at the end of bodily life, the expected gender pattern does not work, because both soul and spirit are female in Mandaeism. Therefore, sexual imagery remains irrelevant in the promised, salvific union of Miriai and Hibil.

While she was Jewish, Miriai had her hand kissed by the Jewish priests and their sons. Now it is Hibil Ziwa who asks for her handshake. His request almost seems to undermine his status as savior. However, Miriai and Hibil rescue one another, and they are equals, both ʿutras. First Hibil saves Miriai from the menace of the Jews, and then she vows that both of them will ascend back to the Lightworld together. The text seems to me to conduct a conversation with itself about the possibly competing roles of priests and saviors. Thus, *John* experiments with different patterns of gender and hierarchy.

A Pious Believer

In sections 21 and 22, *John* offers more information about Miriai.[21] Here are polemical stories featuring John the Baptist in his role as preacher in Jerusalem. Miriai and ʿNisbai listen to his words and weep in response, knowing that John (and/or the women themselves) will soon depart from the city.[22] A bit later, Miriai, Jaqif (perhaps a form of Jacob, Jesus' brother), and Benia Amin ("the sons of Amin," probably a misunderstanding of "Benjamin") speak to John,[23] who has replaced the Torah in Jerusalem with his own teaching. The Mandaeans will disappear from the city, he predicts, and the three inquirers wonder whether the Mandaean message and rituals will cease and the priests be murdered. In response to their anxious query, John predicts not only the dwindling of the Mandaean community and the destruction of Jerusalem but also the rise of Muhammad. Again, one sees the reflection of persecution and migration traditions.[24]

Jaqif, Benia Amin, and Miriai also appear in *GR* 15,[25] in a section concerned with Anuš, the white eagle, which intervenes in the evil plans of Ruha and her planets, the builders of Jerusalem. Anuš declares Miriai to be perfect, and Jaqif and Benia Amin are her descendants, says the text.[26] In turn, the two men give rise to 365 (a much-used mythological number in Mandaeism) disciples in Jerusalem. "Genealogy" leads to "history," for also in *GR*, the Jews are described as destroyers of Mandaeism in their midst. Like Hibil Ziwa in *John*, Anuš calls himself Miriai's healer, and he takes care to mention that he does not demand payment for his services—probably an anti-Christian hint.

Compared with *John*'s story about Hibil Ziwa and Miriai, *GR*'s seems more cautious in terms of gender portrayal, for the ʿutra says that he has baptized Miriai, signing her with the pure sign. In *John*, nothing of that sort happens, perhaps because of Miriai's priestly status. Nobody baptizes Miriai, who already is a priest. In *GR*, John the Baptist's presence does not specifically portray him as a baptizer. Stories such as the one in *Mandaeans*, in which Miriai asks for baptism, stress an initiation ritual, a ritual that probably did occur in Mandaeism long ago, but this is not the regular Mandaean repeated baptism, the maṣbuta.

The materials about Miriai in *John*, *GR* 15, and the oral legends constitute mythological creations and reflections based on admittedly vague and as yet unretrievable, historical traditions. But the notion of a Jewess turned Mandaean seems to give some clues to Mandaean history, which naturally puts polemical issues in the forefront. Elaborations in the mythologies include Miriai's role as a founding mother figure, a sustaining vine, and a priest—all highly positive to such a degree that these traditions appear almost provocative. In contrast, there is the story of Miriai as a demure follower (together with 'Nisbai) of John the Baptist, though here, too, her foundress position is discernible.

Friday and Saturday

In my view, Miriai's most significant appearance in the Mandaean literature is in the weekly liturgy, in two ancient prayers regularly uttered by priests. These are *Prayerbook*, numbers 149 and 162, of the prayer type *rahmas* (devotions), and these two are spoken on Friday morning and Saturday evening, respectively.[27] Each day of the week has its own set of three prayers, and it is significant that the two prayers belong, respectively, to Friday morning, which heralds the Jewish Sabbath, and to Saturday evening, which marks the exit of the Jewish holy day. Both prayers have highly polemical contents.

The first one, prayer 149, recalls the first section of *John*'s Miriai material, in which the young woman ventured outside in spite of her parents' rules. In prayer 149, Miriai's mother meets her daughter at the door of the bit ama, notes her sleepy expression and flushed cheeks, and demands an explanation. Miriai has spent several days in the Mandaean temple, listening to the beautiful service, she says. Her mother replies:

> Have you not heard, daughter Miriai, what the Jews say about you?
>
> The Jews say, "Your daughter loves a man, she hates Judaism and loves the naṣiruta; she hates the door of the bit ama and loves the door of the maškna; she hates the ṭuṭifta and loves the fresh wreath. On the Sabbath (*šapta*) she carries out work; on Sunday (*habšaba*) she keeps her hand (from it)."[28]

In response, Miriai curses the Jews, as she did in *John*, with some of the same expressions used in that text. She declares her love for her Lord, Manda ḏ-Hiia, who will help her ascend from darkness to light. In contrast to *John*, in the *Prayerbook* Miriai plays a more subservient role, suitable for a new convert. She is the female recipient of the male savior's grace, not a bestower of it.

As Mandaean priests speak this prayer every Friday, they remind themselves of and re-create the tradition of their Jewish origins. Miriai is the figure who repeats the statement of Mandaeism's cut ties with Judaism. As a "counter"-day to the Mandaean Habšaba, Sunday,[29] the Jewish Sabbath represents danger, and the prayer can be seen as an exorcism. As in *John*, the text in the *Prayerbook* lists the contrasts between the two religions, contrasts that are too close for comfort.

Prayer 162, the rahma for Saturday evening, puts the Jewish Sabbath in opposition to the Habšaba. Miriai goes to the maškna to perform her prayers, but armed, evil people (presumably the Jews) accost her, demanding to know the character of her savior. She curses them, declares that they will never see what she has seen, and that Manda ḏ-Hiia surpasses everyone else, for the earth trembles before him, he raises the dead, heals, and cures lepers.[30] This prayer takes polemical care of both Christianity and Judaism, and the Sabbath is ushered out, perhaps with the relieved thought of "good riddance." Even as the place is now cleared for the entry of the Mandaean holiday, the Jewish Sabbath is sure to reappear next week. And the weekly round of rahmas begins anew.

Across the Spectrum

To my knowledge, Mandaeism has no tradition in which John the Baptist appears as a proto-convert, like Miriai does. John, simply, is the chief Mandaean prophet, belonging to a prophetic tradition extending back to Adam, according to the Mandaean view. Carrying on the eternal message of the Great Life, John springs up as a timely counter-messenger to the Jewish religion. Nowhere does he baptize Miriai, though he reluctantly baptizes Jesus, who is on his way out of Mandaeism, in contrast to Miriai, who is entering it. If Miriai is baptized at all, it is by an ʿutra, the object of her love, not by a human being. One might have expected a closer connection between John and Miriai, but the two seem to belong to independent traditions,[31] even though they occasionally appear together, as in *GR* 15, 11.

Perhaps the Mandaean adoption of Miriai while denigrating her son reflects a historical development out of Judaism. From the Mandaean viewpoint, Jesus was wrong, an apostate from the true religion, but his mother is a Mandaean heroine. Miriai stands on her own, and her connections are all laudable. She is not upstaged by Elizabeth (ʿNisbai), whose role as mother of John the Baptist puts her in a special position. Traditions such as Luke's gospel (or Islamic reworkings of the story) about the two women seem to furnish Mandaeism with one among several possibilities of distancing Miriai from her pernicious son.[32]

On another note, the intimation of sexual innuendo in the conversion stories finds parallels in Christian apocryphal legends such as "Acts of Paul and Thecla."[33] Swooning to the message by "the alien man," Miriai, like Thecla, converts, and this is understood as sexual seduction, especially by the upset parents who take their daughter's new view as a personal attack on them and on their community.[34] The elevated position of Miriai as otherworldly vine and female Lightworld being, on the other hand, might be related to other Gnostic portrayals of a related kind, such as Ennoia in "The Apocryphon of John."[35]

Mandaeism leaves the road open for depicting Miriai in exalted Lightworld roles because nothing in the religion prohibits such possibilities. Like Ruha, whose portrayals run from the most base and evil to the highest female in the Lightworld, Miriai, too, can be a female ʿutra. Lofty female beings may exist independently, without male counterparts. Miriai leaps from human status upward, to priest and supernatural vine.

Unlike culpable female figures in other forms of Gnosticism, such as the soul who falls, suffers, and finally is rescued by a male and restored to matrimonial harmony, Miriai never sins sexually, needs no pairing with a male, and does not repent. Compared with Ruha, Miriai seems much less endangered. Her "fall" is not one from a heavenly Lightworld down into matter but a horizontal breach with an earthly, religious tradition. In her move from Judaism to Mandaeism, from west to east, Miriai is not brought back into any "fold" but instead, creates her own. Especially in *John*'s account, the daring apotheosis of Miriai makes sense as an illustration of the idea that if male priests are 'utras on earth, so may women be.

Ironically, Miriai breaks out of a religion that seems very close to the one she enters. The polemical dichotomies and similarities listed in both *John* and the *Prayerbook* show that even if Miriai has now joined the better, more"mature" religion of Mandaeism (recall the pun on iahuṭaiia), its features are not that radically different from Judaism's. Both have books, both treasure learning, both have priests with requisite headgear, and Miriai now inhabits an elevated position in Mandaeism—as she once did in her former religion, according to her mother's statement. Miriai has simply made the obvious conclusion that Mandaeism, the fully developed religion, is naturally preferable to the embryonic-abortive Judaism.

The conversion of Miriai seems natural because it is a case of development and replacement, not a matter of an extreme re-creation. The two religious universes are parallel, not totally different, and religious polemical forms of literature gain particular force in such a situation. For battles are begotten not by enormous differences but by scandalous similarities. There is little point in engaging in heated polemics with a religion so different from one's own as to furnish no real common ground on which to hurl arguments. Historically and mythologically, Mandaeism's view is that Judaism and Mandaeism resemble one another too much. The Miriai traditions portray Mandaeism's critical attitude toward its former home.

PART II

RITUALS

6

To the River

In Iran, April 1996

Sightseeing

"Where is the sheikh?" This is the question. On a day's outing to see ancient places, we are waiting at a crossroads in the flat desert countryside north of Ahwaz, capital of the southwestern province Khuzistan. Our party travels in a caravan of several carfuls of people. I am the only non-Mandaean. Suhrab and I take a little walk along the roadside near an orange orchard, carefully keeping a safe distance from a grazing donkey's hind legs. "Behave yourself now!" some of the other men joke to Suhrab as we wander off, talking about lofty matters of "the Truth" (which Suhrab insists must exist), evil, and the limitations of human nature. A goldsmith who has lived almost half his life in England and whose command of Farsi still evokes sniggers from some of the men, Suhrab is one of my interpreters and companions, a serious, thirtyish father-to-be.

We are waiting for two sheikhs, two Mandaean priests, who are with us today: the *riš ama*, (head of the people), Sheikh Jabbar Tawoosie, a magnificent, dignified man of seventy-five in flowing robes, and his older son, Sheikh Salah, dark and intense, dapper in a black suit and white shoes and headgear. Both are long-bearded ganzibras of aristocratic bearing; both emanate indisputable spirituality. To everyone's relief, their car arrives. Maybe they were halted at roadblocks, for the military-looking police might well be interested in taking a closer look at these unusual men. I recognize the fragility of the Mandaean community, how completely it depends on its very few sheikhs, how important it is that no undue suspicion arises at the many roadblocks (conveniently advertised by the signs "Reduce Speed," meaning that seat belts, car, and riders may be checked.)

That morning, before the caravan set itself in motion, I spent more than an hour at the Ahwaz police office of foreign affairs. With Suhrab and Sheikh Choheili—a yalufa and my constant companion, translator, and brother-in-Kušṭa—I drank tea in the police office. In Iran, nothing happens without tea. The officer asked me bewilderingly varied questions while I hoped for a certain piece of paper to whisk me past roadblocks on our sightseeing trip. My chador (full-length veil, self-made, brought from the United States) made a favorable impression on the officer, and I kept it on for much of the day.

It was I, not any priest, who was considered a potential problem at checkpoints that morning. Now, with the sheikhs arrived safely at the crossroads, we speed along, with Suhrab's brother-in-law Hamid at the wheel, sometimes reaching dizzying speeds. Much later that day, after we leave the city of Shushtar, I mockingly slap his wrist and to general amusement call him "bad boy" as he pretends to put on his seat belt when the situation calls for such. I am conscious of my various amulets covering at least three religions; yes, we will be all right. We pass through the desert scenery and green expanses of grass, some of it shorn and carried in towering bundles on truck beds, on mopeds, on donkeys' backs, or on women's heads. On our tape deck Persian music interweaves with Whitney Houston and the haunting tunes by Mr. Askari, Suhrab's father, the first Mandaean to compose songs.[1] One praises Hibil Ziwa; all are his own compositions.

Green parrots and mourning doves fly by, and headtufted gumburras scurry like small roadrunners across our path; vast flocks of sheep with their shepherds and alert, transnational black-and-white sheepdogs trundle along; large trucks and buses emblazoned "God Alone," "Ya Allah," "Ya Ali," and "Muhammad" lumber by. Around noontime, one of them has halted to shed some of its passengers. They stand on the grass to pray toward Mecca, men and women grouped apart. Once in a while, we pass a walled-in village with its blue mosque dome like a community hat.

Our first stop is the tomb of the prophet Daniel in the ancient city of Susa. Formerly, Mandaeans lived here, right by the tomb and by the river, which now has receded so that it no longer flows next to the houses. Enormous, colorful, wet carpets are hung on the second floor banisters to dry. The Mandaean men stroll the tomb's courtyard while I and two of the women, Manijeh and Neda Choheili, shoeless and chadored, enter the holy place. Only women and children are inside, one woman motionlessly stretched out and completely hidden in her black cover on the tiled floor. The honeycombed ceiling and walls blink in thousands of glass mosaic pieces. A fiercely devotional atmosphere reigns, some of the worshiping women have a wild air about them, and I sense that this is a place they seek out for its healing powers. Daniel's coffin is unreachable, enclosed by heavy, gold-painted grillwork. Women kiss the barrier, pray, gaze at the coffin, and put money through the grillwork (I offer my paltry share). Invisible to us, Daniel lies encased in carved marble, surrounded by paper money like fallen autumn leaves.

Days later, I realize that among many other purposes this stop serves a particular, subtle one: as a reminder of our place within the monotheistic heritage. That they be regarded as monotheists is crucially important to the Mandaeans right now, in April 1996, for it is about a year since the Iranian leader Khamenei issued a *fatwa* (opinion), stating that the Mandaeans possess the requisite characteristics to be recognized as a "people of the Book." Since the revolution of 1980, this protection, which the Qur'an does grant to monotheists, has been given to the Zoroastrians instead of to the Mandaeans.[2] For years now, Mandaeans have sought to regain their status. The issue of monotheism is a frequent topic of discussion during my two weeks in Iran.

But now, in Susa and beyond, we dig into another past, first visiting the ruins of King Dareius's palace in Susa. Two guards hover behind us at a discreet distance while we stroll the windblown remnants. The only other visitors to the ruins are a family having a picnic nearby. A few of us climb a ruined but still stately horse statue, and one of the women and I laugh at my clumsy descent, for even without the persistent wind my chador creates problems. I am struck by the presence of the two Mandaean sheikhs here, for they seem naturally to belong to the place, as if they could easily trace an ancient heritage back to this territory.

This impression grows much stronger at the next site, the ziggurat at Choga Zambil, the remains of an enormous and fantastic Elamite castle already very old when Assurbanipal overran it in the seventh century. As the straight road of the flat desert suddenly turns in between narrow, rocky hills and I see the ruin rising like a weird vision on my right, it is impossible not to exclaim. We are the only visitors. The thin, leathery, knowledgeable guide comes with us, and Suhrab translates for me. He points: here virgins were sacrificed; here is the ancient "clock"; out there one can still see the outer concentric walls of the entire complex. Right across the structure appears, once a year, an unexplained green line, pondered over by French scientists who arrive to observe it from the air. Suhrab and I agree that we would like to come back on that mysterious, annual day to see the line.

"Look at the sheikh," Suhrab suddenly says. Sheikh Jabbar seems to have flown like a bird up to the top of the ziggurat, ahead of everyone else. Halfway to the sky, he waves, his clothes like wings in the breeze. He looks like he owns the place, and the sight of him remains one of the lasting, archetypal images of my stay in Iran. We ascend the steep steps. Every tenth row of wall bricks is densely inscribed with cuneiform characters. Sheikh Choheili expresses concern that I might fall off the flattened summit, where I run about, but I tell him that I am used to mountains. He lightens up, "Well, I'll take you mountain climbing in Tehran next week!"

As we circumambulate the ziggurat, I hear that the French archaeologist J. de Morgan was among the scientists who examined the site long ago.[3] I tell Sheikh Choheili that de Morgan procured Mandaean manuscripts in Persia in 1889–90 and that Mandaeans then informed him of severe persecutions about a century earlier. This calamity, de Morgan found, was still fresh and raw in Mandaean minds. As I talk about this, Sheikh Choheili translates for Sheikh Salah, who is walking next to us and now listens intently.

At that time, I do not know that our next site still holds aching memories for the Mandaeans. We are going to Shushtar, dodging traffic around rotaries and aiming first for a sorrowful place near the arches of the old bridge. During the time of Qajar Shah Naṣir al-Din[4] (but not with his approval) Mandaeans were thrown into wells and drowned here, a terrible death for baptists. Some Mandaeans escaped to the village we passed near Choga Zambil, from where Sheikh Choheili's family hails and where Mandaeans lived on good terms with their neighbors. Now, as the probable location of the wells is pointed out, our company grows somber and silent. Because I roam around a bit, entranced by the surroundings, I miss Sheikh Jabbar's prayer for the dead. Suhrab is slightly accusing, "I noticed you did not join in the response to the prayer." He is right; my attention was elsewhere, and because of this I feel guilty.

Next we head for Shushtar's old "Subbi Kush," the Mandaean area, where no Mandaeans live anymore. I recall a number of colophons stating that the scribe did his work in this city, probably in this very quarter. An expanding vista opens up at the end of what is now a Muslim street. Across the valley a dome is gleaming bluish in the far distance. Below it flows the river, crossed by a long, low bridge carrying an ant-sized string of sheep with their shepherd. Hamid takes the opportunity to clean his car, while

The Yalufa Eidan Jizan and the Ganzibra, Sheikh Abdullah in Shushtar, Iran. Photo by author.

Shushtar, Iran. Photo by author.

Sheikh Jabbar, following ancient habits, takes off his robe and heads straight for the river, where he does a ritual ablution and prays. Suhrab, seemingly gripped by a sudden anxiety, turns to me and wonders if local people will harass us. "Relax," I say, "it is not the nineteenth century now." But I sense his worry, and a cloud of unease remains with us until we leave the area.

While still in the bustle of town, we stop on a bridge to admire the dramatic gully with water spouting out of the rocks above the river. Sheikh Choheili, whose affable nature causes him to fall into conversation with locals anywhere—be they taxi drivers in Tehran or fellow passengers on a plane[5]—does just that. We are all ready to leave Shushtar, while Sheikh Choheili still lingers in an animated chat with a man on the bridge. It takes us a while to find the right way out of town. Evening light falls aslant on the flat landscape as we hurtle toward Ahwaz through a rain shower or two, the hazy brown mountains toward the distant northeast. Somewhere in the car lies the enormous padlock used to secure the gas pedal against the "too many Ali Babas," as Hamid has explained to me. But now the car flies, liberated, past the land's manifold vehicles, including Iranian and Toyota pickup trucks crammed with tightly tethered sheep and heifers.

Purity Controlled, Negotiated, Threatened

I would like to import Mandaean cows to the United States. The reason is the yogurt, unpasteurized. I have just finished a bowl of it, like exquisite sour silk, in the house of the gentle, ever-smiling old goldsmith, Mr. Abdullah Tawoosie. Now I want to thank the cow, and we go through a gate to the inner yard, where the cow stands in her shed, a calf nearby, along with numerous chickens, ducks, and geese. Even here, in Ahwaz, a city of 3 million people, people still keep livestock and fowl. Indeed, any time of day or night a neighboring rooster crows next to my hotel. Graciously, I am offered a duck egg and a goose egg, but I have to decline, for how would I cook them in the hotel?

A few days later, when we have spread blankets under trees on the sidewalk in the city of Khorramshahr to have lunch—tea, yellow soda, pistachio cake, mulberries, bread, and so on—the ever-joking Mr. Said Berengi offers me a huge egg. "What is that?" I inquire. "Camel egg," he replies, deadpan. After I have played half offended, we lean over in laughter. The Berengis are a barrel of laughs. One afternoon I spend an hour at their house, in constant merriment, despite our almost total lack of a common language. One of the young sons, Farshad, declared himself to be "my baby" while we were in Susa, so that he could get into the museum, which is off limits to Iranians but not to foreigners. (It was Monday, so the museum was closed anyway.) He has to face military service first, but then he wants to visit the United States. With his jeans and hip sunglasses, he will fit right in.

Now, in Khorramshahr, I have already had another, noncamel egg, and I decline Mr. Berengi's offer. But I am watching Sheikh Najah, who does not eat with us but wanders around with the video camera belonging to Ahmed, the ubiquitous recorder of most of my trip. A younger son of Sheikh Jabbar, Sheikh Najah—who likes to drive fast and who furnishes us with a spiritual presence on this tour to the war-ravaged coastal area—is a tarmida, tall and lanky like his brother, dressed entirely in white, with a coal black beard like a bib. Notably, he neither eats nor drinks on this outing.

Indirectly, I am given several lessons in food. Who eats what, whose food, with whom, where? In the history department at Dr. Beheshti University in Tehran, it is rumored that I am a vegetarian. A whispered question: Would I like the canned tuna cold or heated? I clear things up and eat chicken kebab. But six days earlier, in Khuzistan on our inland sightseeing tour, as we take a lunch break at a sugarcane plantation, I make some observations. Zakia, a Mandaean, works at the plantation, which is why we are invited to lunch there. In the cavernous restaurant, empty except for us, we have an excellent meal. I notice that those who are with us around the table are the ones without special purity rules. Someone sighs about the lack of alcohol—a provocative longing in Iran, a dry country but with very good Islamic beer.

Having leaned back for a bit and decorously picked our teeth, we go outside and then enter a small sitting room with a tea kitchen, like a motel room. There, Sheikh Choheili and Eidan Jizan, the other yalufa in our company, have just finished their meal, eaten off of their own utensils on an oilcloth spread on the floor. They have brought all their food and utensils themselves. Through the half-open door to the next room, I glimpse the riš and notice Sheikh Salah, stripped to his white ritual garments. With a white cloth, he is wiping his empty, clean, tinned food bowl very slowly, very carefully. He catches me watching him. The women of priestly family—Manijeh and Neda, and Neshat, the little girl who skips around and who will later run with Sheikh Jabbar to the top of the ziggurat—have evidently eaten separately. It is clear to me that our lunch has been eaten in different tiers of purity.

In Tehran, later, I play food police and say to a Muslim friend, "Hey, that's not *halal* [pure] for you!"

Mr. Frouzandeh is eating shrimp. I learn that it is clean now, for the authorities, evidently in an effort to boost the shrimp industry, last year declared the food fit to eat. And I, the barbarian from a Christian culture, began to appreciate the Iranian shrimp very soon after my arrival. Another day in Tehran, at lunch in a small restaurant with Sheikh Choheili and Mr. Askari (the singer and shipping company director), Sheikh Choheili has expressed skepticism about the fish. How is it cooked? He eats no meat but will take other restaurant food, which can be risky business. I am surprised to see him eating shrimp one day.

But mushrooms, which I am savoring on that day in Tehran, he will not touch. Mr. Askari gently complains to me, "I have tried to tell him: it is *not* meat. It grows on the ground. Am I not right? *You* tell him. " I agree but must concede that mushrooms have a strange texture, grow in a funny way, and certainly do not look like plants. Sheikh Choheili stands his ground, unswayed. Having listed the mushrooms' suspect features while picking at those remaining on my plate, I am beginning to harbor the more traditional Mandaean attitude toward mushrooms.

That we are separated in thought as in the sharing of food becomes clear in the elegant house of the Tawoosie sheikhs. We spend our time discussing religion (I am the only woman in the company of men). Sheikh Salah, ever the ideologue, and I remain respectful of each other's positions as we sit on opposite sides of the carpet, with Sheikh Choheili interpreting. Both of us are gesturing, acknowledging our differences in the matter of Mandaean origins.

"Our religion is very old. We go back to Adam. You saw the clay *ṭarianas* [trays] in the wedding canopy, like Adam used, everything in natural materials, nothing artificial."

Yes. But I explain that scholars will not accept the historical validity of such statements, that they want proofs, according to *their* scholarly terms. We may *all* derive from Adam, but we cannot prove it historically.

Accepting our separation in views, we finish, and around ten-thirty get up from the beautiful carpet. We, as guests, are invited to take our meal. Throughout the evening, I have not even laid eyes on any women of the house, and only a few young boys have hovered at the far rim of our discussions. Now four men and I sit down at the table laden with a delicious repast of fish, rice, vegetables, and greens. Our hosts are nowhere to be seen, and only toward the end do I notice the passing shadow of one of the sheikhs beyond the sprays of the indoor fountain. Eating seems to be an intensely private affair in a pure house. It feels like an immense honor to eat here at all.

What is clean, what unclean? Cows and fowl stay in their courtyard areas. On Sunday, two hens sleep peacefully a few feet away from the bamboo wedding canopy while the solemn, but festive, ritual proceeds. Except for occasional small birds in cages and goldfish, Mandaeans do not keep pets. Neither do I, having grown up with serious hunting dogs. One morning at breakfast I watch a dust-colored cat lying down to rest in the bed of asters and sweet william right outside the hotel window. Only once does it rise to swat a butterfly. I see no other cats during my entire stay. A few thin dogs slink along the house walls near the hotel.

On my first, dizzying morning in Ahwaz, touring Mandaean workshops and factories,[6] I learn about the distance kept from dogs. In increasing heat and din, we enter an iron-smelting plant. Across the courtyard, I notice three guard dogs pricking up their ears at us from a dark doorway. They actually look friendly, and, following my natural inclinations, I want to greet them, though keeping my distance. But Mr. Kataneh, one of my companions and translators, speaks harshly to them, and they cower and retreat, only their eyes visible. A retired engineer, Mr. Kataneh explains at length to me about the workings of machinery and products, and he also tells me that he once kicked in the teeth of an attacking dog that belonged to a foreigner. Later, at his house, Mr. Kataneh wants to show me something. He reaches up to the top of the air conditioner facing the garden and hauls down a stuffed jackal, its teeth bared. His eternal revenge on that English canine!

Mandaeans seem far away from violent attitudes, however. My blue bag, which holds my daily gear and the plastic bottle of mineral water, Damavand (named for Iran's tallest mountain), evokes the suspicion of the hotel doorman. Am I concealing a bomb? No. Back in Sweden, right before I came to Iran, my Mandaean friend Issam covered his head and shook it when I modeled my chador for him and his family. "You look like a tank! U.S. 's new, secret weapon!"

Naturally, military and war monuments grace city squares and rotaries in Iran, along with huge murals of the leaders, often poised benevolently against a background of clear rivers and flowering fields (tulips and roses seem to be favorites). Young soldiers, mostly without visible weapons, appear just as regularly, and only one bore an expression of such subtle, unspeakable cruelty that I had to turn away. I was unable to shake the impression for several days.

On the trip to Khorramshahr and Abadan, near the Gulf, we visit territory I have seen before on a visit in 1973. However, I now recognize only part of the Khorramshahr city block where Mandaean silversmiths used to have their shops. Aran is no longer here, and Shaker Feyzi went to Kuwait. Mandaeans do not live here anymore, for they all left during the 1980–88 war. We have passed shot-up, rusted tanks on the way, and the areas where heavy fighting occurred are pointed out to me. One of Mr. Kataneh's sons was an officer in the war. The Iranian Mandaeans lost fewer than ten of their own, but more are missing.

We stop at the old, bombed Mandaean quarter in Khorramshahr. I take a picture of Mr. Sobbi's rebuilt house, to show him back in New York. Mr. Kataneh and his wife are in our company, and he tells me where his own house stood. "It must be strange for you to be back," I offer. It is; they have not been here for seventeen years. Behind a brick wall, the Mandaean mandi still exist, cared for by the people who live there. The locals eye us with mild, curious suspicion.

After the lunch of the spurned "camel egg," we cross over to Abadan to look into Iraq. Having arrived at our first vantage point, we leave immediately, sensing that it is safer to go to a slightly different place to ponder the border. Soon we stand meditatively in front of a tall, chain-link fence topped with barbed wire and gaze at the green, seemingly uninhabited marshland on the other side. In easier times, Mandaean priests were able to cross the border to officiate at rituals for their fellows in the neighboring country, but not now. Are there still Mandaeans left in the southern Iraqi marsh country? Yes, a few. Are any of them looking across at us, right now?

In Shiraz, at the dinner table in the Ghilani family's house,[7] I ask if there are differences between Iranian and Iraqi Mandaeans. At first, the answer seems to be no. But the question quickly unleashes a twenty-minute heated discussion, which I wait out. When I surmise the result, it is almost the same as the answer given to me on Long Island in New York: a hesitant "no, but . . ." Perhaps the reaction would be different in Iraq, but the consensus here seems to hold that the Iranians feel themselves to be more careful in keeping to the traditions and the Mandaean language, while the Iraqis are suspected of relaxing the rules, more susceptible to modern, secular ideas.

Without having been in Iraq, I cannot judge. But from my own experience, it seems to me that differences may not be that wide. Some Mandaeans have more money than others, more education and familiarity with other parts of the world, but even the most "Westernized" seem to maintain a sense of identity and commitment to the religion and to its values. My experience now, in Iran, of a persisting community, with leaders and priests, marks a contrast to the mostly priestless groups outside the "old" countries. However, after I return home from Iran, I learn that the Australian Mandaeans have obtained a Mandaean tarmida from Iraq. Later, in the fall, I find out that Sheikh Salah and his family have moved to Australia, too.

Traditionally, at least yalufas may be movable. Several years ago, Sheikh Choheili spent a month in Germany to work with Professor Macuch. He also went to Australia to prepare the way for Sheikh Salah, who traveled there twice to perform rituals for the emigrated Mandaeans and to ready himself for his move. The sheikh's travels astonished me. The risk! On his first air segment, Sheikh Salah ate nothing but stopped over in Malaysia to rest, eat, and purify himself. Coming from Ahwaz, he had entered the Tehran airport carrying two bottles of water from the river Karun, only to have one bottle rendered useless by a customs official who suspected liquor. The presence of Mandaean leaders, with their white clothes and dignified long beards, made a deep impression on the airport personnel, who whisked them through the electronic controls.

I remember that upstairs in my hotel room I have photos of my beloved Florida springs and rivers. I fetch the pictures to show to Sheikh Choheili. He looks at them carefully, and we start to form dreamy plans. Could we obtain regular access to a good Florida river, have a pure place for the priest to stay in, and North American Mandaeans could come there to be baptized and have other religious needs fulfilled? Could the rules be changed so that a yalufa might do the rituals if a priest did not come? (Since then, the Mandaeans in the midwestern United States have obtained a priest and a mandi, as noted.)

"Did you not ever want to become a priest?" I ask Sheikh Choheili at some point. "No." "Why not? " "Because then I could not work with someone like you." I see. One of the many new things I am learning in Iran is the role of the yalufas, the men in the mediating position between priests and laypeople.

Proximities

One of the hardest rules for me in Iran is that I must not touch a man in public. Shaking hands is out of the question, and yet I unthinkingly violate the rule several times. It is especially difficult not to touch Sheikh Choheili's hands, for he quickly becomes like a brother to me. One evening in Tehran, when I notice that Sheikh Choheili is exhausted, I exhort Cyrus, "Take good care of him!" Cyrus is Suhrab's twin brother and a computer virus exterminator. He promises to give the sheikh a good massage. Sheikh Choheili, my trusted friend and soul mate, spends most of his time with me, not only in Ahwaz, for we also travel by air together to and from Shiraz and Tehran. Virtually every morning, he shows up in the hotel lobby, a gray-bearded, alert, kind, slightly built man in a green-gray suit, his woolen beanie on head or in hand. In Ahwaz, his trusty old Ford, with its long-spent suspension, windshield bullet hole, and coarse fake fur on the dashboard, waits outside the hotel.

On Easter Sunday morning he arrives while I am still at breakfast. "Come. The priests are already at the river."

For the first time in my life, I will see a Mandaean baptism. We park on the wide riverbank, and between us and the swiftly flowing, mountain-born Karun full of melted snow water, now brown and muddy, the three priests work like a team. Downstream on the bridge, occasional pedestrians pause to glance in our direction. The yalufa Amin, who is the *šganda* (ritual helper) today, walks about in his rasta (ritual garment), barefoot on sturdy legs, ever watchful, hands mostly clasped behind his back. Once he gently but firmly shoos away a curious little outsider, a boy who sits a bit too close to the action. Amin functions as the religious overseer, directs those to be baptized to their right place, and otherwise makes certain that everything proceeds correctly. (Off duty as šganda, Amin is never without his brown, knitted cap.)

I sit down, but Mr. Kataneh soon alerts me to my scandalous attire: the ever-present scarves, long, voluminous pants, loose shirt—but without a skirt! It would not be good if people reported this. I scurry to the car, get my chador, and soon sit under a fancy white lacy umbrella lent to me by a photographer who is here to take pictures of one of the bridal couples. Today, two such couples are being baptized. In addition, there is one other young man who was married last Sunday, though his bride, due to her period, is absent.

The previous day, I attended the party of one of the couples. Now both the groom, Behzad, and his bride, Shaida, are serene in their rastas. Shaida wears a yellow cloak over her rasta, and her face bears no trace of the previous day's carefully applied makeup. But yesterday was a din of festivities, with singing to taped music, hand clapping, drumming, foot stomping, dancing, women's thrilling cries, and swaying walls of happy, perspiring humanity (women and children) in the room filled to overflowing. Prodded, I shed my scarves and dance with the women. The men are by themselves, in another room. After the ritual applying of rings and gold necklaces on both bride and groom, the two feed each other from the sloping, sweating, three-tiered pink wedding cake. Sheikh Choheili finally appears to extract me from the hot, exhilarated din.[8]

Today is a contrast, the quiet, serene work of baptism moving like finely tuned clockwork. Sheikh Taleb Duragi, with his gray-brown beard and tilted-back head, is older and smaller than the Tawoosie brothers. Sheikh Jabbar, their father, has stopped doing most public rituals. I watch, strangely familiar with most of what I see, so I am not surprised. Here, in the middle of Ahwaz, with the "real" world going about its business in the distance, the baptism scene seems timeless yet completely natural, a vivid image of ancient Gnostic life. I photograph Sheikh Salah smiling, pausing and at ease between two ritual segments, his black cloak for warmth over his wet rasta, a wrinkled, empty Winston cigarette pack on the hardened mud just inches from his sandaled feet.

The three priests are positioned on different "workstations," as it were. While one of the Tawoosie brothers stands in the water, inviting a bride (who is accompanied by female relatives) to descend for baptism, the other stands on land behind one of the crouching grooms and reads prayers from the baptism liturgy. A bit farther back, Sheikh Duragi, his lower face without the *pandama* (ritual mouth cover) and his rasta falling freely and not tucked up into his belt, consecrates his crown, readying himself for his next ritual segment.

A priest at work is never without his staff, his margna. I notice the endearing gesture for keeping the margna in place when a priest ascends from the river.[9] Holding his right, bared arm outstretched—for it is newly cleansed—he will tilt his head to his left shoulder to support the margna leaning there. At this point his left hand holds the water-filled bottle, and his right hand must remain free. When the silk *taga* (crown) is deconsecrated, the priest lifts it to his mouth and eyes in an elliptical motion, rhythmically and with lightning speed.[10] A praying priest places his right hand to the right side of his head, concentrating on his crown.[11] Deactivated several times during the entire event, the taga is secured inside the right, rolled-up sleeve of the priest's shirt.

I watch the praying Sheikh Duragi rapidly count formulas on the three digits of his fingers. Zakia, a layman, hovers about throughout the baptism. Now he crouches and pulls myrtle twigs out of the large plastic bag; he is the man who twists the klilas. The gold ring, Šum Yawar (the Name of Yawar) shines on the priest's right little finger when he pushes the klila in under his crown. Only much later do I realize that no drabša stood on the riverbank. It is used for major holidays, such as John the Baptist's birthday and Dehwa Rabba (New Year's), for masiqtas, priest initiations, and at the five-day-long intercalary feast *Panja*.

Saeed, one of Sheikh Choheili's brothers—all of whom are yalufas—has rolled the legs of his pants up to his knees, and now he helps with the baptism of the cooking gear. A large stack of kitchen pots sit on the riverbank, gleaming, for they were freshly

Sheikh Salah on the riverbank in Ahwaz, Iran. Photo by author.

The baptism ceremony; the groom is crouching in the foreground. Ahwaz, Iran. Photo by author.

The bride and her female relatives participating in a baptism ritual. Ahwaz, Iran. Photo by author.

Two brides crouching in front of the priest in the baptism ceremony. Ahwaz, Iran. Photo by author.

retinned for Panja just a few weeks ago. One woman has carried a tower of pots on her head. Her chador is tied up crosswise for work, and she and the yalufa hand the pots to the priest, who gives them the requisite cleansing.

On and off, I scribble in my notebook, but mainly I watch. For a little while, the grandmother of both bride and groom sits next to me and smiles with satisfaction at the well-made match. A bit earlier, another woman has helped me arrange my chador, for I still have trouble with its symmetry, nearly tripping on the side hanging down too low. Mostly, I sit still during the baptism, chatting with people now and then, and nodding to myself as I observe a ritual gesture so far known only from books. I am satisfied to see that my theory of ritual as work holds up well today.

Afterward, we go up to the house of the Tawoosie sheikhs, and I am invited to take a seat on a log next to two priests by the house wall, in the shade of trees. Sheikh Choheili stands by a truck, chatting with other men. The priests in this household can go right out of their back door, cross the small street, ascend the steps up the low brick wall on the other side, descend behind it, pass on a path through bushes and low trees, and arrive on the riverbank in a matter of minutes.

The worlds I inhabit in Ahwaz are mostly with men, although women clearly dominate the home sphere. Suhrab's sister, Seema, gives me a black elastic band to keep my hair in place under my scarves. The awkwardness of the visiting outsider! It takes me a good while to realize that when I am in people's homes and they say, "Feel free," they mean, "You may take your scarves off now." At first I think that my pale skin and light hair make the children shriek in excitement and surprise when I look directly at them or when I take off my head covers. But no, a woman explains, "it is your eyes." I play hide-and-seek behind my hand, throw a sudden glance in an unexpected direction at the groups of children, and delighted screams erupt from the girls and smaller boys, the older boys being more brave, their gazes steady.

I sense very strongly the immense advantage of a married priesthood. Everyone is naturally comfortable around women, and the priests' attitude toward children is warm and affectionate. An informal, relaxed atmosphere reigns in private. At first wary of shedding my scarves in people's homes, I am shocked to see my own bare head in the video segment in the priests' house. (Later, in the Bahrain Airport, people look naked to me—though some of them almost are, for Hajj season is near). Rules for public appearances in Iran are clear, and to an outsider like me the difference between public and private spheres in Iran is striking. Bejeweled, colorfully clad, exuberant women inside homes don large scarves and long, demure coats or become black bundles on the street (although airs of quiet testing of the limits do occur: a fancy pair of shoes, a touch of earth-colored lipstick, "I-dare-you" gazes). Young men swagger in jeans or black, tight-waisted, loose-legged pants and fashionable shirts, bead strings dangling from their hands. The men show easy affection for one another; they may kiss and hold each other's hands. Only once, in another city, do I see a young Muslim couple holding hands on a street, and then I cannot quite believe my eyes.

A wedding takes days, for a married couple is not made in a hurry. On the day of the baptism, stepping across the blood of the rooster killed that morning,[12] I enter the courtyard of the house of the wedding. Where there was no structure yesterday, an airy bamboo bridal canopy festooned with gladioli and roses stands like the frame of an elegant gift. Inside, soon enough, sit the three priests and the bridegroom, with Sheikh

Salah officiating. Onlookers press on at the edges, videos whirr, and cameras hover. Sheikh Jabbar, off duty, sits contentedly at the canopy's northeast corner. I am particularly interested in the end of Sheikh Salah's long stole (*naṣifa*). For hours, the bridegroom maintains a firm grasp on it, because the creative powers residing in the ganizbra will pass to the groom through the cloth, like nourishment through an umbilical cord.

Two boys are present, white cloths artfully arranged around their heads. Each waits for the cue to smash an earthen pot on the threshold of the canopy and of the door to the house. They each get their chance, for there are two pots. The basket with the mixed clothes of bride and groom stands nearby, the green bridal veil on top. We enter the house to watch the backs of the groom's and the bride's heads being knocked together, nine times in all. A white, gossamer-thin cloth suspended from the ceiling separates their heads. We women sit along the walls, clapping and singing. I munch on pita bread, and outside, an old woman hands me peeled cucumber. We all need our strength. For a while, I sit ringside on the narrow terrace above the canopy, watching and talking to a Muslim woman, a guest and friend of the family.

Sheikh Salah keeps up his readings, whether he is outside in the canopy or inside the house. Where he goes, the groom follows on the naṣifa leash. The sheikh makes his way through the entire wedding liturgy. At some point, I notice that his voice rises to a different pitch. I have long known that Mandaeans do not sing, and so it is not correct to call the prayers "hymns," but they are certainly performed in a kind of chanting voice. Finally, with a flourish the groom throws away the naṣifa and speeds ahead of the priest into the house to shake hands with his bride. A ripple of good-natured laughter erupts at Behzad's hurry.

Public Appearances

My image of a mandi was based on Lady Drower's photos and descriptions of the traditional hut made of straw, bamboo, and mud.[13] But I knew that Mandaeans have larger, modern ones, essentially community houses and administrative centers. In Khuzistan, I see both kinds.

One day we drive out to a remote village, where the traditional hut sits enclosed by a high wall, behind a locked gate. A corrugated tin roof covers the entire mandi area. This is the Mazrieh mandi, in the village of the same name. The Mandaeans can have their holy place here because of Mr. Haial Berengi, who, dressed in traditional garb, accompanies Mr. Kataneh, Sheikh Choheili, and me on this trip. On friendly terms with the locals, Mr. Berengi has enabled the granting of the land for the building. The hut looks old, but it is not. Two ṭarianas (ritual clay trays) sit on its mud roof (others are inside the building). A channel has been dug so that water flows sluggishly into the mud brick–lined pool beneath the earthen steps in front of the hut. The water does not look clean to me; still, Mr. Berengi performs his ritual ablution.

By special, previous permission from Sheikh Jabbar, I cross the *miṣras*, the ritual lines drawn on the ground, and enter the mandi on ritual footgear: wooden sandals. Light comes only from the narrow doorway; the floor is hardened mud. My eyes adjusted, I ask about the location of various activities during the priest initiation. Sheikh Choheili points out the details of the hut's construction, the place where the sacrificed

Ahwaz. Three priests in front of a wedding canopy: Sheikh Salah, Sheikh Najah, and Sheikh Duragi. Photo by author.

The bridegroom holding on to the priest's stole. Photo by author.

The Mandi in Mazrieh, Iran. Photo by author.

dove is pushed in between the roof and the wall, where the ṭarianas stand. Again, as at the baptism, I feel on eerily familiar territory.

Outside, I sit on a huge, upended clay pot to contemplate the place. "This is where Sheikh Jabbar always sits," Sheikh Choheili says, nodding toward my seat. They have just celebrated Panja here a couple of weeks ago, but it is hard to imagine 200 people thronging inside this small enclosure. Singing birds flutter in and out of the space between the corrugated roof and the surrounding wall. I clutch my *himiana* (sacred belt), which Mr. Berengi has given me and patiently tried to teach me to tie correctly.[14]

There is a garden with small fig trees and recently cut olive trunks, for the olive trees had grown too large. Soon we sit down to tea on the floor in the adjacent shed, where we are served by Mr. Berengi's son, a young, recently married man. Mr. Berengi coughs (I brush aside a shade of guilt for having given him American cigarettes) and then sings. I lean against the wall, listen, and gaze out the open door. Mr. Kataneh becomes inspired, too, and drumming on the emptied tea tray, joins in the singing. A peaceful time, a comfortable, cozy lull before taking off into the flat, endless, patchily cultivated desert again. I am struck, as so often, by the contrast between us in a small room and the vast land outside, largely devoid of people.

Crowds show up where least expected, however. I had not been prepared for the large number of Mandaeans coming to meet me at the Ahwaz airport the first evening. As we wait for my luggage on the moving band, Sheikh Choheili says softly, "There are some Mandaeans here to see you." I sense several people behind the glass wall. Outside, a video camera whirrs, and a veritable wall of people surrounds me. A girl with a large bouquet of gladioli, roses, and carnations stands in front of yet another group. I glance back and say to myself that there must have been someone important on our plane from Tehran. But the smiling girl starts moving toward me, and I realize what is happening.

From there on, it seldom stops for long. Many people want me to come to their homes. Treated like a visiting celebrity or a head of state, I am given flowers and gifts; I sign autographs, smile, and shake hands. On my first full day in Ahwaz, I give two conferences in the mandi, the community house with a large hall downstairs and a half second-story level holding an office for business affairs and for the settling of internal disputes. First, in the late morning, shedding my shoes at the door and seeing the large audience of men in the hall inside, I am taken by surprise. Is this the entire Mandaean male population of Ahwaz? Priests and a couple of dignified-looking, bearded older men in traditional dress sit on chairs in the first row. Many men sit on the floor, some lean against the walls (among them is the white-bearded Mr. Moradi, Saeed's father,[15] whom I may have met in his shop back in 1973).

On the lectern, placed in the northeast corner, stands a vase of myrtle, water for me, and a microphone. If I look straight up, toward the window of the mandi office above, I see a serenely depicted drabša under the inscription "Praised be my Lord! with a pure heart." On the north wall hangs an impressive painting of John the Baptist, praying on the riverbank and portrayed in the Islamic artistic manner: his face a protruding flame. Later we will all stand facing north, with our hands outstretched and palms up, as Sheikh Choheili, his eyes shut in passionate concentration, leads all in wall-vibrating prayer.

But first there are solemn introductions, and I speak. On that occasion alone, I have three different interpreters. Scholarship and studies, how I came to these, the origins question, Dead Sea Scrolls, Gnosticism, history, Lady Drower and Professor Macuch, my friendships with Mandaeans in the United States, prospects for the religion—all of this and more. The men's attention does not flag. Afterward, additional issues and questions arise from the audience. I sip water, talk, and listen, waiting for the translator to finish his sentence.

In the late afternoon, I return to find the mandi even fuller, this time with an enthusiastic audience of women and children. By this time, I feel like a veteran and give a wave and a smile as I enter. Two groups of children in rastas give heartfelt recitals of Mandaean prayers. They have been taught by Sheikh Choheili, who tirelessly works to impart the religious traditions to the young. I sit next to Suhrab and listen, almost regretting that I cannot see the childrens' faces, for they have their backs to me (though now I have the video). One of the girls projects such intense sincerity in her powerful voice that I feel certain she will be priest material.

This conference resembles the earlier one, but the atmosphere is looser and more intimate. Now the questions from the audience are written down first, and children and women, weaving their way through the others, come up with pieces of paper in hand. At the very beginning, even before I have said anything, Shahrzad Abadeh Ahwazi, a woman from the Mandaean Association, presents me with a white gold ring with a brilliant. This is the first in a veritable shower of jewelry I receive in Ahwaz.

Days later, just before I head for the airport on my last evening in Ahwaz, there is a farewell session in the mandi's upper office, with warm words, presents, and assurances that I will keep in contact and come back. A young woman, Reema, gives me a beautiful present: her own cross-stitched embroidery, with flowers and the words *Ya Hiia*. Next to me, Shahrzad mercifully prevents me from committing a bad mistake, for I am hot, sigh, and make motions to loosen my chador. Whispering, she swiftly tells me: no, for there is a Muslim present. I had no inkling of this. Now I notice a man in earnest conversation with Sheikh Choheili, and I see them throwing glances in my direction. The authorities have been kept aware of my presence in the Mandaean community. It is certainly important that I behave decently now!

In a letter of January 20, 1995, Sheikh Choheili had ended with these words: "We hope that you will get whatever you want as well as being useful to us in this journey." Then, I could not know how poignant his words would turn out to be. The History Department at Shahid Beheshti University in Tehran had arranged for my visa (a lengthy saga in itself). Without assurance of any set schedule, I had made extensive notes for two academic lectures, one on Mandaean religion, one, based in part on my colophon research, on Mandaean history. On the advice of an American colleague, I had arrived in Tehran thinking that maybe I would lecture, maybe not. But in Iran, people turned out to have firm plans for me.

Mr. Frouzandeh, a rice importer and a student of Sheikh Choheili's, may be the first serious Muslim student of Mandaeism in his generation. For a month, Mr. Frouzandeh worked on my schedule, arranging for my appearances in Tehran. We spend much time together, at tea-drinking sessions in the lobby of my hotel, Azadi, on the northern slope of the city, and in Mr. Frouzandeh's car as he careens through the smooth chaos that is Tehran traffic. Twice, we have a late dinner in a village restaurant up in the mountains. Sitting under a half roof on a carpet-covered table, listening to the rushing stream below, we eat and carry on philosophical discussions. One evening, a few flakes of snow fall as the coals glow on top of the hookah, the water pipe, at the next table. "Ahh, delicious. We are like Sufis, " says Mr. Frouzandeh, leaning back contentedly the next night, after the three of us (Sheikh Choheili is the third) have finished our meal and our conversation.

Untiring in his quest for religious information, Mr. Frouzandeh wants to know the positive versus negative percentage in the personalities of certain ʿutras. Details about Mandaean Lightworld geography interest him so keenly that I have to tease him and ask whether he is planning a trip. Does he have a ticket? But for now, my own movements have priority. Who will be my audience at the planned sessions, where, and when? At the tea-drinking meetings in the hotel lobby, I meet my first interpreter, Mr. Amin, the sociologist, and Sadaf Azimi, the young woman who for Mr. Frouzandeh's benefit has translated my encyclopedia article on Mandaean religion into Farsi.[16] Mr. Askari, the Mandaean singer, often shows up. An energetic man with a lively gait, dancing eyes, and a voice like a burbling brook, Mr. Askari lives in a nearby town, though his business is in Tehran. Sheikh Choheili and Mr. Askari are my constant Mandaean companions in what is decidedly Muslim territory.

Mr. Askari's son, Cyrus, turns up, and, as Sheikh Choheili promised back at Choga Zambil—and I do not let him forget—a mountain trip is arranged. The three of us embark on an unforgettable climb up through the villages in one of the dramatic mountain chasms north of Tehran, an almost Himalayan-looking landscape. Passing caparisoned donkeys carrying cases of soda and supplies for the tiny restaurants higher up the path, Cyrus, Sheikh Choheili, and I make our way slowly above the brown, high-lead-gas-saturated air of Tehran. We never even approach the pristine, shiny snow peaks hovering at 15,000 to 16,000 feet. Villages seem to hang, suspended, off the mountain cliffs; three-log bridges fortified with cement cross the rushing creek; two men lean on the edge of a laboriously built stone terrace hemming in their garden plot. Even up here, Sheikh Choheili befriends a local, a man who hails from Khuzistan. Climbing, the two keep up a running conversation.

But most of my time in Tehran is spent indoors, at business. Dr. A. Khalatbari, the chair of the History Department at Shahid Beheshti University, has arranged for my appearance there. Khamenei's fatwa regarding the Mandaeans is foremost in the minds of Sheikh Choheili and Mr. Askari, the only Mandaeans at my two large public events. What I will say about Mandaeism to the Tehran audiences—students, faculty, and clerics—carries the most serious import.

In the photos taken of the conference at Shahid Beheshti University, Mr. Amin, my translator, is consistently hidden behind the Iranian flag, which sits on the long table with the gladioli arrangement and the microphones. My scarf-covered head is bent over one of them. Alternatively, microphone in hand, I stand gesturing at the whiteboard, felt pen poised. Under the klieg lights, Mr. Amin works harder than I do. The event, in the Rumi Auditorium, to an audience of several hundred, lasts for two hours. I talk about the Mandaeans and, by request, about Manichaeism. At the beginning I am puzzled by the intoned formulas emerging from the rows seating most of the male students. On two occasions when I refer to Khamenei, they pray for several seconds. I think that this is some form of decorous heckling, but later realize that at the mention of the country's leader, the formulas are automatic.

We break for lunch. At the meal, with Sheikh Choheili and Mr. Askari sitting opposite me at the table, Mr. Askari begins to sing two of his Mandaean songs. It is about one o'clock. Outside, the broadcast voice of the muezzin calls to prayer. Mr. Askari continues. I watch and listen as the two voices carry on in parallel. There is a quiet attentiveness in the room, followed by subdued applause around the table for Mr. Askari.

We return to the auditorium for the panel discussion, which lasts for two hours. With Dr. Khodadadyan as moderator, six of us sit down at the podium. Mr. Amin and I hover together, and he goes to work for me again. Now Sheikh Choheili is with us, together with three professors, one of them a philosopher, and on the far right Mr. Frouzandeh's beloved teacher, the delightful elder statesman of religious studies in Iran: Dr. Mujtabai. We spend most of our time dealing with written questions from the audience. A stack of small pieces of paper grows in front of Dr. Khodadadyan. Some questions are in English, some in Farsi. Several are addressed especially to me, and one expresses sincere concern that this might be a tiring experience for me. No matter! We take turns answering the queries, and I refer some present-day Mandaean issues directly to Sheikh Choheili. Everything is translated for my benefit.

Throughout, I feel strongly that this is a very positive event, a sincere and well-received learning experience for all—certainly for me. I hope to have done a satisfying piece of advocacy. It is evidently a long time since anyone has come to give a presentation on Mandaeism to a university audience in Tehran. Later, at home in the United States, the soulful, inward gaze of the artfully turbaned mystic Rumi peers down from a wall. The silk carpet with his image, a gift from the university's president, hangs there, reminding me of that day.

A few days later, we attempt to rehearse what will be a somewhat different appearance. I meet for hours with members of the Ibn Sina Institute, an organization devoted to the philosopher's ideas and to the integrated study of religion, philosophy, and psychology.

The members wish to obtain connections with similar organizations in the United States. Made up of a group of spiritually inclined men devoted to a sort of Islamic New Age monotheism with Sufi overtones, the institute has as its spokesman the unflappably balanced, elegant Dr. Mahfouzi, a clinical psychologist. We have an excellent lunch, and then tea, with Armenian delicacies (Armenian bakers and confectioners are famous).

Then our distinguished visitor enters. He is Ayatollah Sajjadi of Alzahrah University in the holy city of Qum. A candidate for Parliament and a well-known legal scholar, he carries himself with natural authority and seems at ease in our company. His questions to me about the Mandaeans are three: Do they have prayers? Do they fast? Do they allow temporary marriages? I appreciate the practical focus of his queries, and he seems satisfied with my answers.

I spend two hours priming tomorrow's interpreter, Mr. Khoshchashm, a quick-minded young man with a degree in English. The makers of my second conference have arranged for it to be held on neutral territory in Laleh Hotel, rather than at a university. They have asked for a presentation on research methods in the study of religion. In a country like Iran, this topic seems challenging. I decide to tackle it head-on, and I fill Mr. Khoshchashm's head with scholarly terminology. But the Ibn Sina society has its own concerns: Will I attend to the question of relativity, that is, the absolute knowledge of God versus our, incomplete one? I say I will, probably indirectly—but it turns out to be sufficiently direct.

The next day we arrive early, passing through the hotel lobby, which sports an ominous sign on one wall. A stream of professionals with light and sound systems parade into the barely lit conference room. I wonder who is going to show up, for I have seen a rather elegant, printed invitation (there was a notice in one of Tehran's newspapers about my first appearance). Clergy, professors, students, and intellectuals are in attendance. I keep an eye out for "my guys" sitting in the front row: Sheikh Choheili, Mr. Askari, Mr. Frouzandeh, sitting together with some of the professors from Shahid Beheshti University.

There are a number of introductions, one by a scholar from Shushtar, Sheikh Shushtari, who knows the Mandaeans and speaks well of them, to the pleasure of Sheikh Choheili and Mr. Askari. Dr. Mahfouzi makes another introduction. Deplorably, I neglect to start with the formula, "In the name of Allah, the Compassionate, the Merciful." Mr. Khoshchashm works with admirable concentration for about two hours. On the whiteboard, I sketch three positions I call "Pure science," "hermeneutics," and "going native," criticizing the first position, then postmodernism, absolutism, idealism, and the privileging of monotheism. I posit myself in the "hermeneutics" slot, side with Buddhism and the pre-Socratic philosophers on paradox and relativism, and knowingly create a polite stir.

Just as I am drawing in my breath to wrap it all up, Dr. Mahfouzi decides it is time for a break. Talking among themselves, people head for the refreshments—tea, cakes, and fruit—set up at a long table. An enthusiastic young academic immediately engages me in conversation, and I hardly have time to eat half an orange before we start again. The indefatigable Mr. Khoshchashm at my side, I ascend the podium with three men ready to respond to my statements: the literature professor Dr. Awani; the religious leader Hojatolislam Abd Khodaei; and Dr. Tawakuli, a loquacious young sociologist who at first seems quite challenged by my talk.

He believes "going native" is a fine position, and it soon dawns on me that this is of course the conversion position, of eminent importance in a country like Iran. (I recall that at the office of the police of foreign affairs in Ahwaz I had pleaded scholarly objectivity and declined to recognize Islam as the best religion). I defend my position as that of an academic's inquiry into religions, stressing tolerance for native logic, objectivity without meaninglessness, and agreeing to ethical standards. The literature professor, while happy to hear that Americans are now gripped by colonial guilt in the study of "others," twice holds up Augustine as an example for us all. Avoiding what I consider Christian bait, I pay no special homage to the church father. But I am intrigued by Hojatolislam Abd Khodaei, who seems to me a master of diplomacy and evenhandedness. Holding on to his own positions regarding faith and monotheism, he is deft in his defenses, and I find myself frequently nodding to his words. I am exhilarated by this event, our high-wire act between the poles of faith and academic freedom. A shiny-eyed young woman asks me afterward whether I am aware that this was quite provocative. Oh yes.

There, at the Laleh Hotel, my last public appearance in Iran, Mandaeism is hardly mentioned (aside from the Shushtar introducer). This conference probably did not feel very relevant for Mr. Askari and for Sheikh Choheili, who faithfully sat through it. We do not talk much about it, as the event dealt with a different, to them more abstract, side to my religion studies. The Mandaeans clearly welcome my study of *their* religion, and I am now firmly ensconced in what feels like a new, large family. Already two years ago a Mandaean friend on Long Island in New York had said to me, "You are part of us now, and we of you. There is no going back." And this is true.

7

Baptism (Maṣbuta)

When people think of Mandaeism, they might quite rightly automatically associate it with baptism. One might call baptism *the* chief characteristic of Mandaean religion. This runs counter to two traditionally held assumptions, however. The first is that rituals as such are basically superfluous in Gnosticism, and the second is that baptism always marks a ceremony of initiation. With regard to the first assumption—now fortunately fading in research on Gnosticism in general—scholars have tended to think that if Gnostic rituals occurred at all, they belonged either to an early or to a late stage of the development of Gnosticism. Far from being innocent labels, "early" usually implied having a place in a mythological stage of Gnosticism, that is, one unformed by philosophical, abstract ideas, while "late" connoted degeneration, a form of Gnosticism slid into magic from a prior, more genuine stage.[1] In neither case did ritual occupy any rightful position in a "present" tense, but it was seen as part of a once genuine, now lost, stage, or as an embarrassing survival.

Regarding the second assumption: when initiatory baptism is considered as the only valid form, a repeated ritual like the maṣbuta becomes categorized as "atypical," at best. Max Weber shows his distaste for repeated rituals in a remarkably prejudicial manner: "Mysteries purport to produce their effect *ex opere operato* by means of a pious occasional devotion. They provide no inner motivation for any such requirement as the believer's demonstration in his life pattern of a religious norm as rebirth might entail."[2] Weber clearly evaluates an event such as "rebirth," the once and for all transformative experience, as positive, juxtaposing it to negatively judged repeated rituals of salvation. In Weber's view, ethics and sincere religiosity do not fit with repeated rituals.

Scholarly prejudices aside, one must ask what Gnostic baptisms, taken on their own terms, look like. K. Rudolph has soberly observed that there is no common Gnostic ideology with respect to baptism.[3] The Mandaean maṣbuta must be interpreted in accordance with Mandaean cosmology, anthropology, and soteriology. Running water in Mandaeism is the form that the Lightworld takes on earth. Therefore, repeated immersions mark preparations and rehearsals for entry into that world, an entry that properly happens only at the death of the body. If one takes seriously this fundamental Mandaean understanding, a valid interpretation of the maṣbuta cannot insist on a rebirth typology. And stubborn comparisons with early Christian and Jewish forms do not lead to enlightenment, for such approaches leave Mandaeism "lacking" or "abnormal" as it is held up to unavoidable standards taken from these religions.[4]

Rudolph rightly states that "because the baptism furnishes the only possibility for taking part in the Lightworld, its steady repetition is necessary."[5] In other words, were baptism to be abolished, spiritual death would ensue.[6] Stepping into the water, the people are dressed in the required white garment, the rasta. How could they enter the Lightworld in any other way? But the white dress, too, has been a stumbling block for interpreters, who expect an investiture *after* the immersion, not *before*. Freshly immersed, dripping Mandaean people stand on the riverbank and do not wear their regular clothes, nor are they naked. In a sense they are pure already, before they step into the water. In what follows, I will give a brief description of the proceedings in the maṣbuta and then attend to specific interpretive problems in it.[7]

Outline

Baptism takes place in running, "living," water, either in a river or, if the area has a mandi (cult hut), in a channel dug and directed from the river so that the water moves, whether rapidly or sluggishly, in front of the hut.[8] Baptism belongs in many contexts in Mandaeism, but here I will focus on the maṣbuta as it occurs in its simplest form—alone, not in a cluster of other rituals.[9] On Sundays and major holidays, many Mandaeans choose to be baptized. On my 1973 trip to Mandaean territory, in Khorramshahr, Iran, Mr. Feyzi said to me, "Come back at Panja! Then we all go into the water!"[10] Feast days tend to be baptism days for Mandaeans who may otherwise neglect the ritual.

Several priests may be present at a baptism. A ganzibra or a tarmida baptizes men and women in separate groups. They are all dressed in rastas, and women add a cloak for the sake of modesty. The people line up on the riverbank, where several ritual implements are ready. If it is a major holiday, there is the banner (drabša), a length of white, looped-up silk on a cross-barred, wooden pole stuck into the ground. Myrtle is twined where the two poles meet, and an almost invisible thread of gold is tied right under or next to it. Always, the clay table, the ṭariana, sits on the ground, holding incense and fuel. There is flour, salt, and sesame, brass drinking bowls, a bottle (*qanina*), and a bunch of myrtle twigs that are kept fresh in a water-filled container (or in a large plastic bag, as I have seen).

The priest recites the set prayers (rahmas) for the day.[11] He is in full regalia, and he pays attention to each piece of his ritual garb as he blesses one after the other. His chief emblem is his taga, the white silk priestly crown, with which he touches his eyes, mouth, and forehead sixty-one times, very rapidly. Then he burns incense and mixes flour and salt with water to make a *pihta*, a small, biscuit-sized flat bread that he will eat. Later he bakes another pihta, which is to be shared among the baptized people.

If the drabša is present, the people stretch out their right hands to grasp hold of its vertical pole before they descend into the water, one at a time. First they take hold at its bottom, then at the top, and the priest places his right hand just above the hand of each person holding on to the drabša pole. The priest enters the water first, and then the people on the riverbank, one at a time. Each walks out into the water in front of the priest, turns leftward around him, and crouches in the water to make a full submersion three times in the water behind the priest. Then the priest throws water three times on the wet figure. Using his left hand, the priest next grasps the person's right hand and transfers the splashed figure to his right side, placing the person between himself and the priestly staff (margna). Stuck into the river bottom, the secured priestly staff frees the priest's hands.

The priest submerges the person three times and uses his wet finger to draw a line three times across the person's forehead, from the right to the left ear. Again thrice, the person in the water receives a palm full of water to drink. The sacred handshake, kušṭa, takes place between the two. The officiant sticks a klila, a small myrtle wreath, under the baptized person's burzinqa (turban). Protecting the baptized with potent names of Lightworld beings, the priest then places his hand on the person's head and recites these Lightworld names.

Back up on dry land, the baptized crouch, often shivering, and wait until the officiant has finished the ritual in the water for each one. There may be a fire nearby for warmth. If many people are present, the line on the riverbank grows, people waiting for the priest to smear each one with sesame paste across the forehead. As before, the movement is from right to left. The priest gives each one a second kušṭa, and each now descends to the edge of the river. There the baptized, using their right hands, splash water three times over their own right arms. Up on the bank once more, priest and baptized people alike extend their right hands toward the river, taking the yardna as a witness to the baptism.

The meal comes next. Crouching on the ground, the baptized receive a piece of the communal pihta and, in individual bowls, three servings of water, which the priest pours from the bottle. They drink the first two full bowls but throw the third pouring over their shoulder. After a third kušṭa, the priest stands behind the row of crouching people, touching the head of each person while uttering the *haṭamtas* (sealing prayers). Risen, the baptized people exchange kušṭa with the officiant, and the rite ends as each participant extracts the klila from underneath the turban and throws the little wreath into the water, where it drifts off, slowly or rapidly, depending on the current. Finally, the priest performs the deconsecrating rituals. These mirror those that he went through before the baptism, and thus the circle of events is closed.

Details

Throughout the baptism, the priest has kept up a steady stream of words, more or less muffled by the priestly mouth and nose cover (pandama).[12] The prayers called for in each step of the proceedings can be found in the *Prayerbook*. Their contents not only express the significance of the ritual steps but also contribute to creating these steps. I will now focus on the contents of the baptismal prayers, on some of the implements used in the baptism, and on the prescribed movements. Actions and words, as manifested in practice and mythology, mutually reinforce and support one another in rituals, and the maṣbuta is no exception.

A Mandaean consecrated priest is an ʿutra manifested on earth. The officiating priest at a baptism first "opens up" the yardna by reciting prayer 12.[13] The act can be interpreted as activating the channel from the Lightworld to the earthly river. During a specific line in prayer 13, the priest descends into the water while calling on the Lightbeing Piriafil to "give free movement to the limbs of my body!"[14] He continues, "I go down before these souls [i.e., the people to be baptized] whom the Life delivereth and saveth and protecteth these souls from all that is evil."[15] He then asks a number of Lightworld beings to guard and secure the souls of those to be baptized.

Prayer 14 is recited for the margna, which is baptized and, as noted earlier, stuck into the river bottom. Secured in an upright position, the margna stands enclosed within a loop in the *kanzala* (priest's stole). Prayer 14 describes the margna as being covered in light and radiance, which suggests not the white stole but, more accurately, the water, because the water *is* the Lightworld. Removing a tiny klila that has so far encircled his finger next to the one bearing the Šum Yawar Ziwa, the priestly gold ring, the priest slips this wreath onto his margna. The staff, then, is subject to a twofold activity: baptism—a form of investiture—and wreathing.[16] In this very graphic manner, the margna seems to represent a priest or an ʿutra.

Yet another item is a personified Lightworld being, for a drabša on the riverbank receives treatment like a priest. When the persons to be baptized grasp hold of the drabša pole before they descend into the water, the act can be interpreted as a kušṭa. The banner marks the presence of the Lightworld, and its length of cloth must avoid the earth beneath it. This correlates with the rules for a priest's clothes, which likewise may not come into contact with the ground. Both margna and drabša receive a klila. The evergreen klila is a female symbol, a counterpart to the white crown, which is always coded as male.[17]

While he stands in the water, the priest draws three circles in it with his margna in order to bind the forces of darkness. Prayer 15 speaks of seven walls of iron, which in all likelihood refer directly to the priest's activity. He must rid the water of evil, making it suitable for baptism. Only one-ninth of the water particles are pure[18]—the rest are mixed or evil—but the ninth part is, of course, crucial. The central baptism prayer is prayer 18, in which the priest calls on the first person to join him in the water: "In the name of Life! Let every man whose strength enableth him and who loveth his soul, come and go down to the jordan and be baptised and receive the Pure Sign; put on robes of radiant light and set a fresh wreath on his head!"[19]

As noted, the lack of investiture after baptism has been a puzzlement to commentators on the maṣbuta, especially so to Segelberg. He feels that originally there *must* have been an investiture, and that the Mandaeans are now using the rasta symbol ineffectively.[20] Segelberg cannot abandon the idea that all baptisms are initiatory. When he quotes a so far unpublished Mandaean text, which states, "It is the water in which we clothe ourselves,"[21] he is unable to hear the text out, that is, he cannot accept the water as a garment. However, in prayer 18, the expression "put on robes of radiant light" also refers not to actual, material clothes but to the water, which is the Lightworld incarnate, the "garment of light" enveloping the rasta already on the bodies in the water.

Instead of looking in vain for "typological" initiations and for after-the-fact investiture, one must instead recall that Mandaeans prepared for baptism are no neophytes ready to step into a new stage of life, acquiring a new religion, or new selves. The Mandaeans are secure in their identities. In baptism, they seek reaffirmation, consolidation with the Lightworld, and a reintegration with fellow Mandaeans past and present. Like all Mandaean rituals, the maṣbuta re-create and reconfirm the laufa, the vital connection between the earthly world and the Lightworld.

Masiqta Zihrun Raza Kasia, the text quoted by Segelberg, interprets the priest's left-to-right movement when he grasps the person in the water as an act of clothing with the garments of Life.[22] The movement is, indeed, another pervasive item in the Mandaean symbolic universe, and it corresponds to the vertical movement from earth to Lightworld. However, an earthly, human being never fully belongs in either realm. By immersion in baptism, Mandaeans secure the laufa, a connection that cannot be severed as long as ritual life persists.

I suggest that the baptism is a "horizontal death mass," that is, it foreshadows the masiqta, the death mass (to be treated in the next chapter). The movement down into the water symbolizes and prefigures the final, vertical movement, at the death of the body, up to the Lightworld. A rasta is worn at both rituals, and the technical term *to raise up* (*SLQ* I)[23] is used for the activity and the outcome in both baptism and death mass. Horizontal and vertical movements mirror one another, and the right-to-left pattern marks the path from earthly, female world to male Lightworld.

In the water, each person is signed with water across the forehead, and each individual's name is mentioned in the formula "N., son of N., thou hast been signed with the Sign of Life and the name of the Life and the name of Manda-d̲-Hiia were pronounced upon thee."[24] Drinking the three handfuls of water, the celebrant is invited to "be healed and strengthened!" Consuming the water can be understood as a kind of internal baptism. "May kušṭa heal you and raise you up!" says the priest, and this is repeated by the baptized person. The two then shake hands, confirming the mutual wish. According to prayer 19, the name Hazazban and names of other Lightworld entities are spoken over the baptized person. The names seal and protect.

Back up on land, the baptized await smearings with sesame paste. This ritual segment has caused problems for some interpreters, such as Segelberg, who feels that the smearings appear in the wrong order; to him, oil signs should occur before wreathing.[25] But his view seems unduly influenced by ancient Near Eastern royal enthronement ideologies, which are only partially useful for comparison. The baptized person does *not* become a king, and the oil prayers 22–24 nowhere even hint at royalty rites. Instead, the oil is emphasized as healer and protector from illness. It has come down from the Lightworld "to heal, uplift, raise up and ameliorate all pains, diseases, complaints, tumors (and) the seven mysteries that inhabit the body."[26] This prayer has a polemical tenor, for it takes the opportunity to stress that the oil is that of Mandaeism, not of Christianity nor of the Ishtar worshipers.

Polemical issues figure centrally in prayer 21, recited while the baptized step up on the riverbank in order to receive the sesame sign. Here, pihta, kušṭa, and *mambuha* (water drink) are listed among the primary bearers of witness for the newly baptized souls. After the signing, the persons go down to the river to splash water on their right arms, a rite that Segelberg rightly sees as a form of kušṭa with the water.[27]

Like sesame, pihta and mambuha are substances that originally descended from the Lightworld. Salt must be present in the pihta dough, for the celebrants are alive (in the masiqta, as we shall see, the pihta symbolizing the dead person is saltless). At the moment when the third bowlful of water is thrown over the left shoulder, the priest says, "For your left."[28] "The left" signifies Ruha, associated with the female realm and the earth, who in this way is allotted her rightful share.

Let me make a brief aside here. In the film *Mandaean Ceremony*, made by an assistant to Drower in Qalat Saleh, Iraq, in 1954, a small boy forgets this step and instead of throwing the water away, drinks the third bowlful. Nobody reacts.[29] I was thinking of this film as I watched the video of Majid's baptism (see chapter 2). Then I leaned forward and focused especially carefully as Majid, crouching in his wet rasta, is about to throw the bowlful of water over his shoulder, and he does it. I exclaimed, "Thank God you did that right!" The others laughed, and I explained to them that in the film, the little boy does it incorrectly.

On that occasion, Majid's wife, Abir, watched with interested amusement (she was not with him in Iraq at the baptism). "Why are they taking so long?" she asked me. I told her that they have to get all the evil off her husband and all the good spirits on him. "Oh, I see," she replied, laughing and leaning back in the sofa, "there's a lot to get off him! No wonder it takes time!" "No," I said, "it's like that for everybody."

Now I return to the sequence of the baptism ritual. After a third kušṭa, the priest recites the four haṭamta (sealing) prayers 25–28 over each person. These prayers protect them from evil powers, and their souls are now "bound and sealed," immune to attacks by illnesses and curses. Following a number of prayers, a fourth handshake occurs after the recital of numbers 71 and 72, an especially powerful combination of prayers. Prayer 72 is Mandaeism's "chief sacramental formula,"[30] asking forgiveness of sins for past and present Mandaeans. In addition, it specifically mentions the food provided for the baptism ritual. Indeed, the prayer's enigmatic title,"Good is the good for the good" (*ṭab ṭaba lṭaba*), shows the importance of the effect of food on the good people, for ṭaba refers to the food benefiting "the good people" (lṭaba), who are partaking of the food and those who are commemorated in the ritual. This is a good example of Mandaean fondness for wordplay.

The four appearances of the kušṭa occur at these points: (1) after the baptized have been signed with water across their foreheads, (2) after the sesame smearings, (3) following pihta and mambuha, and (4) at the closing of the sacramental prayer 72. I interpret them as a reconfirmed laufa with alive and departed Mandaeans and with the Lightworld. Laufa is chiefly expressed in terms of food, the prime symbolic means of exchange across the realms. In all four instances of the kušṭa, the celebrants have just received some kind of life-giving substance ultimately stemming from the Lightworld. These four are water (twice, externally across the forehead), the mambuha drink, sesame, and pihta. Both externally and internally, the baptized have been fed by the Lightworld. The food purifies, revives, and sustains them as Mandaeans.

The well-worn term *realized eschatology* would seem at least partially legitimate with respect to the maṣbuta. Salvation is already at hand. Still, the constantly created redemption remains incomplete, for it must be balanced at the end of earthly life with the final liberation from this life. While it persists, life on earth is neither free nor automatic but must be continuously reconfirmed in its dependence on the Lightworld. The example of the maṣbuta demonstrates the human responsibility for keeping up the laufa. It is not just a matter of the Lightworld benevolently sharing its bounty.

Becoming Who You Are

Again, I wish to emphasize the importance of an already existing, communal Mandaean identity, as exemplified in the baptism ritual. Mandaeans (like Manichaeans and doubtless other ancient Gnostics) belong in clearly defined communities. Identity is chiefly a communal matter. But scholars tend to remain fascinated by the singular initiation ritual, its lone subject, and the ritual's concomitant dramatics of personal transformation. Thus, individual identity is overemphasized. The conversion model featuring a reborn person, a neophyte, seems hard to resist. As indicated, such a pattern, with its narrowly viewed "ideal-type," initiatory form of baptism, may derive from scholarly Christian biases. However, this model has limited use in Mandaeism.

Any study of ritual needs to establish what the ritual accomplishes and means to its practitioners. Native exegesis must be consulted, above all else. If no such direct exegesis is available, it should be teased out of the text—or out of other forms of evidence. A ritual such as the Mandaean baptism creates and re-creates meaning, reconstituting and undergirding the realities discernible in the ceremonial goings-on. One might say that rituals reconfirm consensual realities.

From a scholarly viewpoint, rituals of course do not fall from heaven but are human creations. Needless to say, repeated rituals are created in order to be performed more than once in a person's life time. But the mere fact of repetition appears to be disagreeable to scholars who—consciously or not—operate with an ideal model of baptism, a model based on initiation. As noted in chapter 1, I consider rituals to reflect a particular understanding of work, emerging from everyday experiences of labor. Creators of rituals find their models in work, and as in ordinary life, some tasks are once-and-for-all, while others require cyclical or seasonal reproductions. Regular intake of food is necessary, but one may have to be inoculated against a certain disease only once in one's life. Mandaean baptism is understood according to the food model, while a priest initiation fits the once-in-a-lifetime pattern.

When Sevrin states that rituals in Gnosticism are "in disagreement with its most profound character,"[31] he seems to subscribe to an abstract, so-called spiritualized view of Gnostic religiosity, one disproved by many forms of Gnosticism, and certainly by Mandaeism. On the other hand, when Gnostics themselves criticize rituals, they do so primarily for two reasons: either the (orthodox Jewish or Christian) non-Gnostic practices are seen as useless and impotent, or the traditional rituals are considered to be in need of new modes of understanding. Very rarely is the idea of rituals as such rejected. To make Gnosticism into a kind of abstract philosophy deprives the religion of its basis in concrete reality.

A lived, practiced religion presupposes rituals. To view rituals along a time spectrum from the "once-and-for-all" through "occasional" to "frequently repeated productions" is a line of scholarly inquiry that has not yet been fully explored. Any examination of rituals in a given religion must take that religion's basic cosmologies and mythologies into consideration. If the religion has both initiatory and repeated rituals, an analysis of them will yield, among other things, information about that religion's understanding of work and production.

In this chapter, I have presented maṣbuta as a specific example of a repeated ritual in Mandaeism. I have argued that the ritual is best comprehended within the greater horizon of Mandaean cosmology. As one of the means to constantly re-create the laufa, the maṣbuta has its natural place in Mandaeism. The next chapter will investigate another laufa creation, one particular form of the masiqta, the death mass: the "masiqta of the Parents," the *Ṭabahata* masqita.

8

The Ṭabahata Masiqta

In her introduction to *Haran Gawaita*, Drower says:

> To [the Mandaean] the immutable and sacro-sanct elements of his religion are the ancient rituals, baptism and the various forms of the sacramental meal. It does not worry him that there are a number of creation stories, contradictory to one another or that there is confusion in his heterogeneous pantheon of spirits of light and darkness. What does matter is that no rule of ritual purity be broken, and that every gesture and action prescribed for ritual shall be rigidly observed.[1]

The Mandaean masiqta (death mass) is performed three days after the death of a person, unless an astrologically "bad" (*mbaṭṭal*) day interferes. It is an extremely complex ritual, focusing on the spirit (ruha) and the soul (nišimta), the two upper elements constituting the human being. Because the body (*pagra*) cannot rise to the Lightworld, it receives little or no attention in the masiqta. The emphasis rests on the joining of spirit and soul, for these must accompany one another upwards in order to be incorporated into a new, Lightworld body, the *'usṭuna*. This is the masiqta's goal. In addition, the ritual aims to incorporate the newly deceased into the community of the Mandaean ancestors in the Lightworld. Like the baptism ritual, the masiqta effects a re-created, reestablished laufa.

Death masses differ somewhat with respect to prayers and numbers of required priestly participants.[2] The masiqta I present here is the "masiqta of the parents" (*Ṭabahata*), an event occurring only once a year, on the last day of the five-day intercalary period Panja. It is a double masiqta,[3] performed in two parts, the first of which has two segments. I will describe the masiqta in three sections, relying on Drower's fieldwork accounts and on her editions and translations of Mandaean texts. Prayers, priestly instructions, commentaries, and activities will be laid out in conjunction with one another to show the complex interactions of religious thought, imagery, and ritual proceedings. I start with the preparations for the Ṭabahata masiqta, then move to the three descriptive parts, and end with a short interpretive section.

Preliminaries

In its entirety, a regular, single masiqta takes about twelve hours,[4] but the annual Ṭabahata masiqta requires even more time. Of the several priestly celebrants, at least one must be a ganzibra. As usual, an ašganda (helper) supplies the priests with certain materials for the ceremony. Preparations begin the day before the masiqta. On the day of the ceremony itself, the celebrating priests perform minor ablutions and partake of two ritual meals, *zidqa brikha* (blessed oblation) and *dukhrana* (commemoration). During the second meal, the priests begin to impersonate the dead person(s) for whom the masiqta is celebrated.[5] The presence of laypeople, as spectators, is required during these public rituals, but the masiqta proper is conducted inside the mandi (cult hut), unseen by anybody but the participating priests.[6]

Before they enter the mandi, however, the ganzibra, assisted by the ašganda, kills a dove outside the hut. The two men imitate the two primordial ʿutras who first carried out a masiqta, the masiqta for Adam, the first man.[7] Impersonating "Pure Ether," Ayar Dakia, the ganzibra puts the dove under his foot, lays the knife against the bird's throat, and, watched by the ašganda, intones:

> "'In the name of Life and the name of Knowledge-of-Life"' is being mentioned over thee! Ptahil summoneth thee and Hibil-Ziwa commandeth thy slaughter.'" And then he drew the knife across the mystery of its throat and said 'Thy flesh is pure for souls of those *masiqtas* who are called on (*by name*). With thee, Adam shall rise to the Light, and any who eat of thee shall live, be made healthful and well-established. The name of Life and the name of Knowledge-of-Life is mentioned upon thee.'[8]

The dove, called Ba, symbolizes the spirit, and the priest assures it that it will rise with the soul.[9] After the killing of the dove, the ganzibra and the ašganda immerse themselves in the river. The ašganda brings the sacrificed dove with him into the water. Back up on land, the ganzibra takes the bird, plucks away some of the feathers on the right side of the bird's breast, cuts out a piece of flesh, roasts it in the fire burning on the precincts, dips the piece in salt, and shreds it into tiny bits. Later these pieces will be distributed to the celebrating priests as they arrange their ritual trays (ṭarianas). The fragmented bird flesh is called "the portion of the Ba." Drower describes what happens next: "The *ganzibra* wraps the body of the dove (the *Ba*) in palm-fibre, enters the cult-hut and pushes it into the space between the roof and the northern wall, so that it will face the celebrants during the *masiqta*."[10]

In the meantime, the other priests have purified themselves, prepared ritual foods, and cleansed their ṭarianas. *Faṭiras*, small, round, saltless biscuits, are half baked, and a certain number of these are distributed to each of the priests. Now each priest arranges his clean ṭariana with the following: a small water bottle; a cup of miša (sesame oil mixed with pounded dates); the allotted faṭiras (the total must be sixty, or fifteen biscuits each for four celebrating priests); a drinking bowl containing four raisins; a twig of myrtle; and, finally, shreds of these foods: Ba, seeds of grape, pomegranate, quince, dates, coconut, almond, walnut, and citrus. All the trays are placed within the mandi. A second tray for each priest holds a fire basin with fuel and a stand with a cube of incense. In full ritual garb, the priests enter the mandi and remain secluded there until the end of the masiqta.

The First Part of the Masiqta: The Sixty Faṭiras

Each celebrant stands inside the mandi in front of his two trays; the one to the left, with the foodstuffs, represents the spirit, the one to the right, the soul.[11] After reciting a prayer for his mouth cover (pandama),[12] each priest picks up the bottle and the sprig of myrtle

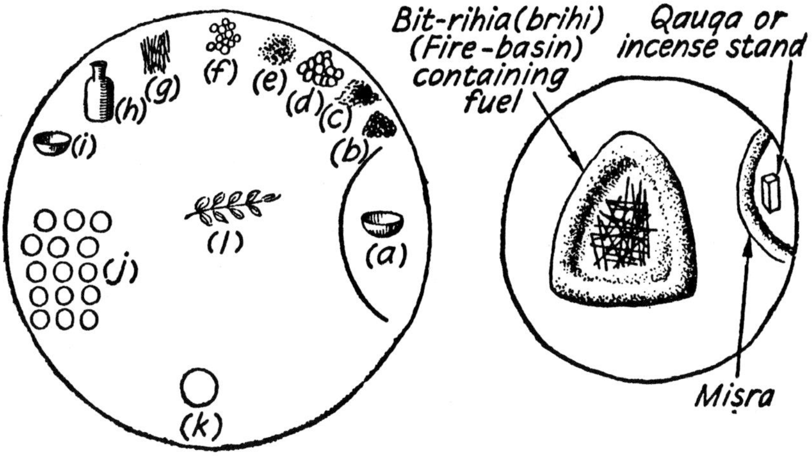

The two *ṭarianas* at the *masiqta*. From Drower, *Water into Wine*. Used by permission of John Murray, publisher.

on his tray and pours some of the water from the bottle over the four raisins in the bowl. Kneading the raisins in the water, he turns the liquid into *hamra* (wine).[13]

While he is doing this, he recites prayer 33, the first of the masiqta prayers. This prayer addresses the life-giving "water of Life," which has come from the Lightworld, and which erases evil. Also:

> As the water falleth on the earth, so shall their sins, trespasses, follies, stumblings and mistakes be loosed from those who love the name of Truth (*kušṭa*) and from the souls of this *masiqta*, and from (the souls of) our fathers, teachers, brothers and sisters who have departed the body, and those who (still) live in the body.[14]

Next, the priest lifts the incense cube from the right tray and salutes the First Life in this manner:

> Hail Yuzaṭaq, *Gnosis* of Life, Source of Life; He who unveileth the silence, giveth hope and keepeth the prayers of the spirits and souls of the righteous and believing men into the Place of Light. . . . Pray ye from there for us and we will pray from here for you. All fruits wither: all sweet odours passeth away, but not the fragrance of *Gnosis* of Life, which cometh not to an end nor passeth away for an age of ages.[15]

Like prayers, incense rises toward the Lightworld, maintaining the laufa. Incense is now thrown on the fire, and the smoke wafts toward the left in order to envelop the items on the left tray in the fragrance of the Lightworld. *1012* explains the effect of prayer and of the wafting onto "the Mystery of the Mingling" (i.e., the liquid in the hamra bowl) as giving the soul a hand, purifying her, lifting her up, and mingling her with "the mystery of the Water."[16]

The next, very long prayer, number 35, includes these words toward its end: "Spirits and souls sit (*here*) as guilty, (*yet*) by thy name they shall rise as innocent."[17] After that, three other long prayers follow, numbers 75–77. The first one describes how the Lightworld messenger causes joy but also wreaks havoc when he enters the world. Even the evil ones, "sitting on thrones of rebellion," are overpowered by the forces of the Light and end up praising these.[18] When the priest reaches the words "Turn back, push back, remove and make impotent Angels of wrath, frost and hail from my land and My house" in prayer 75,[19] the effect is that "spirit and soul are estranged from hatred, envy, dissention and evil thought."[20] At the very end, prayer 75 asks for the soul's successful establishment in the Lightworld. And at these words, says *1012*, "soul and spirit take hands and are heartened."[21]

The next prayer in the segment, prayer 76, mentions the Perfecter of Souls, who gives the soul a radiant garment and a wreath made of victories. The soul's own good works while on earth, including proper partaking in commemorative meals for the dead, will precede the soul on its way upward and make the soul perfect. Just as the priest will now eat for the benefit of the ascending soul, so that soul, while on earth, ought to have observed the duties of dukhrana and zidqa brikha.

At the recital of prayer 77 the foods on the ṭariana are illuminated.[22] Before the recital prayer 9, which follows, there is a formula that begins, "May there be laufa, solace of Life, and forgiveness of sins for me." At these words, "the spirit moveth towards the soul and saith to her, 'By thy life, my sister in kušṭa, this is my day of days! Mine eyes are no longer dazzled and fleshly sloth is removed from my heart.'"[23]

Prayer 35 now reappears, and during its recital the priest purifies the soul's "eyes and ears, the portals of the brain, and bones, heart and liver."[24] It is worth noting that prayer 35 is an extremely versatile; it is called "good for all occasions."[25] Indeed, the reappearance of prayers—at different times, in the *same* ritual—is an important feature of Mandaean rituals. The prayers may have different effects depending on where they appear in a ritual sequence. As tools, prayers perform functions that vary according to where the ritual worker, the priest, is posited in the ritual production toward the construction of a complete ritual edifice. To give an example: frame carpentry is different than fine cabinetmaking, but the builder is still in the construction business, using the tools of his profession. Repetition of prayers and specific, set prayer sequences surface regularly in Mandaean rituals, and I shall have more to say about the significance of these features later on.

The Great "First World," commenting on the proceedings during prayer 35, reminds the priest to insert the *zhara* (warning, i.e., the name of the deceased). Thus the formula in prayer 35 is individualized, adjusted to the present moment: "barred to this the soul of [name inserted] of this *masiqta* is the gate of sin, and we will open to him the Gate of Light."[26]

All through these prayers the priests have wafted incense toward the left onto the foodstuffs and other items on their ṭarianas. Drower explains:

> Throughout this opening part of the ritual [the priest] has held myrtle in his left hand. He now twists it into a tiny wreath. Meanwhile, the *ashganda* has left the hut and goes to the *yardna*, taking flour with him. He mixes this with a little water in the palm of his hand and makes a saltless dough. As he goes by the fire on his way back to the hut, he passes the dough thrice through the flame, saying, "The name of Manda-d̲-Hiia is pronounced on thee." This is called "the testimony of the fire." On the *ashganda*'s re-entry into the hut, bearing the dough, each celebrant takes a pinch of it from him.[27]

This dough fragment becomes the pihta. Eight pihta prayers follow, the first of which opens "the great Door of Nourishment to the soul and spirit."[28] Together, the eight prayers symbolize the eight months of pregnancy.[29] In this manner the gestation of the Lightworld soul is foreshadowed.

Each man dips his priestly gold seal ring, Šum Yawar Ziwa (the name of Yawar Ziwa), into the hamra bowl and recites the two prayers for the mambuha. (In this case the mambuha is identified with the hamra in the bowl, but mambuha usually refers to the ritual drink of river water.) The last sentence in the second mambuha prayer is "(Like) the mingling of wine with water, so may your truth, your righteousness and your faith be added to those who love your name of Truth."[30] This mingling, by those who love the name of Truth, the priests, is threefold: *in* the priests themselves, mediated *through* them as activators for the ascending spirit and soul, and *in* the spirit and soul.[31] The hamra bowl is a womb, now fertilized by the priests' actions.

Prayers 46 and 47 are klila prayers, which interweave spirit and soul, and the klila is set on the head of the soul. The next prayer, 48, an oil prayer, clears the soul's vision.[32]

The masiqta has now reached a crucial stage. If errors in the ritual are committed at this point, at prayer 49, the proceedings must be halted at once, and severe penalties are due. Carefully, each priest puts down the klila and the pihta on the ṭariana, and he places his right hand on the first of the faṭiras (as seen in figure 1, there are fifteen faṭiras to a tray—the total number of faṭiras must be sixty). Prayer 49 begins, "This, the glory and light of life, is to bring forth the spirit and soul from the body and to clothe the living soul in a living garment."[33] Further, the prayer invokes Ṣauriel, the angel of death, and the soul is said to acquire vestments of light after all bodily components have been removed from it.[34] Envious but impressed, the hostile planets behold the soul's radiant clothes, but they can do nothing to harm the soul at this point. Ascending, the soul reaches the scales of Abatur, where the soul and spirit are questioned "as to their names, their signs, their blessing, their baptism and everything that is therewith."[35]

Each priest now sits down, pulls off a shred of the pihta, and folds it over the klila but makes certain that the two ends of the dough fragment do not meet. This act is called "clothing the wreath."[36] In his left hand the priest holds aloft the klila with the pihta piece, and while he holds it, he uses his right hand to move the first of the faṭiras to the front of his tray. Next he picks a little of each kind of fruit, seed, and nut and a piece of dove flesh and puts these fragments on the faṭira. It is now an "arrangement" (*qina*). He then dips four fingers, tips pressed together, into the oil and signs the faṭira with oil three times, from left to right.

The triple smearing takes place three times, so that there are nine passes of oil for each biscuit. These passes are required at specific lines in prayer 49: at "that which is with her of the body," at "the House of Abatur," and after the phrase "the spirit of N. [zhara] of this masiqta hath gone and become of (*the same*) nature as the soul."[37] As a result of these passes paired with the required words, the soul gazes at the spirit, reaches out for her, and embraces her.[38]

Risen to a safe position, the soul sits in Lightworld splendor. At the requisite prayer, number 50, another triple sign of the faṭira is due. And again, at prayer 51, at the words "When this, the soul of N., casteth off her bodily garment, she putteth on a dress of life and becometh like unto the Great Life in light."[39] At prayer 52 a triple pass also occurs.

Returning to the rest of his faṭiras, the priest deals with each one in turn, beginning all over again with prayer 33. His acts are identical to those for the first faṭira, with one exception: the very last faṭira, the fifteenth, receives no sign at prayer 52. This omission leaves an open-ended situation, and the point of this will become clear later. Next the treated biscuits are piled into a stack, on which the priest puts his hand while reciting prayer 53, the "seal of the masiqta."

The crucial part involving the prayer sequence 49–53 is now finished, but prayer 49, alone, is repeated, with the difference that at the phrase "the House of Abatur" it is not the name of the dead person that is inserted but the word *ṭabahatan* (our ancestors).[40] This is most fitting, for the stack of biscuits now invoked represents the assembled ancestors, whom the risen soul will join.

Lifting his hand from the pile of faṭiras, the priest repeats the first mambuha prayer, 44, which invokes the source of living water, Biriawiš. Having held the pihta-wrapped klila in his left hand for a long time, the celebrant finally separates the dough from the klila and puts the wreath down on the pile of faṭiras. Mysteriously, the wreath is called "an inner heart situated in the breast."[41] This exegesis associates klila and the dove, the Ba, whose breast meat has been distributed onto each of the faṭiras in the stack. Both klila and Ba are spirit symbols.

"Should the slightest error be made at this point, the entire *masiqta* is invalid; moreover, the soul for whom it is celebrated may be injured. The priest who made the mistake is automatically disqualified from his office," says Drower.[42] The priest must say "One and two and three" as he separates klila from pihta. Then he breaks off a piece of the top faṭira in the stack and one from the faṭira on the bottom.[43] This breaking off marks a mouth opened for the soul.[44] Obviously, the soul, as a kind of fetus handled by the priest, is now ready to take nourishment. The priest presses the two separated pieces of faṭiras and a sliver of the dove meat into the pihta and then pours water from the water bottle into the hamra bowl. This mingling of water and "wine" is "the union of the cosmic Father and Mother, a union previously sanctified by the dipping in of the priestly ring. The Divine Womb, represented by the hamra bowl, is now fertilised."[45]

"Eating in the Above, drinking in the Above and casting incense in the Above," the priest utters, while he folds the pihta around the foodstuffs pressed into it and dips it into the bowl, while reciting prayer 54.[46] The effect of this action is that spirit, soul, and body are now firmly integrated, the soul being clothed with the mystery of the cosmic parents: the Father, water, and the Mother, the hamra.[47]

Prayer 55, short and to the point, follows: "The Great Life spoke and revealed (opened) with His mouth, in His own radiance, light and glory."[48] Each priest now imitates the Great Life, for he "pushes aside his *pandama*, opens his mouth and drops the *pihta* into it, swallowing it whole. Then he drinks the *hamra*."[49]

The mediating ašganda enters the mandi with a water bottle that has so far been kept outside. This is called the "outer bottle," to distinguish it from the bottle on the ṭarianas. The "outer bottle" contains *halalta* (rinsing water), which the priests use to rinse their bowls. They then drink that water, for nothing of it must be spilled. Prayers 56 and 57 follow, and throughout the rest of the prayers, numbers 58–72, the priests extend their hands above the heap of faṭiras. Prayer 91 is the last prayer for this part of the masiqta. At the end, they all exchange the kušṭa, saying, "May *Kušṭa* strengthen you, my brother-ʿuthras! The living have been joined in communion, just as ʿuthras in their *škintas* are joined in communion. Pleasing is your fragrance, my brothers, in your innermost, that is all full of radiance!"[50]

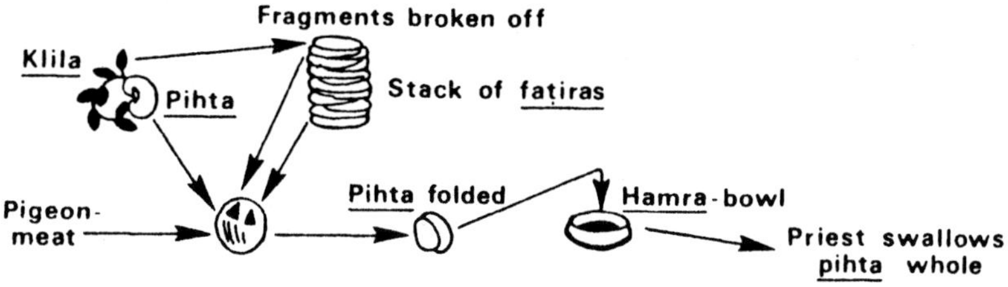

Procedure for creating a Lightworld body (ʿuṣṭuna) for the soul. Drawing by author.

The Second Part: The First Treatment of the Six Faṭiras

Six faṭiras (not shown in figure 1) have been left untreated on each ṭariana. Each priest's attention now turns to these. Drower admits that she fails to comprehend why these six biscuits now require a full, separate treatment.[51] There are differences in the masiqta for these six, and *The Great "First World"* gives the best account of how these six faṭiras are handled.

As before, the action begins with prayer 32, and it continues, as in the masiqta for the batch of sixty faṭiras, up to prayer 49. Then a voice of warning is heard from the Lightworld regarding the phrase "that which is with her (ma d̲-bh̲)': 'Be heedful lest (*thou signest* a sign (at) the *Ma d-bh* (or) the soul will not enter.'"[52] If a priest errs by making a first sign on the sixth faṭira with sesame oil at prayer 49 in this second round, he resembles a date palm consumed by fire. In addition, his own right eye and the left eye of the rising soul suffer injury, and the priest himself is polluted.[53]

Only the first sign—of three, as in the masiqta for the sixty—appears to cause destruction at this point. The two other signs at prayer 49 seem to produce no harm. Prayer 50 follows, with no signs this time. At prayer 51, the priest must again be on guard against signing. At prayer 52, also, the priest must restrain his hand, making no pass at the conclusion of this prayer. A sign here would seriously stain the soul.

After this section, the prayers run as before, in the masiqta for the sixty faṭiras, up to prayer 91, which concluded the first round. But a whole new series of prayers now ensue, twenty-four in all, ending with the large Ṭabahatan, the genealogy prayer 170.

So far, one notices that neither the sixtieth faṭira in the first round of the masiqta nor the sixth biscuit in the second treatment has received a sign during the recitals of *prayers* 49–52. This has left an open-ended, suspenseful situation. *The Great "First World"* explains regarding the first sixty faṭiras that they "keep the (*unborn*) babe safe: thirty for the days, and thirty for the nights during which it breathes not (yet) the breath of life."[54] And *1012* considers the six faṭiras to be the head of the so far headless body created by the sixty biscuits.[55] It now becomes clear why there is no sesame oil sign at the sixtieth faṭira at prayer 52 in the first round of the masiqta. The reason is that the sixtieth faṭira keeps the headless body ready for the creative act of attaching the "head." This head is the sixth faṭira, to be added to the body already created by the sixty biscuits. But the question still remains why an open-ended situation, the lack of oil signs at prayers 49–52, still exists for the head.

This question will not be answered until the third section of the Ṭabahata masiqta. Having completed the second round, the priests now deconsecrate themselves and prepare and consume the same two meals that preceded the first part of the masiqta. Symmetry rules.

> The *ashganda* collects the piles of *faṭiria* from the *ṭariania* and takes down the dove from the north wall. He wraps bread and dead bird together in a white cloth and places the bundle reverently aside somewhere in the *bit manda*. . . . the bundle is interred by the *ashganda* in the sacred area. Any part may be chosen except ground lying east of the cult-hut.[56]

The Second Treatment of the Six Faṭiras: The Ṭabahata Masiqta

Now, finally, comes the answer to the puzzle of the open-ended acts, the lacking oil signs. As noted, only at the festival of Panja, the five days between the old and the new year, does the entire sequence, the "masiqta of the Parents," take place. The third section of the ritual ties up the "loose ends" of other masiqtas performed throughout the year and completes the lacking oil signs so far. At Panja, when access to the Lightworld is open and unimpeded, the time has come to bring everybody who has died during the old year safely to the goal.[57] Masiqtas are also celebrated for Mandaeans who have died impure deaths during the past year. This is so because the Ṭabahata masiqta takes care of any evil effects of such deaths, and it helps those souls stuck in the maṭartas since bodily departure.

One may safely say, therefore, that the Ṭabahata masiqta constitutes an annual closing up of necessarily incomplete death rituals performed during the past year. Spirits and souls wander about until they are liberated by the Ṭabahata, for this masiqta functions as the final sealing of the united body, the ʿuṣṭuna.[58] *1012* warns against the error of performing the Ṭabahata masiqta at times other than Panja.[59]

The Great "First World" instructs the priest in the following manner: the Mother masiqta, that is, the ritual of the sixty faṭiras and the first treatment of the six faṭiras, is different from the next component. This is the Father masiqta, in which the six faṭiras are treated for a second time, now smeared with sesame oil.[60] Together, then, the first two treatments mark the Mother masiqta, while the Father masiqta stands separately, concluding the work. The fifteenth faṭira in the section for the sixty, and the last biscuit in the first treatment of the six are now signed at the requisite places in the central prayers, numbers 49–52.

The sequence of prayers for this section varies from those in the preceding two sections. The difference begins with prayer 91, which concluded the masiqta of the sixty. After a segment of ten other prayers, at prayer 9, the soul becomes enveloped by the mysteries of the Father to such an extent that the purgatory dwellers are unable to block her way.[61] The two klila prayers, numbers 46 and 47, are omitted. This is a telling feature, for the klila marks a spirit symbol, and a reference to it is avoided at this point, in all likelihood because the spirit has become one with the soul.

As noted, at prayers 49–52 all six faṭiras—not just the last one—receive signs. At this point, *The Great "First World"* takes care to note that the myrtle on the pile of faṭiras is the seal of prayer 52, for the myrtle is "clothing which preserves the soul. So she goes and puts it on, rejoices in it and is enveloped in it, for it is a body into which she entereth."[62]

Even though the seals of the soul are now concluded, the soul has not yet arrived at its goal. It obtains a letter from Abatur at prayer 53 and enters his scales at prayer 54.[63] Judgment and prosecution of the soul are finished thirty prayers later, at the second occurrence of prayer 71, and the prayer sequence now parallels that of the first treatment of the six faṭiras. The masiqta finishes with prayer 170, as did the first round of the six.

Prayer sequences of the three parts of the Ṭabahata masiqta; numbers refer to prayers in Drower, *Prayerbook*.

1. Sixty faṭiras	2. Six faṭiras (= 6, 1)	3. Six faṭiras (= 6, 2)
		91
		96
		79
		80
33	33	33
		81
34	34	34
35	35	1
75–77	75–77	75–77
9	9	9
35	35	35
36–45	36–45	36–45
46–47	46–47	
48	48	48
49 signs	49, no sign at sixth	49, all six signed
50 signs	50, no signs	50
51, signs	51, no sign at sixth	51, all six signed
52, signs, *except* for last	52, no signs at sixth	52, all six signed
53, seal of the masiqta	53	
49, with ḏ-abahatan	49	
44	44	
54, pihta in hamra	54	54
55, pihta swallowed	55	55
56, drinking halalta	56	56
57–72	57–72	57–72
91	91-99	91-99
	71	70
	100	102
	71–72	71–72
		80
	101-3	101-2
	63	63
	108	58
	3	3
	9	
	58	58
	65	65
	71	76
	170, Ṭabahatan	170, Ṭabahatan

Final Interpretation

Spoken prayers accompany pertinent acts, both endeavoring to lift the soul and spirit upward, to join them into one, and to incorporate them into the company of the ancestors, the "Parents" (Ṭabahata). The sheer mass of tangible materials and the meticulous rules for the masiqta may strike an observer as most mystifying. Drower, for example, admits that she is put off by the initial dove sacrifice, an act she considers unnecessary, for, in her opinion, the Mandaeans are "above all things, baptizers," not sacrificers.[64] But the dove is the body most appropriate for the spirit in its ascension aspect. Ba is a pun for the indicated spirit. It means "with it," that is, "with the soul," a euphemistic way of mentioning the spirit without directly invoking it.

As the priest handles the various elements on his tray, one notes a consistent right-to-left symbolism. Incense is wafted from right to left, that is, from Lightworld to earth, and the food elements are cloaked in the fragrance from the upper world. Klila and pihta remain in the priest's left hand. The wreath and the piece of dough are still in their earthly modes, but through the mediating stage of qinas they aspire to become faṭiras, the heaped-up ancestors on the right side. Appropriately, these are treated with the priest's right hand. The clothed wreath—a soul-wrapped spirit—is moved from left to right.

The faṭiras play the double role of ancestors and rising soul. One notes that the signings on the biscuits are performed, or emphatically *not*, while the pihta is held aloft in the priest's left hand. I see the treated qinas, which are faṭiras-in-the-making, half baked, as being both "here" on earth and "there" in the Lightworld. They manifest the soul's final goal. So, these biscuits move back and forth between signifying ancestors safe in the upper worlds and symbolizing the rising soul being led upward, step by step, seal by seal, and, most important, by *withheld* seals when required. Seals in the wrong place would impair the soul's development in its temporary home in the symbolically created wombs of the priests. For thirty days and thirty nights, neatly corresponding to the sixty faṭiras, the body will mature. Its head is provided by the six in the second round. (By any computation, this is a speeded-up pregnancy.) Full integration of the completed body occurs only with the second treatment of the six faṭiras during Panja, an auspicious time when deaths turn into perfect lives in the Lightworld.

When, in the two first parts of the masiqta, the phrase "our ancestors" (Ṭabahatan), is inserted into prayer 49 at the appropriate spot, the prayer focuses on the ancestors, not on the soul. Only the ancestors can assure that the rising soul achieves its goal. The pile of faṭiras is the laufa made manifest, and all ascended Mandaeans are present in the heap. Thus symbolized, they are finally buried with the dove.

What about the klila on top of the heap? The wreath is called "the inner heart,"[65] and when it is disconnected from the pihta and placed on the pile of biscuits, it invigorates the ancestors with the myrtle's evergreen life force. Even if the spirit must be overcome, in the sense that it will be subsumed by the soul, the klila as spirit symbol still holds a positive value both for the "raw," ascending soul and for the "half-baked" ancestors. These ancestors feed the soul when a piece from the top and one from the bottom faṭira are broken off. *1012* calls this "the opening of the mouth of the soul."

When the priestly ring is dipped in the hamra bowl, the liquid becomes fertilized. A birth is going to take place. But how? The priests turn themselves into wombs by swallowing the wetted pihta holding food fragments. One notes that they do not chew it,[66] for the pihta must remain an unmangled fetus, soon safely incubating in the priestly "wombs." The "male" people par excellence, the priests, have become women!

In *The Great "First World,"* Pure Ether (Ayar Dakia) approaches the king of the Lightworld with a question about the lack of sealings in the two first parts of the masiqta. The king's answer is lengthy, and it includes the following:

> If thou signest (at the *ma d-bh*) . . . the soul perisheth and is destroyed.
>
> Look at that salt yonder, which is (*symbolises*) the soul! (*Salt*) when covered with water, a stole of water covers it, a tunic (*ksuia*) of water is placed on its shoulders, a girdle of water is bound about it and it putteth on leggings of water! When it cometh out of its (*watery*) dress, and is clothed in air (ether) it becomes changed! It (*salt*) may lie in the earth a thousand thousand years and yet not be spoilt, but when water reaches it, it goes wrong and is destroyed!
>
> Behold! the soul is sealed with sixty-six seals . . . see, (*therefore*), that signing (*performed*) at the *ma d-bh* destroys them and spoils the whole Body (*ʿuṣṭuna*).[67]

A sign at "ma ḏ-bẖ" would ruin the sixty-six seals of the soul, which is here depicted in its baptismal rasta. Drawing a parallel between soul and salt, the king states that just as water dissolves salt, so would a seal at "that which is with her" destroy the newly formed ʿuṣṭuna, the Lightworld body of joined spirit and soul. Attention drawn to the spirit alone at these points (in prayers 49–52) would demolish the entire ritual construction. An interesting point in the king's speech is that water, normally an undisputedly positive symbol in Mandaeism, is detrimental to the soul understood as salt. The explanation delivered to Pure Ether also contains an explicit "physics" lesson on the effects of the elements water and air on the soul.

The carefully choreographed three-part Ṭabahata masiqta frees the souls caught in the maṭartas during the past year. The final part of the ritual (6,2) closes the open-ended acts, sealing the ascended Mandaeans into the community of the ancestors above. General scholarly consensus rules that the masiqta liturgy, as found in the *Prayerbook* and also partly in *GL*, belongs in the oldest strata of Mandaean literature. There is therefore no reason to assume that the time-consuming, meticulous, step-by-step character of the ritual is the product of more recent times. What Drower saw and then described in *Mandaeans* and *Water into Wine* from the 1930s on can be correlated without difficulty with *Prayerbook* liturgies extending back at least to the third century and probably beyond. The origins of ritual commentaries such as *Exalted Kingship*, *1012*, *The Great "First World,"* and *Coronation* appear to be very old. Despite their linguistically younger features, the texts offer information that may be nearly as ancient as the liturgies themselves.[68]

Most chief Mandaean rituals remain the business of priests. Without this class the religion would not have been kept alive throughout the centuries. How the Mandaeans create their officials will be the topic of the next chapter, which centers on the creation of the tarmida, the lower ranking priest.

9

The Initiation of the Tarmida

To make a new Mandaean priest of the first level, a tarmida, is an extremely complicated matter.[1] Most taxing, for initiator (*rba*) and novice (*šualia*) alike, is the week they spend sleepless in the initiation hut (*škinta*). The entire ritual takes sixty-eight days and requires set clusterings of rituals and ritual segments. Here I will give as simple a presentation of these proceedings as I can, trying not to violate the initiation ritual by oversimplifying it. In addition to offering a description of the sequence of events, I will focus on two particular issues, first, the relationship between the novice and his teacher, and second, the emphatic instructions regarding including or excluding certain words or formulas at specific points in the ceremonials.

Similar to the masiqta, the tarmida initiation ritual can be seen as arranging building blocks in order to construct the new edifice, which is the new priest. The proceedings show a kind of logical progression that should, by now, have become familiar to the reader. In the ritual, the novice is gradually transported from the earthly to the Lightworld realm, a goal that necessitates nothing less than a re-creation of the man.[2]

Preparations

Any Mandaean man of pure (not necessarily priestly) family can become a priest.[3] He need not yet be married, although this is the desirable Mandaean state. In all likelihood, the novice has trained as a šganda since childhood and is familiar with the priestly activities. He will be ready for initiation after puberty.[4] His teacher, a ganzibra, gathers as many priests as can be found for the initiation ceremony. The priests baptize the initiate, who is then closely inspected, for he must be perfect of body and mentally fit.[5] Next a ritual slaughter of a sheep both wards off evil and furnishes a *fidwa* (ransom) for the novice himself.[6] The mutton feeds the community, in anticipatory parallel to the new priest, who will soon serve his people.

The priests construct a reed hut (*andiruna*) and throw a blue cloth, the "little sky," over it as a roof. This symbolizes the earthly, female world, ruled by Ruha, in which the novice will first sit, and then leave. Sacred books are placed in the hut, and the texts

The Great "First World" and *Exalted Kingship* must be present; otherwise the initiation will be invalid. [7] The rba prays the rahmas, the prayers for the day, inside the hut. Outside, the novice sits on a chair, receives his silk taga (crown), and is publicly tested in his knowledge of the baptism liturgy. Spectators are grouped around him. Drabšas stand on his right and left, as do two *kintas* (ritual clay receptacles).

Holding myrtle (*asa*) in one hand and the closed book of the part of the *Prayerbook* called "The Book of Souls," the baptism liturgy, in the other, the young man recites prayers 1–103 from memory. If successful, he joins the other priests in the andiruna. They pray, and soon the other priests leave, and only the novice and his rba are left inside. Before night falls, the other priests, helped by laypeople, construct another reed hut, a škinta, to the north of the andiruna.[8] This hut, named like the heavenly habitations, symbolizes the Lightworld, and it receives a white cloth roof, in obvious color contrast to the blue roof of the other hut, blue being Ruha's hue.

The novice and his rba spend the night in the andiruna, and the hatchling priest must not fall asleep. Outside, the laypeople keep up a din of festivities; inside, the teacher instructs his ward. Neither man must leave the hut during the night, but at dawn they emerge, and the hut is taken down. Now the novice stands between the two huts—suspended, as it were, between earth and Lightworld—and recites the baptism liturgy again. He is watched by his rba and the other priests, who stand inside the škinta, waiting to receive him into their company. Two laymen witnesses, who have already given the postulant a piece of silver and one of gold to put on his stole (naṣifa) bring him inside.

Baptism and Crowning

The priests in the škinta have been praying and consuming a meal of pihta and mambuha. Now they greet the novice with the word *Asuta*! (health). He sits down. The others address a prayer to him, in which he is praised as a pure mirror, an enlightener, and an ʿutra.[9] At the line "Rise up, thou great ʿuthra, to thy feet," the novice stands up, and "the ʿuthras and kings who sit in this *škinta*," the priests, welcome him as one of their own.

For the third time, but now inside the škinta, the novice recites the baptism prayers.[10] He has already given the chief ganzibra (a man other than his rba) "The Book of Souls" and has also kissed his head. A brief antiphonal scene ensues, for prayer 324 is spoken by the priests, prayer 325 by the laymen witnesses, and prayer 326 by all in unison. Together with the already recited prayer 323, these coronation prayers praise the novice's new status as king (*malka*).[11] A myrtle-smelling segment follows, during which the rba takes the myrtle from his pupil's hand and utters prayer 327, which praises the primordial myrtle. All inhale the scent of the plant. Then the novice kisses the heads of both his teacher and the senior ganzibra.

After he has twisted the myrtle into a tiny klila, the rba asks the other priests for permission to baptize his pupil. Having obtained consent, the rba and his charge go outside, and during the baptism the teacher takes care to remember the zhara, the name insertion for the candidate, at designated points in the accompanying prayers, for the whole baptism must be with zharas. For instance, there are zharas in three places: in prayer 18,[12] "Behold this soul (N.), who quits destruction for construction, (goes) from

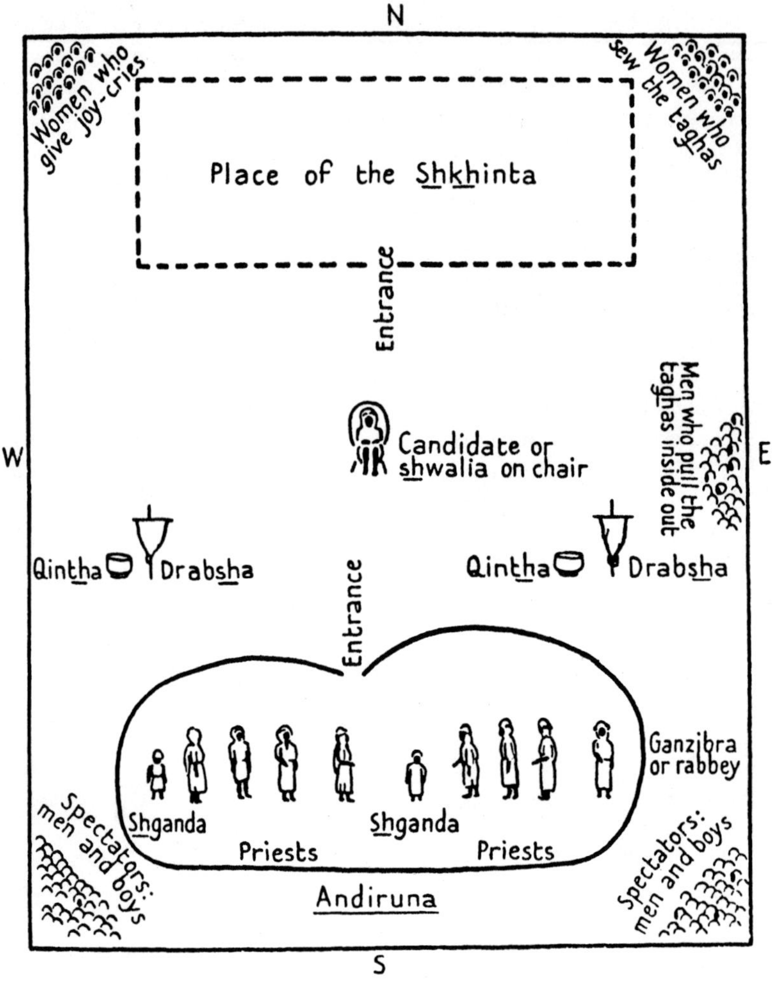

From Drower, *Mandaeans.* Used by permission of Brill Academic Publishers.

error to truth and (leaves) the abode of fear"; in prayer 35; and in prayer 77, "Make victorious and raise up this soul of N."

After the baptism, kušṭa is exchanged among all the celebrants, and several prayers are recited before the utterance of two conjoined prayers, numbers 71 and 72. These two almost always appear together, and they usually conclude a ritual segment. It is important to keep track of their appearances throughout the initiation because of special features in these prayers. Prayer 71 promises that "a wreath from the vine Ruaz" will be placed on the head of the soul of the person for whom the prayer is uttered, and also for the souls of "our fathers, our teachers, our brothers and our sisters, of those who have departed the body and those who are yet in the body."[13] The clause "of our fathers" should more correctly be rendered "our Parents," as the phrase is d-abahatan.

This inclusive term is used for all Mandaeans, past and present. It occurs in many prayers and is sometimes (though not at this moment) avoided if a zhara occurs in the same prayer.

Prayer 72 is recited with bent knees, a gesture indicating that the prayer focuses on the Lightworld and not on the particular person indicated by the zhara. In fact, at this point the rba is instructed to substitute the phrase d̲-abahatan for the otherwise expected zhara in the slot where the prayer pleads, "[F]orgive him his sins, trespasses, follies, stumblings and mistakes."[14] This changes the focus of the prayer from a concern with a specific person to an emphasis on the ancestors in the upper world. Such tailoring of prayers is required in specific ritual segments.

As noted, these two prayers, numbers 71 and 72, when recited in sequence, always conclude a ritual segment, and they are followed by a meal of pihta and mambuha. The meal completes the circle of events beginning with the postulant's entry into the škinta. Honoring his crown by removing it from his head, lifting it from his lips to his eyes, and mumbling *mqaimitun* (be raised up!) sixty-one times, the rba next recites the requisite prayer 178 for his taga. The text *Coronation* utters a dire warning against reciting the wrong prayers at this moment. Should the rba forget himself and mistakenly recite prayers 2, 4, or 6, which are *širiatas* (loosening prayers), these prayers would annihilate what has been created, deconsecrate what has been consecrated.[15] Even if a segment has now been concluded, a complete break, which a deconsecration would signify, is out of place. One might say that events are simply going into another round, for one group of building blocks is now in place, and another set will follow.

A veil is held over the postulant as his baptism dress is removed. He obtains a brand-new garment, and his rba recites the main Mandaean prayer formula over him:

> My Lord be praised! In the name of the Great First Other-Worldly Life! From far-off worlds of light that are above all works may there be healing, victory, soundness, speech and a hearing, joy of heart and forgiving of sins for me [zhara insertion], through the strength of Yawar Ziwa and Simat Hiia![16]

At the rubric for the zhara in prayer 1, the rba inserts both his own and his pupil's name, making two zharas. This is the first indication of a significant point in the initiation: that the ritual affects the teacher, too, not just his novice. While he recites the formula, the rba holds his hand to his head, a gesture that emphasizes his taga.

Two women appear, each to wash one of the novice's legs.[17] A banner prayer, # 345, comes next, and, in precise parallel to the prayer's content, the priest in charge moves the drabša into the hut. He also brings in the *Ginza*, and all celebrants reenter the škinta. A series of prayers called *kd azil bhira dakia* (When the proven, pure one went) follow.[18] These twenty-four prayers describe and praise the new priest, who is now included among his fellow ʿutras. He is invited to take his seat among them (prayer 246), kušṭas are exchanged, and, according to prayer 253, the priests admonish the novice to remove himself from passions and to achieve identity with the priests.[19]

Eighteen prayers for the drabša ensue (# 330–47), and the priests and the rba exchange kisses. Each of the others receives a sprig of myrtle (asa) from the rba. Prayers 1, 3, 5, and 19, which constitute a recurring sequence, are recited by all. In the first of these four prayers, at the words "Then that Lord of Lofty Greatness took a circlet of radiance, light and glory and set it on my head,"[20] the priests crown the novice with the silk taga and place their hands on his head. After a number of prayers from both the baptism and the masiqta liturgies, the priests end with the sealing (haṭamta) prayers, numbers 25–28.

Marriage and Insignia

Pouring a quantity of hamra, water mixed with macerated dates and raisins, into a bowl, the postulant prepares to "marry" a Lightworld spouse. He does this by drinking from the bowl seven times, at the end of each of seven prayers: 181–87. [21] The other priests—the novice himself is not included here—recite these prayers, which describe Manda d̲-Hiia, who was consecrated as priest at the beginning of time. Drinking the hamra unites the novice with his *niṭupta*, his "cloud," the designation for a female spouse in the world above. Because he will now become a citizen of that world, he needs a wife from that realm, even if he may already have one (or more) on earth. Like all priests, the new one will belong to both worlds. The novice is enthroned, invested with his priestly regalia, and joined to the Lightworld beings.

A series of antiphonal coronation prayers follow, numbers 305–18, which are exchanged between the rba and the other full-fledged priests. The rba starts with prayer 305, the other priests respond with prayer 312, which is answered by the rba uttering prayer 306, the priests continue with prayer 313, and so on.[22] Then the priests place their hands on the novice's priestly golden seal ring, the Šum Yawar Ziwa, as they recite prayer 319, which bestows Lightworld strength on the novice.

The priests distribute additional crowns to the novice, an act accompanied and described by prayers # 320–21. The novice arranges his ritual tray, the kinta, which holds the paraphernalia for burning incense. Putting his hand on his own head, touching his crown, he recites the salutation prayer, Asiet Malkia,[23] which asks for health and victory for a great number of Mandaean Lightworld beings (including some female ones), John the Baptist, and the reciter himself. After finishing the devotional prayers, the rahmas 106–109, the novice removes his hand from his head, indicating that he now stops praying expressly for himself. He throws incense into the fire at the incense prayers 8 and 34.

Another set of rahmas follow, prayers 113–17, then the very long prayer 77, and finally a repetition of the prayer sequence at the crowning ceremony, the prayers 9, 35, 15–18 (a frequently recurring series from the baptismal liturgy), and 25–28, the sealing prayers. At prayer 35,[24] the postulant again puts his hand to his head and keeps it there until he has finished the sealing series. It is worth recalling that at the first recital of this series, at the crowning, the priests put their own hands on the novice's head. But now that the novice possesses a crown of his own, he uses his own hand, having achieved another level in the step-by-step work of becoming a priest.

Having "sealed" himself, the postulant rises up, praises the First Life, throws incense, and utters number 65, a masiqta prayer. At this point in her translation of *Coronation*, Drower makes a confusing decision. She introduces a parenthetical "not," with a question mark, into her translation, so that it reads, "(but) without the 'of our fore-fathers' because these *rahmia* of the *škinta* are (not?) with *zharas*."[25] It makes sense to leave out Drower's inserted "(not?)" in the text's instruction, for the point is precisely that *inclusion* of zhara(s) *pre*cludes d̲-abahatan. The first part of this prayer reads, "Ye are set up and raised up into the Place where the good are established amongst *manas*[26] of light, the souls called upon and raised up and signed by this masiqta and (the souls of) our fathers, our teachers, our brothers and our sisters."[27] Leaving out ḏ-abahatan, the reciter instead emphasizes the ascent, which refers to the masiqta in the strict sense of the word, of his own soul. Just as his prayers and incense rise upward, so, too, shall his soul.

A series of rahmas ensue, and the postulant ends this round with prayers 71 and 72, the second concurrence of these prayers so far. In prayer 71, he is exhorted to leave out ḏ-abahatan. Why? In my interpretation this is a conscious parallel to the lacking oil signs in the second part of the masiqta, the part for the six faṭiras, as noted in chapter 8. Recall that in the initiation's first concurrence of prayers 71 and 72, the phrase was included, but not now. In parallel, the masiqta of the sixty faṭiras had oil signs at specific points in prayers 49–54, but not in the masiqta for the six. Lest this sort of correlation seems utterly far-fetched, I must emphasize that the esoteric commentary texts themselves support such an interpretation.

For the moment, it is important to keep in mind the open-ended acts, the lack of oil signs in the masiqta for the six faṭiras, a lack that now, at prayer 65, correlates with the omission of the phrase ḏ-abahatan in the present ritual of priest initiation. Still, prayer 65 is a masiqta prayer, and the priest initiation implies a sort of death, a movement from earth to Lightworld. As in the masiqta, one might expect the open ends in the priest initiation to be tied up. Indeed, the immediately ensuing prayer 72 marks a certain closure, for here ḏ- abahatan is included, and the prayer is uttered with bent knees, a gesture that stresses the ancestors and the Lightworld rather than the praying individual.

As in the first instance of prayers 71 and 72, these prayers are now, in their second round, followed by a pihta and mambuha meal. Rising to his feet, the novice utters the appropriate prayers for the water and bread, numbers 36–45, eats and drinks, and concludes with numbers 59 and 60, prayers for the food. Now the sequence follows roughly the same pattern as after the baptism of the novice, with the mqaimitun formula sixty-one times, and prayer 80, in which the novice calls upon a number of Lightworld beings. Kušṭa with the rba follows, and the novice keeps his hand on his head during the rahmas afterward.

At this point the other priests leave the hut; only the rba and his charge remain. They will stay there for seven days in all, without sleep. Outside, the laypeople keep up their joyful noise to help the men stay awake. Each day the novice obtains a new dress, prays the rahmas at the three designated prayer times (the seven days of the week require different sets of rahmas), and receives pihta and mambuha.[28] While he is still praying the rahmas for the last of the seven days—the novice is now probably in an exhausted state—other priests accompanied by laymen enter the hut. The laymen attended the beginnings of the ceremonies in the škinta, and now they witness the end of the škinta period. The novice prays the loosening prayers, the širiatas 2, 4, and 6,[29] which separate the priestly insignia from their ritual uses. Laying aside his crown and wreath until the next day, the novice has finished another level in the creation of his new self.

Baptism of Rba and Zidqa Brikha

It is Sunday morning. Priests are praying the rahmas outside the hut, and the novice is preparing to baptize his rba. *Coronation* says that this baptism must be without zharas in prayers 35, 18, 168, and 169, "because the baptism 'of the sixty' is that of the postulant, but the baptism of the *rba* is *d-abahata*."[30] Moreover, *Coronation* continues to associate the baptism and the faṭiras of the masiqta, for the foodstuffs (ginzas: "treasures") in both sections of the masiqta symbolize spirit and soul, elements that cannot be separated from one another.

Coronation's cryptic and esoteric statements may need explication. To begin, the text links maṣbuta with masiqta, for both are rituals that connect the believers with the Lightworld. As noted, flowing water (yardna) is how the Lightworld manifests itself on earth, and therefore baptism marks a temporary immersion into that world. This constitutes a correlate to the final, eternal immersion in it when a dead person's spirit and soul are conveyed upward by a masiqta. One could call a baptism a repeatedly performed forerunner of the masiqta. The two rituals express the same goal, and the verb *SQL* (raise up) is used for both.

Second, *Coronation* virtually identifies the masiqta for the sixty faṭiras with the already performed baptism of the novice (as seen earlier in this chapter). The number of faṭiras, sixty, causes *Coronation* to interpret this fact as a clue to the baptism of the novice. In addition, to these two correlates is supplied a third, the spirit, so that all three items belong in one category, according to the esoteric exegetical system of *Coronation*. These three are the sixty faṭiras, the baptism of the novice, and the spirit. All are correlated to their higher parallels, which signify a more elevated level of creative work: the masiqta of the Parents. As described in the previous chapter, in that ritual, six faṭiras are all signed with oil, and *Coronation* now associates these six with the baptism of the rba and with the soul.[31]

The reason for *Coronation*'s mystifying aside (apart from sheer delight in esoteric correlations) appears to be a pressing need to explain why the impending baptism of the rba must *not* contain zharas—while the baptism of the novice *did* contain them. My interpretation is this: the rba functions as a personification of the ancestors, the parents, and therefore the baptism does not, strictly speaking, concern the rba personally but emphasizes the Lightworld parents. A zhara, then, will be substituted by the formula d-abahatan.

After the baptism, a "blessed oblation" (zidqa brikha) meal follows, and, in contrast to the baptism just performed, this is eaten in the name of the rba, who does not take part in the meal. The food furthers the laufa, the life force between the earth and the Lightworld, and among beings in both realms. The *ṣa*, a rolled-up piece of flat bread containing nuts and raisins (an obviously phallic emblem), takes central stage in the zidqa brikha.[32] Eating the ṣa in the name of the rba and asking forgiveness of sins for him, the other priests and the postulant invoke the power of Yawar Ziwa and Simat Hiia, the prototypical Lightworld couple.

A šganda appears and recites prayer 348, a prayer that mentions primordial šgandas. To this the ganzibra responds with prayer 349, "Come, come, lofty messenger. . . ."[33] and takes a bottle of hamra and a sprig of myrtle out of the šganda's hand. One notes here that the acolyte plays the role of a Lightworld emissary, bearing life-giving symbols of that upper world. The zidqa brikha ends with the sealing prayers and the priests' blessing of the novice by placing their hands on his head.

The next day, Monday, the novice must include d-abahatan in prayers 58, 65, and 71,[34] because these prayers belong to the škinta and to the sixty faṭiras, while the rahmas of the sixy days connect with the parents.[35] This does not contradict what was said previously, for the mention of the sixty days point forward to the sixty-day seclusion period now imminent for the novice. Here it is important to avoid making a connection between the number sixty concerning the faṭiras and the sixty days, for *Coronation* wishes, instead, to emphasize an opposition. To clarify: the present rahmas, those of the škinta, are of a preliminary nature when compared with those of the sixty-day period, for in those sixty days, the rahmas take on the nature "of the Parents." Prayed during the seven days in the škinta, the first set of rahmas can be compared to a temporary wall or scaffolding, not the final construction. Only the rahmas prayed during the upcoming sixty days will complete the edifice.

Again, let me sum up: the rahmas of the sixty faṭiras correspond to the baptism of the sixty, the baptism of the postulant. Zharas are omitted in the prayers for these two rituals. In contrast, the baptism of the rba is a ritual focusing on the ancestors, a focus characterized by the rahmas of the sixty days, too. One might say that the baptism of the rba eases the transition into the sixty days, for the attention will now increasingly dwell on the Parents.

The Sixty Days: Masiqta for the Rba

Returning to his own home, the novice stays secluded from his wife and his family for sixty days. He cooks his own food, keeps strict purity, prays a total of 180 rahmas, and exchanges kušṭa with a šganda who arrives every day for that very purpose. Impersonating a Lightworld being, the šganda is the only person allowed to come into contact with the novice during these days. *Coronation*, reveling in esoteric computations, explains the 180 prayers during the sixty days as three evenly distributed sets of 60 each for soul, spirit, and body.[36] Essentially, the task of the novice during these days is to pray his own new self into being. According to *Coronation*'s previous statement, these rahmas would include d̲-abahatan, and not the zhara, despite the focus on self-creation. However, that self cannot be constructed without the strength and evoked presence of the ancestors.

The first seclusion period, the seven škinta days, culminated in the novice baptizing his rba. Now, after sixty days' isolation, the new priest emerges and performs a masiqta for his rba. The most striking feature is that this masiqta is read for someone still alive. In the part of this masiqta treating the six faṭiras, the novice includes both the zhara for his rba and the clause d̲-abahatan. No one is excluded. Toward the end, the prayers in this masiqta follow partly the pattern of the two segments of the regular masiqta of the sixty plus six faṭiras, the Mother masiqta. But the sequence also follows part of the Ṭabahata masiqta. For this reason, one might see the masiqta for the rba as compressing and combining the goals of the two masiqtas.

After kušṭa with the šganda, the postulant puts his hand to his head and recites prayers 3, 35, 58, 99, and 71 in his own, not the rba's, name. But at prayer 72, which follows 71, he bends his knees and inserts d̲-abahatan. In this third, and last, occurrence of prayers 71 and 72, d̲-abahatan is present in both prayers, securing and sealing all who are implied in that clause.

Having arrived at the end of his initiation, the novice drinks mambuha and eats pihta, closing the circle begun by the priests eating and drinking at the very start of the novice's initiation.[37] He deconsecrates himself, gives the šganda the handshake, and leaves the škinta where he performed the masiqta. Separated from the other priests, the novice eats the zidqa brikha in the name of his teacher, while the other priests consume the meal in his, the new priest's, name. Reading the very long blessings, prayers 374–79, the new priest is allowed to use the book. He removes his taga, an act accompanied by the requisite prayer 178. His final act is to baptize his rba, and only then is he "authorized to (celebrate) all rites."[38] The sixty-eight days have come to an end.

Concluding Remarks

Moving and being moved through the clusters of rituals and ritual segments, the novice has become a new priest, qualified to serve his community. He travels from the public layman space to the Lightworld environment, from the "female" earthly realm to the upper, "male" one. The varying emphases on him, on his rba, and on the ancestral Parents demonstrate a construction and reinforcement of harmonious interdependencies. On the "female" side belongs earth, laypeople, the left, silver, myrtle, and the andiruna; on the "male," Lightworld, priests, the right, gold, crown, and škinta. The rba seems to be the most "movable" actor in the proceedings, for he alternately is himself, impersonates the ancestors, and exhibits the envisioned status of the novice. In the masiqta read for him, he in a sense "plays dead." but he also acts as the father making possible the novice's rebirth.

The šganda plays the role as Lightworld emissary, despite his status as acolyte; he is not a priest. But in his Lightworld aspect, he paradoxically inhabits a level higher than the novice. The laymen who come into the škinta at the beginning and the end of the novice's week in the hut function as representatives of the "female" world that the novice is leaving. And yet, as long as he remains on earth, the new priest of course partakes in that world, while still occupying a role as ʿutra impersonator.

The inclusions and exclusions of zharas or the phrase d̲-abahatan, the instructions regarding bent knees, kisses, whose hand(s) on whose head, kušṭas with whom, meals, specific prayer series, the symbolism of numbers, and so on, all segments possess their own logic. In some prayers, both zharas and d̲-abahatan may be present. But regarding others, admonitions grow adamant against including one or the other. Rahmas, in particular, are regarded as construction prayers, for the verbs used for them convey the meanings "construct," "build," and "establish,"[39] rather than "speak" or "recite." Rahmas build a mental universe. Obviously, it would be detrimental to build with unsuitable phrases, with wrong materials and tools.

Gradually, the initiation constructs a new priest through a ritual that reinforces the mythological universe already envisioned. The thrice-recurring conjunction of prayers 71 and 72 has a special significance, comparable to the oil-signs (and lack of such) of the faṭiras at prayers 49–54 in a masiqta. The first time prayers 71 and 72 occur in the tarmida ritual is after the novice's baptism, before he enters the škinta. D̲-abahatan occurs in both prayers. This I take as a parallel to the sealings of the faṭiras in the masiqta prayers (where only the last one of the treated sixty biscuits remains unsealed). As the novice is about to leave the škinta for the sixty days of isolation, prayers 71 and 72 appear again, but now with the exhortation to leave out d̲-abahatan in prayer 71. This corresponds to the lack of seals in the first treatment of the six faṭiras. But in the third concurrence of prayers 71 and 72, at the end of his initiation, d̲-abahatan occurs in both prayers. This correlates with the act of securing and sealing all faṭiras in the annual Ṭabahata masiqta. Recall also that toward the end of the priest initiation, the novice's prayer sequence intermingles the Ṭabahata masiqta prayer sequence and that of the first treatment of the six faṭiras.

Little breads (faṭiras) symbolize ancestors in the masiqta, and the tarmida initiation correlates the phrase d̲-abahatan with these. "Ṭabahata," in the sense of "the masiqta of the Parents," should be kept separate from the phrase d̲-abahatan (of our Parents), though both certainly point to the same entity. Calling the baptism of the rba "d̲-abahatan," *Coronation* juxtaposes this ritual to the baptism of the novice, which is called "of the sixty," and which includes zharas. For the novice's baptism belongs to "the Mother," the "female" realm—like "the masiqta of the Mother," the two first parts of the masiqta.[40] But the rba belongs to the Parents, and his baptism is linked with the Lightworld and with the Ṭabahata masiqta. His baptism by the new priest falls quite outside of this pattern, for this act can be seen as a first "test case" for the new priest. It therefore symbolically moves the rba, who earlier played "ritually dead" in the masiqta performed for him, back to earth, so to speak.

For this treatment of the tarmida initiation, I have not used *Exalted Kingship*, another text that deals with this ritual. This text pays much more detailed attention to sections of the tarmida initiation than does *Coronation*. The latter looks like a list, offering a virtual "telephone book" format with respect to the proceedings, whereas *Exalted Kingship* considerably expands on the treatment of certain parts of the initiation. *Exalted Kingship* soars in seemingly extravagant loops of esoteric exegeses. Later, in chapter 12, I will give a sample of this text's dizzying interpretive style by showing how it understands the effects of the novice's recital of the liturgy when he sits in the škinta, watched by the priests. In the figure I offer in parallel columns the sequence of prayers for the tarmida initiation, according to *Coronation* and to *Exalted Kingship*.

Prayer sequence in the tarmida initiation.

Coronation	*Exalted Kingship*
323[41]	323
1-103 (novice's recital in škinta)	1-103
324-27 (coronation prayers)	324-27
3, 5, 19	3, 5, 19
79, 81[42]	79, 80, 81
preparation for baptizing novice	
1, 3, 5, 19	1, 3, 5, 19
32	32
8, 34 (incense prayers)	8, 34
75-77[43]	75-77
35 (with zharas)	35
baptism of novice begins	
	10-13
	18
	414

	19
	first kušṭa
	82
	20–24
	second kušṭa
	36–45 (pihta and mambuha)
	third kušṭa
	25–28 (sealing prayers)
	29, 30, 83–86, 88, 90
	71–72 (first concurrence)
	fourth kušṭa[44]
	18, 109 (rahmas)
58 (with zhara)	58
65	65
168–69	168–69
71–72	71–72 (second concurrence)
	36–45 (pihta and mambuha)
59–60	59–60
31, 8	31, 8
72	72
	171
mqaimitun (sixty-one times)	mqaimitun
80	80
kušṭa with šganda	fifth kušṭa
63 (masiqta oil)	63
178	178
1, 3, 9, 15	
344–45	
233–56 (kd̲ azil)	233–56
330–47 (drabša prayers)	
novice crowned	
1, 3, 5, 19	1, 3, 5, 19
35, 9	35, 9
15–17	15–17
25–28 (haṭamtas)	25–28
hamra ceremony	
180–99	180–99[45]
305–21 (antiphons)	305–21
škinta period begins	
	72, 31, 8, 94, 63, kd̲ azil[46]
106–8	106–8
1, 3, 5, 19	1, 3, 5, 19
8, 34	8
	165–69
113 (a Sunday prayer)	113
114–17	114–16
77, 9, 35	77, 9, 35
15–17	15–17
25–28	25–28
58, 65	58, 65

119-22	
165-69	165
71-72	71-72 (third concurrence)
36-45	36-45
59-60	59-60
72	72
	171
80	80
kušta	kušta

PART III

NATIVE HERMENEUTICS

10

The Ducks That Came to the Marshes

New York

Voices of the Present

The jewelry store on Seventh Avenue in Manhattan looks like many others, shining with bright lights and glass, and gleaming merchandise displayed everywhere. Two Mandaeans work here. One of them, a younger man named Saeed Moradi, greets me warmly after I am buzzed inside (this is in 1995). He says he thinks he remembers me from 1973, when I visited his father's jewelry store in Iran. The other Mandaean is Nasser Sobbi, a seventy-year-old man with a thin white mustache in a broad face under short, sparse, white hair. He is square and compact of body, which he moves with surprising speed as we leave the store and set off toward the subway that will take us to Flushing. Mr. Sobbi hails from Khorramshahr, where he still owns property. He has been in the United States since 1970, and he is one of the few Mandaeans on this continent who speaks, reads, and writes Mandaic. Lamea in San Diego had put me in contact with him.

On July 16, 1989, Mr. Sobbi finished copying an entire *Ginza* at his home in Flushing. At the end of the work he has written a message in Farsi, Arabic, and English. He tells who the owner of the original is, says for whom it was copied, gives his own maṣbuta name, and thanks the owner "for giving me the opportunity to rewrite, by lending me the holy book - sidra and pray for all Sobis (Mandaei) the good health, prosperity and have patience when facing difficulties. Melka rama denhoora wa mari d̲rabotha alitha ('the great King of Light and the lofty Lord of Greatness') protect them all. Almeh wa Heyee Zaknen ('The world and Life be praised!')."

It is strangely moving to see this inscription, to know that such a work has been done on these shores. Mr. Sobbi's wife, Shukrieh, tall, black-haired and striking, with a drabša around her neck, tells me that when the copying work was going on, for four months, the apartment had to be quiet. I wonder about the enormous gray parrot, squawking and fixing me, one eye at a time, a bird approachable only by the family's son, Issa, who alone is exempt from his bites. Was the parrot quiet, too, during those four months?

I see Mr. Sobbi's books and scrolls, stashed away in drawers and cupboards in the living room. He has Lady Drower's works, too. He tells me that he has found 800 errors in Macuch's *Handbook of Classical and Modern Mandaic*. "Still," he says, "Macuch did very good work." We agree that he was the best, *the* scholar of the Mandaic language. It is news to Mr. Sobbi that Macuch died in the summer of 1993. The two never met, but when Mr. Sobbi was a boy, he did see Lady Drower once when she came to Iran.

One evening Mr. Sobbi and I sit side by side in the sofa, each with our *Book of John*, he with his Mandaic one, I with my tattered copy of Lidzbarski's translation. After some searching, we correlate our texts to the tractate I have asked him to read aloud on tape. The text is "Hibil's Lament." I want to hear how the Mandaic sounds. Across from us, alert and perched on another sofa and on chairs, sit the others. They are all Mandaeans: Mrs. Sobbi and one or two of her daughters; Mamoon Aldulaimi, a fiftyish engineer originally from Baghdad; his wife, Shafia, pretty and delicate; and Shafia's mother, Bibi Um Aduan, who arrived from Iraq only ten days ago, a black-clad woman with a broad, wise face and a large gold pendant bearing the image of her deceased husband.

"Ready?" I ask.

"OK," says Mr. Sobbi.

He reads. We all listen. Throughout the reading, Mr. Sobbi hesitates only at a few words that he does not understand. I follow the Mandaic text, nodding, humming, and clucking a few sounds of sympathy to the sections where Hibil Ziwa complains bitterly about his tasks.[1] I am so entranced that I forget to look at the others across the table. How did they react? Later, I ask Mamoon, who says that they were happy to listen but wished that they could understand the language. At the end, there is applause for Mr. Sobbi, and soon my tape is awash in a mayhem of intermingled voices: Mandaic, Arabic, English. When the doorbell rings, I turn the tape off. But Mr. Sobbi ponders what he has just read. "It is very deep," he remarks. "I want to read it again, study it." He does not recall having read this story earlier.

On my previous visit, in October 1994, Mr. Sobbi and his wife engaged in a small conversation in Mandaic for my benefit. Many Iranian Mandaeans, especially of the older generation, speak Mandaic, while the Iraqi ones, in general, do not. Now he talks to his wife about getting his flu shot at the hospital recently. With us are Mamoon and one of his friends, another Mandaean engineer, Zuhair Jenab. I strain my ear and recognize only three or four words of the conversation in Mandaic. I look at the engineers. "Did you understand?" "Not a word," says Mamoon emphatically, "not a *single* word!" I am surprised.

I first met Mamoon and Zuhair when they joined Mr. Sobbi and me for dinner in an Afghan restaurant in Flushing. On the way there, we stop to play the lottery. Mr. Sobbi plays every day, and he initiates me, a complete novice, into the mysteries of filling out the form. (Do I still have an unchecked ticket?) The two of us head down the street enveloped in international aromas and populations: Korean groceries, Indian sari shops, vendors with tablefuls of crystals and incense. We repeat this trip four months later, but this time we dip into a liquor store for a bottle of Johnnie Walker Black Label. Mr. Sobbi tries to fit this into his inner jacket pocket but the bottle is too large. "Let me," I suggest, opening my purse. I manage to force the bottle down into it. The Korean girls behind the counter laugh and say, innuendo heavy in their singing voices, "Have a *good* evening!" Out on the street, Mr. Sobbi mutters, "Let them think what they want."

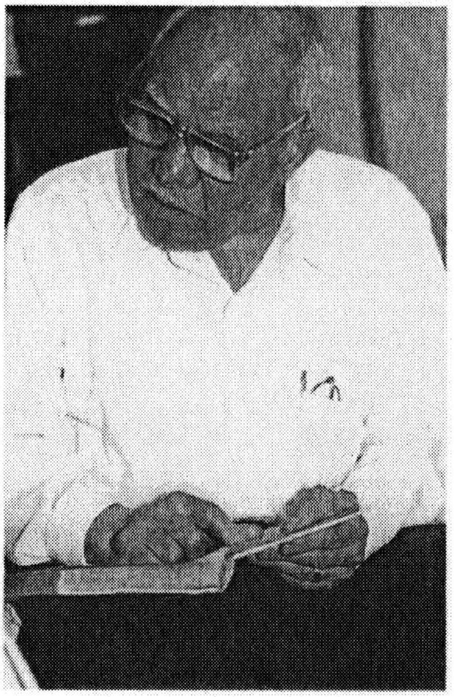

Mr. Nasser Sobbi. Photo by Jesse Buckley.

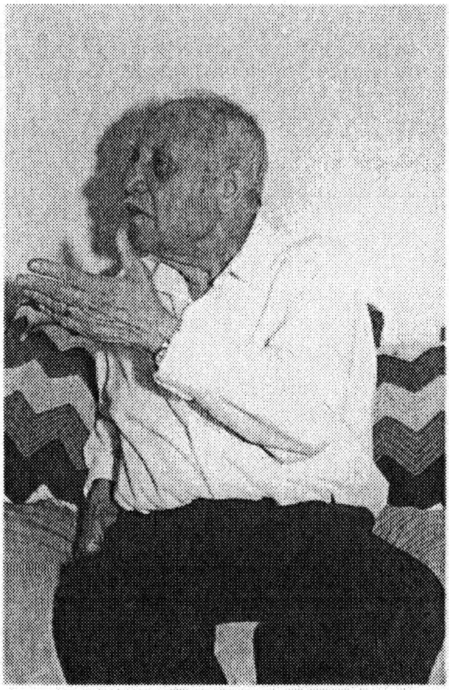

Mr. Nasser Sobbi. Photo by Jesse Buckley.

We enter the Afghan restaurant. Gradually, a whole table fills with Mandaeans. Mamoon, smiling, passes around copies of the first issue of his newsletter, *Almandi*, which he has produced in his basement office at home on Long Island. His parents arrive, as well as his wife and mother-in-law plus two couples. Food appears. Bibi eats only a little yogurt and some vegetables. Shafia explains to me, "She is very religious. She cannot eat restaurant meat." I understand; in fact, I think that she is brave to eat in a restaurant at all.

Even before we eat, the conversation turns to religion, especially to the questions of origins and identity. Afifa, a vivacious redhead, and Fawzia, Mamoon's stepmother—a woman with an intense, alert expression and a square face framed in dark hair—are listening to Mr. Sobbi expound on one of his favorite topics, John the Baptist. Fawzia follows him step by logical step and concludes, "OK. If John's mother was Jewish, and John's father was Jewish, doesn't that make John Jewish and not Mandaean?" Mr. Sobbi, however, waves this aside. But Fawziah has not forgotten, for she brings it up again with Afifa and me a few days later.

In the restaurant, I have a conversation with the two women about the eternal problems of how to deal with the "Jewish origins" question and with the Mandaean mythology and traditions versus the scholars' views and modern, scientific notions. "What is true? What are we to do, to think?" asks Fawzia, widening her immense eyes and throwing up her hands. For Afifa, too, these are difficult subjects. I decide to use an approach I sometimes try with students. Divide your brain into two compartments, I suggest, one dealing with the scientific views, the other with the religious traditions, the stories. Do not worry about the truth being only of *one* kind. Respect the traditions, the stories, because they are *yours*; they are true for you. Accept the rationalistic explanations, too, but realize that these have no monopoly on truth; they are another kind of "stories." One can operate with different areas of truth, I conclude. The women listen to this, attentively, and appear content that there may be some way to deal with these intractable questions.

Mr. Sobbi wants to leave. The Johnnie Walker is all gone, distributed into glasses of water for the men (and for me). We all repair to Mr. Sobbi's apartment, where we are served fruit, liquor, coffee, and tea. A beautiful color photo, taken in 1992, hangs on the wall. Three Iranian Mandaean priests, father and two sons, stand side by side in ritual action, praying and handling their white tagas. They are Sheikh Jabbar Tawoosie, the ganzibra, and Sheikh Najah and Sheikh Salah, both tarmidas. The youngest son is in the middle. All three are stunningly handsome, of unquestioned dignity, and seem utterly unperturbed by the photographic moment.[2]

Pretty soon, the voices of two (I think) of these priests boom on the sound system, a tape made by Mr. Sobbi's brother, who took the photo, too, and whom I will meet later. I try to find out where the reciters are in their prayers, but I cannot. Mr. Sobbi leaves through his book of prayers, the ʿnianas, also without luck. After a while, the prayers stop. I take out my *Book of John* and show Mr. Sobbi the Mandaic writing in the back, Lidzbarski's own calligraphy. This is not typeset Mandaic. "Wow!" says Mr. Sobbi. "I should become as good as he is!" As we handle this and other books while we talk, I sense Bibi contemplating us. I know she must wonder, particularly about my handling these holy books as though they were ordinary ones. Still, her expression is warm, accepting.

Suddenly, while we are all talking at once, in three languages, the sound system erupts without warning, and Mandaic prayers fill the room. How did the tape suddenly come back on? All laugh and wonder aloud, but I point silently to the ceiling and look at Bibi. The voice of the Lightworld! She laughs happily, understanding my gesture.

The Elders

"That wasn't a very kosher lunch you had," I gently reprimand Mamoon one day as we exit a restaurant. He has eaten clam chowder. "I know. My mother-in-law says, 'How *can* you?' when she sees me eating shellfish," Mamoon admits. He has taken good care of her, however, for he went to a neighborhood farm on Long Island to get a chicken, and he cut its throat with the ritual iron knife, the one I have seen in his basement. I shake Mamoon's hand when he tells me about the correct slaughter. "Well done! Congratulations!"

Respect for the elders shows in many ways. I sense that Mamoon considers Mr. Sobbi almost to be a spiritual father. On my first evening in Mr. Sobbi's apartment, I notice that the two engineers, Mamoon and Zuhair, called the older man by a name I did not recognize. I decide to ask Mr. Sobbi about this later on. Right now, however, he insists on riding with me all the way on the Long Island Railroad back to Penn Station in Manhattan and walking with me from there to the entrance of General Theological Seminary, where I am staying with friends. As we argue about the necessity of this chaperoning, both of us stubborn, I find myself naturally imitating his gestures of hunched-up shoulders, elbows to the side, hands flitting in the air, raised brows. We stand flapping at each other, and of course Mr. Sobbi wins.

On the train, I bring up my question about his "other" name. "Yes," he explains,"it is a form of honorary address; that is how you speak to an older person. I am Abu Issa, Father of Issa, because Issa is my son. If I had more than one son, men younger than me would address me by using the name of my oldest son. This form of address holds for women, too, so that Lamea in San Diego, for example, might be called Mother of Zaki, as he is her oldest son."

Another elder I meet among the New York Mandaeans is Mr. Sobbi's brother, Dakhil Shooshtary. He is ten years his brother's junior, also a goldsmith, but an entirely different type physically: tall, with a powerful brow over deep-set eyes and a prominent mouth in a square face. A stunning photo hangs over the sofa in his living room. It shows Mr. Shooshtary and his wife, Noona, who now sits next to him on the sofa. A distance of about four feet separates the image above, taken thirty-seven years earlier, and the couple beneath. Noona is a striking beauty, and her husband sports a mass of black hair. My gaze travels up and down. As in the photo, he sits at her left.

I have already noticed Mr. Shooshtary's belt loop. A double-sided drabša, made of white gold and diamonds, hangs from it. Mr. Shooshtary made the drabša himself. He slips the piece off, and I turn the drabša carefully in my hands. I have never seen anything like it.

Soon we descend—Mamoon, Mr. Shooshtary, and I—to his office in the basement. A real Mandaean workplace! On the wall hangs a checklist of manuscripts copied and those still waiting to be copied. Mr. Shooshtary has learned copying from his brother,

Mr. Sobbi. The two have different last names, I am told later, in order to confound the military. A drabša the size of a table flag stands on the desk. It is knitted, made of pure, white wool. Behind the desk are shelves of books and papers.

On the wall hangs a picture that I recognize as a larger print of one in Mr. Sobbi's apartment, an old, brown-and-white photo taken in Iran in the early 1930s. Only Mandaean men—and one boy, Mr. Shooshtary himself! All are in local garb, unrecognizable as Mandaeans; and that is the point. The Mandaeans were forced to look "generic," for Khuzistan had just been ceded to Iran from Iraq, and the authorities demanded that the Mandaeans dress like everyone else. This is the proof. The leader wears a large cap; there are no priests in the photo. Mr. Shooshtary can name every man in it. The impressively dignified men gaze directly, even defiantly, at the photographer, as if to say: no matter the garb, our identity is still our own.

There are two sticks in the corner by the desk. They are margnas (priestly staffs), cut off from olive trees in Arizona and sent by Mamoon's brother via mail. These sticks caused a certain stir in the post office, with the mailman who delivered them asking Mr. Shooshtary, "Excuse me, what exactly are these?" "As you can see, sticks."

Mr. Shooshtary carefully lays out a white cotton garment on his desk. It is the rasta that was made in Iran, the one I saw on Majid's video in San Diego. The very same rasta! In the video, the men sat along the walls in a room and watched raptly as the priest cut the fabric with scissors and explained each step in the proceedings. It was Mr. Shooshtary's video, for he took a trip back home and there obtained the rasta, which he took halfway around the world back to New York. I admire the fabric, very soft and delicate to the touch. Mr. Shooshtary speaks about the rasta's features: the stitched-on pocket (*daša*), where the "passport" will be put, and the places near the clavicle, where the gold will be fastened to the right, the silver to the left, when the shirt is used for a dead person. He points out the naṣifa (stole), which is separate from the shirt. Flipping the shirt at the shoulders, he shows me that it is correct, without seams. He folds the garment and reverently puts it away.[3]

I receive many gifts in Mr. Shooshtary's office: a Mandaean calendar that he has made; a copy of a primer in modern Mandaic, made by Sheikh Salem Choheili;[4] a photocopy of a sheet showing a Mandaean magical bowl, with its customary, outwardly spiraling script. I tell Mr. Shooshtary and Mamoon about a particular letter that I have, one that the young scholar Cyrus H. Gordon, who was studying such bowls, sent to Lady Drower in 1938. Professor Gordon typed on one side of the paper, then turned it around and continued upside down on the back. Having realized what he just did, he added, in black ink, "I notice that I inverted the page in starting this page. Perhaps the cause is to be found in the bowls that I have been turning around and around of late."

Mamoon and I return to Mr. Shooshtary a series of color photographs, which he took in Iran of Mandaean ceremonies in 1992. Mr. Shooshtary himself, ready for baptism, appears in at least one of the pictures. Mamoon and I have already made color photocopies, of surprisingly good quality, on sheets of paper. We enlarge one photo of the three priests at prayer, tagas in hand, and we also make a copy of the picture hanging in Mr. Sobbi's living room in Flushing.

No one has said anything, but I have a strong sense that the rasta and the margnas are there to be used. Maybe a priest will come to New York, someday. People do die, and, according to their traditions, Mandaeans need a priest to perform the rituals for the dead.

The Laufa

Death is a difficult issue. I have asked Mamoon, carefully, whether it is possible for me to see a Mandaean grave. So far, four Mandaeans have passed away in New York and have been buried in local, non-Mandaean cemeteries. Mamoon calls his cousin Kareem, whose father died ten years ago in an accident. Now the three of us drive in some hurry to the cemetery, hoping that it will not close early this afternoon. Kareem—fortyish, serious, and of a mystical bent (he tells me of visions and dreams)—drives, with me in the passenger seat, and Mamoon in the back with a large bouquet of flowers and a bottle of water. We speed along, and our fears have been justified, for the cemetery is about to close. But we drive inside, Kareem calling urgently to an official, "I have to! I have guests from overseas!"

Flat grave markers lie on the ground (to facilitate lawn mowers, I suspect). We stand at the grave, and Mamoon informs me about the burial, "It is done correctly, facing north." I nod. Kareem flips up the metal vase, fills it with the carried water, and puts the flowers in it. With the rest of the water he washes the marker and kisses it. I read aloud the dead man's name and the years of his life, "Jalal Jawdat 1928–1985," embossed on the marker. I am overwhelmed by the feeling that any Mandaean who dies here perilously diminishes the group's number, that the deaths point mercilessly to what the Mandaeans fear: that they will not be able to continue as a religion, that they will die out—plants cut down, on a foreign soil.

I thank Kareem for letting me come here. Mamoon sniffles behind me, I am on the verge of tears myself, while Kareem sighs deeply and weeps very quietly. Mamoon and I embrace Kareem without words. We step into the car and drive away; only after a long silence does Kareem ask me why I wanted to see the grave. "Did you want to write about it?" "No," I say," I only wanted to see the grave of a Mandaean buried here in this country." But now I have written about it, too.[5]

Three weeks earlier, a Mandaean died in Iraq. New York Mandaeans will have a ceremony (*fateha*)[6] in Flushing, a gathering of many Mandaeans, to sit together, to eat, to pay their respects to the mourning family. A couple of the sons live here, with their families. Do I want to come? Of course.

We dress up, those of us who are women in black. Fine jewelry flashes on the Mandaeans. In the car, on our way from Long Island to Flushing, Mamoon tells me the story of the ducks that came to the marshes of Iraq earlier in this century. Bands on the ducks' feet showed that they came from America. The ducks stayed; they did not fly on but became residents. Hunters trapped them and sold them to the Mandaeans for food. Even now, Mamoon tells me, these ducks are eaten only by Mandaeans. It is a strangely poignant story, I feel, almost prophetic, for by traveling to America the people closed the circle that the ducks began.

The first Mandaeans came to the World Exposition in New York in 1939, to show their silver and gold art. There were five, Lamea's father among them. They stayed, some for a long time, and the war intervened, too. Mamoon has a photo of these five men standing by a river in Queens, which they found suitable for their ritual ablutions.

Now, stories told, we enter a street lined by two-story apartments. Shafia and Mamoon are a bit distressed when they realize that the men and the women are separated—the reason given is lack of space. But this is, in fact, the old-time, traditional arrangement.

Together, we decide that I will go with Shafia and Bibi, briefly, to meet the women, who are in an apartment diagonally across from where the men sit. Afterward, I will become a kind of "honorary man" and be with the men. This sometimes becomes my role as a scholar, a position between the male and the female spheres.

We go upstairs. Food activities rule in the kitchen, and in the living room about twelve or fifteen women line the walls. I know only Fawziah and Afifa from before. I shake hands with everyone. One of the mourners is a desolate-looking young woman with dazed eyes and a limp handshake. Some of the women look hardy and robust; others seem decidedly urban and could fit into any cosmopolitan setting. I sit for a while, contemplating the womens' faces. Bibi is greeted with special warmth, the most recent breath from "the old country."

Shafia takes me across the street to the men in a similar apartment, with food preparations made by men and women in the kitchen. About forty men sit along the walls, and I shake hands all around. Ghazi is there, and I meet Majid's brother Raad, larger than his sibling in San Diego. I sit by the window, between Mamoon and his father. A young man comes around with coffee, and I take a small amount in the bottom of the tiny cup. Cigarettes lie fanned out from open packages on napkins. Six or seven men are working their strings of beads. Subdued, mumbling conversations, greetings, handshakes and embraces. A couple of little boys run to and fro throughout the afternoon, orbiting to their affectionate fathers.

Discreetly, I watch the men, who are of all types. The day before, Afifa has asked me, "How come we Mandaeans have so many different looks? Some of us are light, others darker, I'm a redhead"—here she lifts her hand to her hair—"some are shorter, some taller. And some have blue eyes, too!" She turned to Mr. Aldulaimi, who has blue eyes. I said, "I don't know, but an old theory held that the blue eyes hinted at a Caspian Sea influence." Around 1930 the American anthropologist Henry Field and his researchers measured Mandaeans' heads in Iraq, finding nothing conclusive to support that era's theories of physical anthropology.

Now, at the fateha, I watch. On and off, Mamoon and his father converse quietly with me. We sit. Aldulaimi senior says that there probably will not be a *lofani*, the special meal for the dead man, because no one is clean enough, there is no priest present. But I have heard that there will be such a meal, and indeed, soon enough, Mr. Sobbi ascends the stairs in his dark suit and strides purposefully, most likely in the role of ritual official, into the kitchen. Things begin to be moved from the kitchen to the bedroom of one of the children. I sit conveniently positioned, observing these activities. Young men and one young woman hurry back and forth carrying food and white cloths into the room in the back, it seems according to Mr. Sobbi's directions. Something is about to happen.

Mr. Sobbi says to me, "We will do the lofani; do you want to see?" Yes. I enter the room and sit down on the edge of the bed, with one of the young women perched behind me. Mr. Sobbi, holding one large and one very small piece of paper, sits at the other end of the bed. In the doorway stand a couple of young men and some children, riveted by the scene in front of them on the bedroom floor. A white sheet arranged to form a large, shallow pure area on the floor holds many items for the lofani: a bowl of water; a filleted, broiled fish; a lemon; an orange; an apple; a banana; an onion; shaved coconut in a heap; scallions; pita breads. In front of this arrangement sits a small, slender man, with a white cloth napkin on his head. This is the most pure man in the assembly, baptized three times, with enough priests in his family to make him the best suited for the hallali (pure layman) task. He will be the conduit to the deceased man.

Watched by all in the room, the man on the floor tears off a piece of pita bread and puts fragments of each kind of food on a piece of bread first, and then in his mouth, one kind of food at a time. This is not as easy at is sounds, for the man uses only his hands, no knife. He tears open the lemon and the orange with his hands, and a piece of onion is sent flying as he squeezes the translucent meat under the thin skin. Now Mr. Sobbi looks at his large piece of paper, which has the requisite prayer in Mandaic on one side and Farsi on the other. He reads, pausing after each word, and the hallali repeats each word separately. When the place for the zhara appears, Mr. Sobbi glances at the small piece of paper that bears the dead man's maṣbuta name. Next the hallali eats the pita with the food on it. He speaks no word except for the prayer. The prayer ends. "Now he can eat what he wants," says Mr. Sobbi, mostly to me, as a commentary. And Mr. Sobbi rises up and leaves the room. The attentive, mourning family in the doorway immediately move to join the hallali at the sheet, and with an air of intense concentration they sit down and eat with him. I have no place here now, and quickly follow Mr. Sobbi out of the room. This is strictly family business.

I take my former seat in the living room, where tables are set up end to end, by the young men. Trays of food materialize as if out of thin air: fish, olives, dates, parsley, pickles, hot green peppers, scallions, huge mounds of saffroned rice with raisins and nuts, and a delicious, salty mango pickle. The food is arranged in such a way that no one needs to stretch to obtain anything. "Stand next to me," instructs Mamoon, sotto voce. I have never eaten like this. We stand shoulder to shoulder around the table eating, with very little talk, without knives or forks, fingers only. (The man across from me does give me a plastic utensil, probably because of my culture's well-known clumsiness in matters of eating.) We eat quite fast, with great intensity and concentration, for the dead man, for ourselves. It feels more like a communion than any meal I have ever consumed.

Only Mr. Sobbi (with his bad knees) and a couple of other older men, after a while, take their paper plates and sit down on chairs. Toward the end of the meal, Mr. Sobbi comes by and decides to test my Mandaic. "What is that?" he points to the dates. "Sindirka." He beams to his neighbor. "See?" Some of the men have apparently expressed doubt whether I know the language. But I fail on the "bread" question posed by the man next to me.

A more relaxed mood sets in as we sit down. The food-laden dining tables vanish as speedily as they materialized. Men come around with coffee and tea. Platters of fruit appear on side tables. Some men smoke, and strings of beads dangle. There is a debate about collecting money for needy Mandaeans in Iraq. I watch, understanding very little.

After the discussion, Mr. Sobbi comes and sits down next to me and explains the hallali. "Many of the others are not baptized, not clean enough." He looks around. "I'll ask," he says, for my benefit, and turns to a younger, brown-haired man next to him. "How many times have you been baptized?" "Three." Mr. Sobbi does not ask anyone else. Things are not *that* bad, I think to myself.

Then Mr. Sobbi tells me about his mysterious spiritual experiences and dreams. In one dream, he posed some questions to Muhammed, who was sitting inside a 1954 Buick in the desert. Muhammed shook his head at Mr. Sobbi's questions. Widening his eyes, Mr. Sobbi assures me, " I believe in all of them—Buddha, Jesus, Muhammed." Earlier, in October, he told me how on his visit to India he was completely overwhelmed by the poverty, the life, and the pervasive religiousness in Bombay. "They are so religious!" he marveled.

Before we leave the fateha (which will go on for hours still), I shake hands with the men again. We descend to the street, and as we wait for the women in the gathering dusk, Mr. Sobbi clarifies for me the issue of the lacking knife in the lofani. "Not good; it is used to cut meat, you know." I had already guessed that a knife, an instrument of death, would be out of place in a situation that emphasizes feeding and laufa. But I had also wondered whether the hallali was not to use his teeth, but to swallow the food fragments whole. "No, no, he can chew," says Mr. Sobbi.

In the car, Bibi offers us refreshing cardamom seeds from her cloth wallet. We return to Long Island, and Mamoon sighs, "*Ya*, Hibil Ziwa" as he turns off the ignition in his driveway. We mutter assent.

Politics of Religion

On another day, Mamoon tells me how he called on Manda d̲-Hiia and Hibil Ziwa in a specific case. The ʿutras stepped in to help in an otherwise impossible situation, enabling Mamoon to maneuver his car on an ice-covered driveway. I am reminded of Issam, too, who told me how he invokes Hibil Ziwa when a task requires extra strength. Once Issam was cutting wood with an American friend. Each heaved his axe, drew his breath, and with all his might brought the axe down on the wood. Issam called on Hibil Ziwa to give him strength. Hearing this, the American friend, who was soon to go to Vietnam to fight in the war, thought it might be a good idea to try the Mandaean spirit. He began to call on Hibil Ziwa, too, but Issam put a stop to that, protesting that non-Mandaeans had no right to do this. I imagine these two men in the Swedish woods, Issam defending his religious boundary.

It is a few years since I have been invited to Iraq by the Highest Spiritual Council of Mandaeans in Baghdad. The invitation still stands, but I keep postponing the trip. (By this time, early 1995, I have also been invited by Sheikh Salem Choheili in Ahwaz, to visit the Mandaeans of Iran.) If I travel to Iraq, I will have to go to Jordan and then overland, unless air travel is reinstated to Baghdad. Will it be safe? It seems so, at least as long as I stay in government-controlled areas. "Right now, it is not dangerous, but not comfortable," I am told. Mr. Aldulaimi was part of a delegation from the United States to Baghdad, one week before the Gulf War began, to try to prevent that war.

We talk about these things as we sit down to dinner in Mr. Aldulaimi's house. We eat delicious fish, eggplant morga, vegetables, shrimps, the usual mound of yellow rice, scallions, watercress, and another, quite spicy leaf available in Chinese stores. As we are about to eat, Afifa turns to me, alarm in her voice and demeanor, "We don't know how to pray! Teach us!" I am bewildered and do not feel like taking over in this particular matter. Shafia rescues the situation by nodding towards her daughter Hind next to her. "She knows," says Shafia to Afifa, who now seems satisfied because Hind possesses this knowledge. Almost everyone is eating anyway, and no one waits for the prayer. However, the formula is not lost.[7]

After dinner, cognac appears, and dates from Baghdad, plus an impressive, artistically arranged pyramid of fruit. I am assuming that Ghazi will address me, for he called Mamoon in advance to tell him that he disagrees with something I wrote *in Exalted Kingship*. I have brought the book to confront the trouble head-on. But we settle it, Ghazi and I, for it turns out to have been a result of a misunderstanding of terms. Ghazi is a retired accountant for Scandinavian Airlines Systems. Offhandedly, he says, "I read in the paper today that the library in Kristiansand (my hometown in Norway) had to close." "Oh, how come?" I reply, playing along. "A book was stolen." At this, I gesture to *Exalted Kingship* resting on the back of the couch. "Probably a red one, eh?" Ghazi laughs appreciatively.

He turns his beads in his hands. Each bead carries one of Allah's names. Ghazi starts to read them out loud, one after another, translating some of them for my benefit. "Oh wow, beautiful," says Afifa, his wife. We all listen to the names. Pretty soon, Mr. Aldulaimi gets up to bring Qur'ans. One is large, encased in a red carton. The book is a work of art, with stunning blue pages and golden script. "A special gift," remarks the owner, "not to be bought in stores." The book is handed around reverently, much admired.

We are on to holy books now. Discussion turns to last night's debate in which Mr. Sobbi insisted that there is a reference to the Mandaeans in the Bible, in 2 Samuel 14:47. Among his other enemies, king Saul fights "the kings of Zobah." Mr. Sobbi thinks this is "Subbi."[8] Mr. Aldulaimi gets up again, this time to fetch Arabic Bibles. They scour the *taurah* (Torah), and Ghazi reads a part from the Book of Esther. We lose track of the kings of Zobah.

This is getting positively interreligious, I think, and I catch myself before I make a tasteless joke about how the Mandaeans are now above any reproach, engrossed, just minutes ago, in the Qur'an. But Ghazi has evidently pondered along similar lines, for he remarks, "Well, we were Muslims, reading the Qur'an. Now we're Jewish, reading the Bible!"

He asks me a question that is on the minds of many Mandaeans: How are they going to deal with current and prospective spouses who are not Mandaeans but who wish to convert? Mandaeans prohibit conversion. I suggest that the priests may at some point have to change the regulations, to make new rules. This is greeted with doubt and head shaking. But Mamoon agrees with me and imagines that the priests will say some words to purify the non-Mandaean spouses in order to let them into the religion. He makes up a word based on the Arabic *nadhif*, "pure" for "to purify." I recognize this word, which I learned in San Diego. Mamoon says "to nadhifize," which meets with general amusement.

However, this sets off a serious, animated debate about what *can* and what *cannot* be "nadhifized." How? By deeds, or by sheer words? Voices mingle, hands flutter, and shoulders rise up to earlobes as arguments are exchanged. They remember the ice. The ice? Blocks of ice delivered to Mandaean houses. Priests wash the ice and "say some words over it to make it clean," Mamoon tells me. Does this work? Do the words work, alone? General disagreement and confusion. Ghazi shakes his large head. Fauzia widens her eyes and throws in an additional problem: What about the water used to make the ice? Is is clean? These are impossible problems. Impurity lurks wherever you look.

Ghazi asks whether they, the Mandaeans, can baptize me 360 times to make me a Mandaean. I say that I don't think so. Months before, Mr. Sobbi had phoned me from New York, asking my opinion on virtually the same issue.

"We're sitting here, discussing religion," he begins.

Hearing eager voices in the background, I can well believe it.

He continues, "Is it possible to make a Jew a Mandaean by baptizing him 360 times?"

"You mean, to undo the circumcision?"

"Yes!"

I think hard, hem and haw, and then reply, "No, I don't think so. I have never encountered this in any text. That number of baptisms is required for certain serious ritual errors, but you can't use that ritual to convert somebody."

Mr. Sobbi is pleased, for this has been his opinion, too. "See?" I hear him exclaim to his fellow debaters. "That's what *I* said!"

Mr. Sobbi enjoys it when I appeal to texts to deal with thorny issues in the religion. The first time I meet with the Mandaeans in New York, Mr. Sobbi and I have dinner at Mamoon's. Mamoon's father is there, too. The religious discussion intensifies toward the end of the meal. The women clear the table and repair to the kitchen, and the three men and I are left at the table. Mr. Sobbi, who has long since finished his meal, wipes his mouth, clears his throat, sets his face, folds his hands on the table in front of him, fixes me with his brown eyes, and says, "Now, Professor Buckley, let me ask you something." And the questions come rolling one by one, piled up in a heap, as if this is Mr. Sobbi's single chance to put them to me.

John the Baptist, Noah, Abraham, the "origins" question, the Dead Sea Scrolls, the differences between the religions—all the enduring questions are here. Mr. Sobbi has written down (in Farsi, I assume) the most puzzling queries. "What is this secret little book you have in your pocket?" I inquire, half in jest. But it is no joke. In the tattered little notebook are Mr. Sobbi's questions, those he ponders endlessly. I answer as best I can. When he gives me a quote, I say, "Well, that is in text *x*, and because it is in context *y*, it probably means *z*." To this, Mr. Sobbi lights up, throws his hands in the air, and looks at Mamoon and his father, "See? She knows! She knows!"

Mr. Sobbi and I have in common our knowledge of the texts, for the others do not know them, not in the same way as we do. At times, Mr. Sobbi becomes impatient with the questions of the other men, and he tries to steer the attention back to himself and to the topics in his little book. I tell him the pun about yahṭa (miscarriage) and yahuṭaiia (Jews).[9] This wordplay is news to him, and he becomes quiet, buries his head in his hands, and thinks for a while. Then he lifts his head and smiles, "I like that. I like that a lot."

"Seek and Find; Ask and Be Heard . . ."[10]

I ask about the Ašuriyah, the mysterious annual Mandaean commemoration of the Egyptians who drowned when the sea closed on them in the wake of the fleeing Jews. The Mandaeans side with the Egyptians. Mr. Sobbi says that the festival has to do with Noah, while the Aldulaimis insist that it is a lofani for the drowned, who were Mandaeans.[11] I know of no textual evidence for any of this. Mr. Sobbi is keenly aware of the problems with the incongruities between what one could call "folk Mandaeism," the oral, folkloric traditions, and the written texts. He would like to be able to combine these into a coherent system, but it is difficult. To his attempts, I repeatedly emphasize, "But it is not in the texts!" without intending a denigration of the oral traditions. The written texts do carry greater weight, and Mr. Sobbi shrugs his shoulders and waves his hands as he agrees with me, though still eager to systematize them all.

Seeming a bit pained, Mamoon asks a serious question: "Do we worship directly or indirectly?" I decide to take a risk:

> Mamoon, this question comes from the outside; it is a loaded question, and impossible to answer. I bet this is leveled at you, Mandaeans, by others, for it is about the status of intermediaries, whether they exist, whether they are human or divine. If the person who asks you this is a Catholic (or, in a more remote historical perspective, a Harranian Sabean, say), it is different than if it is a Protestant or a Muslim who asks. These two groups tend to show disdain for intermediaries, and if you say "indirectly," they will have a negative view of your religion.

Mamoon and the others are all ears, and they understand my point. I feel relieved to be safe enough in their company to answer in this way. Four months later, I notice that Mamoon twice declares, "We worship directly" in conversation with others. His statement is not aimed at me but is an attempt to reassure fellow Mandaeans, to "legitimize" his religion vis-à-vis skeptical or competing views.

At one point Mamoon reads through the letter of invitation (in Arabic) that I have received from the Highest Spiritual Council of Mandaeans in Baghdad. He smiles but looks a little embarrassed. "There is something funny at the end." It is about the mbaṭṭal days, the inauspicious days of the calendar when my presence among the Mandaeans would not be possible. I should avoid visiting during such days. I already know this and say so to Mamoon, without implying that astrology should be considered to be outdated or unworthy of being taken seriously.

After dinner, Mamoon and I descend into his basement office to look at his books relating to Mandaeism and to Arabic history. He has many documents, and there is a large plaque with a medal on blue velveteen, a grateful recognition given to him by Iraqi Mandaeans. Mamoon is building a whole research center containing information, from Arabic and Western sources, on Mandaeans and their history.

Later, the two older men, who have remained upstairs, come down the steps to say farewell. Mr. Sobbi looks around. I think that he must be reminded of his own house and its library, now gone, blown to smithereens during the war, in Khorramshahr. The two men leave. Mamoon says to me, "Now they will talk until midnight."

"Really?"

"Yes."

The two are good friends and spend much time together. I have already sensed this, yet I am also struck by their differences. The Iraqi, Mr. Aldulaimi, is taller and blue-eyed, a dignified lawyer with a degree from Columbia University in New York, a man of the world, and quite secular in many ways. The Iranian, Mr. Sobbi, short and still muscular from his wrestling and boxing days, is pondering and brooding, a speaker and reader of Mandaic, knowledgeable about the tradition and deeply steeped in it.

That same night I ask about the fire in front of Majid in the video I saw in San Diego. What is that all about? A Zoroastrian intrusion? I do not recall it from Drower's

Mandaeans. "No, no," Mamoon says. The fire is there because it is cold; in fact, the shivering, dripping Majid crouches right by it. And the black-clad woman hovering about, hands clasped on her back? Who is that? This is not in the book, either. She is the ganzibra's wife. She blesses Majid, says Mamoon, and this is a Mandaean adoption of a Muslim custom, a protection of the newly born. I think of *Exalted Kingship*'s insistence that the ganzibra's wife in priest initiations has a symbolic share with her husband in the initiand. But here she is at the baptism, too.

To my knowledge, no in-depth study of the ganzibra initiation exists, only Drower's description in *Mandaeans.*[12] The ritual remains mysterious to me. Why must the postulant perform a marriage ceremony for a priest colleague (who already has at least one wife) as part of his initiation? No one knows. There is agreement among the three men—Mamoon, Mr. Aldulaimi, and Mr. Sobbi—that this question should be posed to Sheikh Abdullah in Baghdad.

A few months later, in Mr. Sobbi's living room, we discuss the ganzibra initiation again. Drower did not quite explain (maybe did not comprehend) why another priest takes a second wife for the sake of his colleague, who would otherwise be stuck in limbo as a sort of unborn fetus caught between the status of tarmida and ganzibra. Also, there must be a reason for the rule that the initiation can only take place when a pious, priest-family member of the community is close to death. I think the new ganzibra becomes a kind of conduit for a special connection between the "outgoing" soul and the additional wife of the other priest. What Drower does *not* mention, but the Mandaeans here in New York tell me, is that the imminent death is that of a woman. I want to know: Why a woman? The question hangs in the air. Our conversation shifts to another topic.

Surreptitiously, right behind my elbow, Mr. Sobbi is on the phone. To Iran! To ask the priest in Ahwaz! I am floored. It is six or seven in the morning there. Pause.

"No one home. In the river, washing," explains Mr. Sobbi, cupping his hand over the mouthpiece. Then he speaks Mandaic. The right person has arrived at the other end. Mr. Sobbi turns to me, "What shall I ask?"

What indeed? I am taken by complete surprise. "Ask if they take converts." Immediately, I regret this, for Mr. Sobbi, again with his hand over the mouthpiece, looks at me with quiet disapproval, as at an unreasonable child, and says, "I cannot ask that."

Of course not. I feel stupid. Still, he does ask, and the answer is: no, no converts, because it would mean influence from the outside. Mr. Sobbi then asks about the nature of the death in the ganzibra initiation, and he receives the answer that the required death before a ganzibra initiation is that of a woman. I am assured that in Mandaean history so far, this has always been the case, though the death could, theoretically, be a man's. I am suspicious about the theoretical part, and I am almost willing to bet that a dead woman's soul, for the sake of gender symmetry, is necessary for the ganzibra's initiation and his colleague's taking of a second wife.

On one occasion the dying woman designated to enable a ganzibra initiation did not die but revived. The ritual was called off, ruling out that particular priest's possibility of becoming a ganzibra—ever. Word of the approaching death got around to the Muslim authorities, and the case came to court, for it was said that the Mandaeans had strangled the woman, tried to kill one of their own. The incident supplied fuel to the fire of anti-Mandaean feelings, and the case reached the newspapers. "Very bad," says Mamoon, shaking his head.

Shafia Aldulami. Photo by Jesse Buckley.

Mr. Mamoon Aldulami and his daughter Hind. Photo by Jesse Buckley.

Hani Aldulami. Photo by Jesse Buckley.

Mr. Sobbi tells me a story from his time in Kuwait, where he had a jewelry business. He met a man who said he was a Zoroastrian. Mr. Sobbi was not so sure. The two men ate together; all was well. After the meal, Mr. Sobbi fetched a Qur'an and gave it to the man, who immediately kissed it and lifted it up to his forehead. "Hah! No *Zardusht!*" says Mr. Sobbi with relish, as he relates this to me. By his action, the man had shown that he was, indeed, a Muslim and not a Zoroastrian ("Zardusht," in Mr. Sobbi's expression).

Shafia emphasizes her children's interest in and commitment to their religion. She took her daughter Hind, who had suffered a cut, to the hospital. Filling in the form, she put "Baptist" in the religion rubric (Mandaeans very often do this on official documents—with full right). But Hind protested afterwards, "Ma! Why did you do that? We are Mandai!"

"Have you seen your son's picture?" I ask Mamoon. He is not sure what I am talking about. While visiting, I sleep in Hani's bedroom, for Hani is away, a student at Cornell University. His childhood drawing, hanging on the wall, struck me immediately as I first looked around the room. It is a watercolor, done when Hani was eleven.

"It is a very Gnostic, very Mandaean picture," I explain to Mamoon. It shows heaven, with a globe floating in blue space, and a confluence of two golden rivers, like branches, above the globe. A glowing, light-filled sanctuary stands where the waters meet, and underneath a comet zooms by. At the bottom is Hani's poem, defiantly stating that heaven exists, despite what his friends say. The Gnostic tradition seems to continue in the younger people, giving hope for future life and generations.

Watching a video taken just a few years earlier during Mr. Shooshtary's visit in Ahwaz, I notice that canned music plays as background to the filmed ceremonies. (Was this added later?) The modern world! The priest's prayers are almost drowned out by the music, but he prays on, unaffected. People are milling about right in front of him, chatting, some of them carrying cameras. The bank of the Karun River is muddy, clayey, and slippery, and the lower parts of the priest's garments are wet and stained by the reddish water. Next the priest stands in the water, fishing bottles out of the pocket of his rasta and filling them for each person who is to be baptized. On this occasion, it is a bridal couple. The bride wears a coarse, yellowish cloak. Three or four older, black-clad women stand by her, and one of them helps her into the river. Just as Drower describes it in her *Mandaeans*, the bridal couple, later, sit back-to-back with a thin cloth between them, their heads knocked together, softly, three times. Mandaean life seems to go on. In the spring of 1996, in Iran, I see this for myself.

11

An Inscribed Mandaean Body

In *The Great "First World,"* an odd figure appears.[1] This document, along with its companion text, "The Lesser 'First World,'" has obtained virtually no scholarly attention since its publication in 1963. Mandaean priestly esoteric literature, the category into which this text fits, is hardly studied these days. A number of other illustrations appear in the part of the scroll "The Great 'First World,'" but the identity of the depicted figure is not specified. Depicted in the same style as other Mandaean Lightworld beings and priestly prototypes in illustrated documents, the figure is nameless. Drower, the translator, hazards no guess.

A reader may consult the original scroll's facsimile, which is rolled up in the carton cylinder that accompanies the book. On the figure's head appear some of the letters of the alphabet, though the letters are not in alphabetical sequence, as Drower observes. Read together, the four letters under his eyes—two under each—spell the word *shad*: "he testified." The figure's body seems separated by a sort of spinal column that divides it into a right and a left side. I give my own translation of the text on the body:

> Lower, right side of the trunk:
>
> In the beginning: waters, fountains of Life. Three škintas are on them. Watchers, watchers that are sublime; blessed for ever and ever.
>
> Lower left side:
>
> I came forth at the beginning. I went there. I dwelled and empowered them, standing (*mqaimia*) for ever and ever.

On top of the trunk the following is written "upside down," as if the figure might be able to read the text on his own chest,

Right side:		
Sublime and incense	Š	T
They twine your wreath	P	Ṣ
Two twigs	M	N[2]
In the precinct of the cult hut	Ṭ	I
Hibil flourished	H	U
When myrtle	G	B

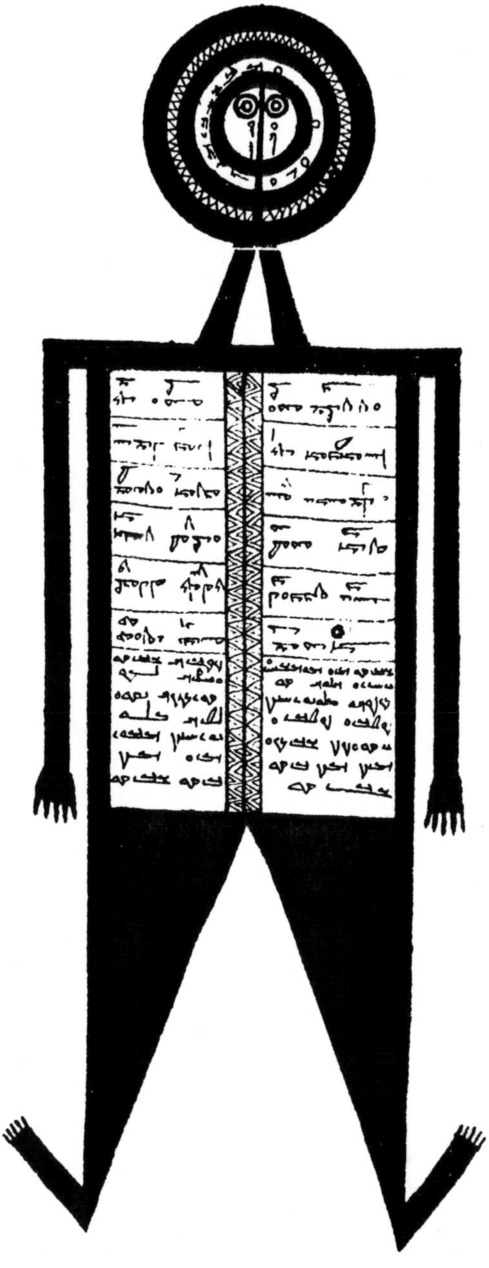

From Drower, *The Great "First World,"* facsimile (in scroll). Used by permission of Brill Academic Publishers.

Left side:		
Fragrant	Ḏ	A
The river which is	Q	R
A twig from it	S	ʿ
Who gave it to me	K	L
When marjoram	Z	Ṭ
Myrtle in the gardens	G	D

Drower makes no comments on the two inscriptions, but she wonders whether both reflect some kind of mnemonics.[3] Note that the Ṭ and the G occur on both the left and the right side.

The Mandaean alphabetic sequence is: A B G D H U Z H̱ Ṭ I K L M N S ʿ P Ṣ Q R Š T Ḏ. Pondering the inscription and Drower's relative silence on it, I noticed, in the inscription on the top of the trunk, that each letter appears with its alphabetical neighbor—except for Ḏ and A. However, these two are the last and the first letters of the alphabet, and so nicely loop the list together in the middle, making a pleasing circle. The only missing letter is H̱, the final third person pronoun suffix, which in a sense is not a "real" letter. Leaving out H̱ and including the G *twice*, at each of the figure's clavicles, the list succeeds in reaching the correct number of letters of the alphabet: twenty-four. By including the Ṭ twice and giving it a different alphabetic neighbor in the two sets of text, *The Great "First World"* avoids the H̱.

Convinced that the words on the left must be found in a prayer in the *Prayerbook*, I leafed through it and soon halted at the translation of prayer 79.[4] After I had consulted the facsimile text in the back of the prayerbook, things suddenly became clearer.[5] Except for the well-known formula "In the Name of the Great Life!," all the words on the figure's chest occur in prayer 79, but the prayer is totally scrambled. Prayer 79 reads:

> In the Name of the Great Life!
> When the myrtle, the myrtle, flourished
> In the gardens of Hibil;
> When the wild marjoram grew in the precinct of the *manda*
> They gave me two twigs of myrtle
> From which they twisted a wreath for the jordan
> For it is wondrous and fragrant is its perfume![6]

The "deconstruction" of prayer 79 in *The Great "First World"* appears to be an example of those word games for which the Mandaeans are famous. But it still remains a mystery why the depicted figure wears the words of this particular prayer, which belongs to the category of "response" (ʿniana) prayers. Every Mandaean priest must recite prayer 79 as he twists a wreath of myrtle for his staff in preparation for conducting a baptism.

So, as the priest prepares for the baptism, he might conjure up the image of the prototypical priest, who is Hibil Ziwa. The figure may be just this mythological person, despite the lack of an expected priestly staff. Support for the idea that Hibil is depicted can be found in the first part of the inscription, on the lower side of the trunk. The words in this textual segment, too, give the impression of being those of a scrambled prayer. Indeed, they are. "In the beginnings: waters, fountains of life," and so forth are the words of prayer 82, which also belongs among the ʿnianas. The text is:

> In the name of the Great Life!
> I went out to the waters;
> at the source of the springs I went (there).
> I founded three škintas, and set over them guardians as rulers.
> The guardians I appointed to rule over them are Sublime, blessed, and trusty, for ever and ever.[7]

As with the other text inscribed on the figure's body, the words have been rendered haphazardly, though every word of prayer 82 is present.

In his introduction to *GR* 4, Lidzbarski notes the presence of liturgical material in it and concludes that the text has been used in rituals.[8] Among the liturgical pieces in *GR* 4 is prayer 82, which is quoted in its entirety, and in *GR* 4's story, Hibil Ziwa utters it. He declaims this prayer after he, along with a number of other Lightworld denizens, has been baptized in the heavenly Jordan. Mythologically superior to Hibil Ziwa, the Lord of Greatness (mara d̲-rabuta) is present, and Hibil Ziwa will soon be sent out to the lower world, the world of creation.

It makes sense, therefore, to suggest that the depicted figure in "The Great 'First World'" might be Hibil Ziwa, and that the speaker in *GR* 4's quoting of prayer 82 is this very figure. Unsettled remains the curious fact of two sets of text, one facing the figure, as if he might look down on his chest, and one set facing the reader. Perceptive readers familiar with Mandaean mythology might think of *GR* 6's mysterious Dinanukht, the half book, half man who sits by the waters, reading in himself.[9] Perhaps the enigmatic figure in *The Great "First World"* intentionally invites both interpretations: both the priestly prototype Hibil Ziwa and the mystic sage Dinanukht.

12

Interpretive Strategies in The Scroll of Exalted Kingship

Along with texts such as *Coronation*, *The Great "First World,"* and *1012*, *Exalted Kingship* belongs to a category of Mandaean texts one might call esoteric priestly documents.[1] *Exalted Kingship* is a large scroll, consists of 1,363 lines, contains drawings (with additional text inside the illustrated panels), and in rather elliptical fashion describes the initiation of the tarmida (this ritual was the subject of chapter 9). *Coronation*, a short text on the priest initiation, tends to march ahead at a brisk pace, while *Exalted Kingship* proceeds much more slowly. It pauses and delves into lengthy dissertations on topics it deems suitable. In this chapter, I will limit myself to dealing with selected sequential passages from among the beginning of *Exalted Kingship*, lines 7–225.[2] In this section the text plumbs the mysteries of the effects of the novice's words while he sits inside the škinta on the second day of the initiation. My presentation of lines 7–227 in this text may be correlated to the relevant parts of chapter 9.

According to *Exalted Kingship*, while the postulant is in the škinta on the second day, he utters the first 103 prayers of the Mandaean liturgy—not just the baptism liturgy, as *Coronation* and and Drower's *Mandaeans* seem to imply. The prayers comprise the baptism and masiqta liturgies (1–31 and 32–72, respectively), the two ʿngirta prayers (73 and 74), three prayers of praise (75–77), and the ʿnianas (78–103).

What makes this recital special is that all these prayers are uttered without their expected ritual contexts, for there are no baptisms, death masses, or call-and-response settings. Still, *Exalted Kingship* comments on the effect of every one of the 103 recited prayers. In doing so, the text interprets not only the inner meanings in those prayers but also the novice's words. The interpretations appear to follow unstated exegetical principles evidently taken for granted as embedded in an esoteric scheme. The text accounts neither for any such scheme nor for any underlying, native theory about ritual. Nevertheless, this chapter tries to offer a glimpse into both. Five themes running through the limited piece of text under consideration are:

1. an attention to the mythological figure Ruha as contrasted with the spirit ruha in the novice's body
2. the text's focus on evoked time—past, present, and future—in the novice's recital

3. a characteristic strategy of "tailoring" prayer contents from the *Prayerbook* to *Exalted Kingship*'s specific interests
4. the relationship of the novice's soul to his spirit
5. the connection between the novice and his rba

To begin, we need to think back to chapter 9 and halt at the point at which the two laymen accompany the postulant into the hut. These two men give strength to his body, says *Exalted Kingship.*[3] He will need it, for it is not just the novice's soul and his spirit that are involved in the present enterprise; his entire body will be re-created. This is the text's primary concern. The novice's old layman self will have to yield to a new, priestly self, and this replacement, understood as a new creation, begins to take place already during his recital of prayers 1–103. He is like a moth developing within a cocoon, a chick maturing in its egg.

Mandaeism usually understands soul and spirit as female, as sisters, elements that need to be merged at the death of the body. In the present case of priest initiation, the death is of course symbolic, for the ritual includes no human death. But, peculiarly, *Exalted Kingship* lets the soul present herself as "male" vis-à-vis the female spirit. This is a far from typical Mandaean view, but it makes a certain sense in this case, where the female, layman world must be overridden by and subjected to the male, priestly one. Even without a death the initiation can be said to emphasize salvation insofar as a predominance of the "male" world marks a redemption from the "female" one. A chastizing soul, assuming a male role, will lord it over her spirit companion, whose gender remains female but who ideally should change to become male.

Like all human beings, the new priest will have a body and an independent spirit, in addition to his soul. But because of his enhanced soul element, his Lightworld citizenship will be stronger than that of laypeople. The entire initiation ritual can be seen as an effort to secure a balance in the new priest's life between his "female" inclinations and his emotions and passions, which are ruled by body and spirit, to his Lightworld soul. Lay status is consistently coded as "female" over against priests, who belong to the "male" domain. As we shall see, even in this limited section of *Exalted Kingship*, the text's vertiginously detailed description of prayers and actions in the ritual emphasizes the necessity and ramifications of the priest's double citizenship. Being simultaneously "here" and "there," the priest must know how to play on this dynamic, to move between the realms, to symbolize and to live the laufa.

I now turn to lines 7–225 in the text and deal with the prayers in sequence. In a short, third section, I will focus on the text's mental universe.

Lines 7–225

When the priests in the škinta offer the novice their greeting "Asuta!" (Healing!), its effect is immediate, for all knots and seals of *mandaiuta* (lay status) are loosened in him.[4] This "exorcism" from the constrictions of lay status opens up the conditions for the possibility of the Naṣoraean, priestly level of the religion. As seen in chapter 9, the priests then recite a long prayer over the seated novice, who rises, kisses one of the chief priests on his head, and, after certain formulas, is ready to recite prayers 1–103.

When the novice speaks the formula right before prayer 1, his own soul, whose armor is the crown (taga), rejoices in its anticipation of that priestly emblem. Crowning lies further ahead in the proceedings (as noted in chapter 9), but the novice's soul already looks forward to the event. Soul and crown dominate as preeminently priestly features. Parallel to the crown soon to encircle the top of his head, the priest's soul shall reign over his spirit and body. *Exalted Kingship* presents the soul as a sort of independent, internal knower attuned to the future event of the crowning.

In a jarring contrast to the soul's just-expressed, jubilant expectation of coronation, prayer 1 points out a lurking danger, according to *Exalted Kingship*'s interpretation. The reason is the following section of prayer 1:

> At that time there was no solid earth and no inhabitants in the black waters. From them, from those black waters, Evil was formed and emerged, One from whom a thousand thousand mysteries proceeded and a myriad myriad planets with their own mysteries.[5]

As anyone checking prayer 1 will see, the mythological figure Ruha is not explicitly named, but she belongs to the dark forces just evoked. It is she who stirs up at the novice's recital of this prayer, says *Exalted Kingship*. Her awakening clearly threatens the novice.

This is the kind of trick liturgies may play on reciters, for mere mention of the dark forces immediately evokes them. Ruha is the most dangerous enemy the new priest will have to contend with, and her presence is regularly summoned in the prayers, either as a teasing device or manifesting real danger. Battles with evil are pointless if evil is not made present. Liturgies conjuring up dark powers do so in order to contend with them. Moreover, the pernicious ones understand the prayers, for they hear when called upon, especially Ruha, who originally belonged to the Lightworld and is contentious and homesick (as seen in chapter 4). The apparently naive question of how evil rears its ugly head as it does during prayer 1 is logically answered: through the reciter's own words!

Next, prayer 2, as a step up from prayer 1's stirring of the soul and its anticipation of the taga, awakens the "inner" crown, a sort of "Platonic" image of the crown that the novice will obtain later on. Texts such as *Exalted Kingship* assume this kind of dualistic typology because a material item is inextricably tied to its dmuta, the upper Lightworld image that vivifies the concrete item. The "inner," that is, Lightworld, image is put on alert, readied for action in the near future. "Inner" in this case equals "upper." While dwelling on prayer 2, *Exalted Kingship* launches into a little lesson on companionship, a further elaboration on the typology just noted. Everything is part of a pair, for the external, concrete crown has its inner counterpart, and the two relate to one another as husband with wife. Neither part can do without the other.[6]

The mystery of the "Father" (as opposed to the lay status symbol, the "Mother"), awakens at the novice's recital of prayer 3, a prayer for the burzinqa (priest's turban). The text's association is suitable, for the prayer praises "the Great Mystery of Radiance" in the Lightworld. At the utterance of prayer 5, whose title is "Let there be light!," "the springs of living waters awaken, from which he wishes to receive a sign."[7] Activated by prayer 5, this sign belongs to the baptism awaiting the candidate after the present round of recitals.

Prayer 8 awakens the incense that belongs in another baptismal segment later on; this time it is the baptism for the rba. These two examples, prayers 5 and 8, show a concern with calling on items that belong to specified, future strata, to two different baptisms. Two of the "tools of the trade," water and incense, awaken to their future tasks, not the performer reminding himself of what he will need later on. That the tools take precedence over the worker here shows *Exalted Kingship*'s inclination to stress human humility in a work context. The ritual implements are "alive."

At prayer 14, "that adhesive which supports him and his whole body palpitates, stands up, and sunders the mysteries of mandaiuta from their inner protective cover."[8] The text's exegesis relates directly to the contents of the prayer, but one must note the lack of a baptism context in the present situation. Prayer 14 directs itself to the priestly olive-wood staff, the margna, stuck into the muddy river bottom as the officiant descends into the water up to above his knees. The dramatic "sprouting," the palpitation taking place in the novice's body, according to *Exalted Kingship*, seems related to the olive-wood staff. The staff's work is to raise up souls to the Light, as the prayer states. Notice how the candidate literally sheds his lay status, like a plant reaching a new stage in its development.

The seven walls of iron evoked in the protective prayer 15 surround the novice at the moment of his recital, and the seven magical sounds in this prayer—*ma*, *ya*, *baz*, *aziz*, *as*, *asin*, and *as*[9]—obviously parallel or name the walls. The novice departs from the mystery of mandaiuta at prayer 18, which ends in the bestowal of numerous protective Lightworld names on the novice. Prayer 19, next, evokes time in a way that is different than in prayers 5 and 8. These were future directed. But now, at prayer 19, the novice's recital awakens the water sign of his own first baptism as an infant. Retroactive, in a sense, prayer 19 calls up an action long past, one that nevertheless remains in effect.

Prayer 26's clause "Bound (*together*) and sealed are these souls that went down to the jordan . . . secured with bonds of righteousness and with the bonds of kušṭa,[10] and with the bonds of Zhir, the great light of Life!" produces this interpretation in *Exalted Kingship*: "the spirit is secured in the fetter of the soul."[11] This is the first example of a specific strategy that *Exalted Kingship* applies to its exegesis of the *Prayerbook*, namely, *Exalted Kingship*'s liberty in transferring roles given in the *Prayerbook* to actors that concern *Exalted Kingship* at a given moment. So, the souls bound to righteousness, truth, and Zhir in the *Prayerbook* become the spirit bound to the soul in *Exalted Kingship*. I can find no particular pattern to this kind of exegetical play (perhaps it is typical of religious intellectuals). In the present case, the text clearly tries to link the spirit to the soul in a manner that does not unduly weaken the spirit but that places it under the power and tutelage of the new priest's soul.

Prayer 31 begins, "Radiance goeth up to its place and Light to the Everlasting Abode. On the day that Light ariseth, Darkness returns to its place."[12] According to *Exalted Kingship*, Ruha (who is unmentioned in prayer 31) reacts to this recital by weeping, complaining that the soul has ascended and that she, Ruha, is turned back to dwell in her place.[13] Unable to ascend, she has lost a human companion. One might say that this prayer, or baptism in general, hints at what is in store for Ruha at the end of the world: loss of Mandaeans under her sway. When no Mandaeans are left in the world, it will end.

The association between soul ascent and the conclusion of the baptism, reached with prayer 31, depends, as already noted, on the equation of baptismal water with light, for baptism becomes a temporary access into the Lightworld. Final entry comes only at the end of human life. At the novice's initiation, his very utterance of prayer 31, without a baptismal context but still able to conjure it up, causes Ruha to grieve over lost territory.

Finished with the baptism prayers, the postulant launches into the masiqta liturgy. Prayer 33, a mambuha prayer, is addressed to the waters of Life, which refreshes the good but causes the evil ones to express anxiety about their eligibility for salvation. *Exalted Kingship* is interested in a liquid more directly related to the novice's body, however, for at this recital, the text says, the postulant's semen "awakens and multiplies into 360 streams (or: "veins") and expels from the purity the pollutions that dwell in them."[14] Semen is a correlate to mambuha, according to the text, and it acts as a cleansing "medicine" in his body. But if the seed is impure, that impurity will rule out any righteousness in the veins of the novice, says *Exalted Kingship*. In prayer 33 the wicked ask whether there is no room for them in the place of Light, and the answer is obvious no. "As water when poured out falleth on the earth, so (too) doth evil fall abased before good," says the prayer.[15] But *Exalted Kingship* takes liberties with the prayer contents and shifts the emphasis onto the reciter's own body.

At the uttering of prayer 35 ("good for all occasions"), Ruha and her seven planetary sons sit in lamentation, curling their lips in disappointment and disdain at the prospect of the soul and the spirit leaving the body, according to *Exalted Kingship*. One of the expressed promises in prayer 31 is "(Though) spirits and souls sit (*here*) as guilty, (*yet*) by thy name they shall rise as innocent, (*thy name of*) Yuzaṭaq-Manda-ḏ-Hiia."[16] Here, as elsewhere, *Exalted Kingship* makes a sharp distinction between the spirit ruha in the human being, which is eligible for ascent, and the mythological mother of the planets, who is left behind with her sons. This emphasis, again, suits the specific interest of *Exalted Kingship*, namely, the priest initiation, which, to the greatest extent possible, must free the postulant from the clutches of Ruha.

During prayer 49 the celebrants of the masiqta would, at another stage of the ritual, begin the complex work of joining spirit and soul as they prepare to depart from the dead body (see chapter 8). But at the moment, mere recital is in order. The intoned prayer affects the planets, who at the sight of the ascending soul, clench their fists, beat their breasts, and exclaim, "Woe on (us) planets! for they (we) are powerless, but the works of Their [i.e., the priests' ʿutras'] hands are victorious!"[17] According to *Exalted Kingship*, Ruha and her sons react in a similar way, but they also add, "Why did we plan to have a company (for ourselves) in this world? He has been saved from beneath our hands and it (or: 'he') will be our downfall."[18] In the text's interpretation, the salvation does not mark a path out of this world, but from layman to priest status. Already at this early stage of the initiation, the planets' influence over the postulant is waning.

Prayer 51 states:

> I beheld Life, and the Life beheld me
> And in the Life I put my trust.
> When this, the soul of N., casteth off her bodily garment
> She putteth on the dress of life
> And becometh like unto the Great Life in light.[19]

According to *Exalted Kingship*, the effect of the first quoted sentence in prayer 51 is that the soul accuses the spirit of having persecuted her. The soul specifies, "See, (you) spirit, that I am a master whose mistress takes off her female dress and puts on a male garment."[20]

This is the first time *Exalted Kingship* portrays the soul casting herself in a male role. She insists that her "mistress"—the spirit, subjected to the male soul and master—must also don the male garment. Such a garment is required for the move from "female" lay level to "male" priest level. Note that the *Prayerbook*'s ungendered "dress of Life" and "bodily garment" turn gendered in *Exalted Kingship* 's exegesis. Because the soul has changed her clothes in prayer 51, the spirit must do so, too. The switch also implies a continued gender consistency, for now both soul and spirit ought to be male, whereas usually, both are female. Again, we see that *Exalted Kingship* freely interprets a prayer's content to suit the specific purpose of priest initiation.

Ideally, a new priest should possess a male soul and a male spirit. This is a view that opposes more common exegeses not only in Mandaean literature in general but also in other parts of *Exalted Kingship*. In a masiqta, for instance, the elements remain sisters, female. But *Exalted Kingship* has a different agenda, a need to press for a movement from female to male, while the text nevertheless must concede that the new priest, by dint of also being human, still remains subject to "female" forces.

Prayers 49–53 form the nucleus of the masiqta. It is only natural, perhaps, that the effects on soul and spirit—by means of the artifacts of the faṭira ritual—would be reflected at the recital of these same prayers now, in a quite different setting. Alluding to the handling of soul symbols in the masiqta, *Exalted Kingship* warns the novice against the danger of making a mistake further on in the priest initiation, when the same prayers are used. At the present moment, during his recital of prayer 53, the initiate is warned not to fail in a future, repeated segment of the ritual. Regardless of what mistakes he might commit later on while reciting the same words in that future context, he will still, at the present moment of prayer 53, "create, call forth, vivify, heal and establish"[21] his own body.

Exalted Kingship offers a peculiar combination of anxiety provocation and consolation, it seems. The warning constitutes an explicit command to associate the use of the same prayer in two different contexts. Present, nascent fear is rapidly consoled, and our text issues a warning to be alert in the future recital of prayer 53. Creative activity now will not be annulled retroactively by ritual mistakes later on, the text says. But even raising this question acutely demonstrates a keen sense of acts and their effects. If the candidate now creates his own body, and then, about two months hence, makes a mistake in his rba's masiqta—which will create a new body for the teacher—will the novice's own body, as he has created it so far, be destroyed? The answer is no. But he may ruin his teacher's body and his own in the future ritual if he does not at that later point pay close attention to his work.

What map can we obtain of a religious mentality expending energy on such notions of mistakes and their results? What is the understanding of cause and effect, of time, of tools and their employment? What is the precise relationship between the novice's and the teacher's body? Answers to these questions would demand separate studies, and I can only make the issues explicit here. Clearly, the dangers of Mandaean priestcraft are overwhelming.[22]

The two-line prayer 55, "The Great Life spoke and revealed (opened) with His mouth, in His own radiance, light and glory,"[23] has the pleasant effect of raising the curtain that separates spirit and soul, according to *Exalted Kingship*.[24] The opening of the mouth, then, becomes interpreted as a raised barrier in the second text.

At prayer 68, which depicts the ascending soul being questioned by the tollhouse watchers about its heritage, *Exalted Kingship* launches into an invective against Ruha. She is described in the following words: "She lives in horrid darkness, sits in the company of devouring fire, and drinks red waters. She wears garments of many colors."[25] The text goes on to laud priests, who in contrast to Ruha dress in white silk, enjoy living waters, and are delivered from "horrid darkness." Prayer 68 makes no direct mention of Ruha herself. Neither was this the case in prayer 1, as seen earlier, for sheer association evidently suffices. Ruha may be loosely linked to the soul's interrogators. In any case, the context of priest initiation makes it imperative to emphasize dissociation from Ruha. *Exalted Kingship* stresses that the soul's father is the yardna, but that her nourishing mother is Ruha, the earth, from whom the soul has now escaped. Here is a conscious effort to distance a "real" birth—that of a human being into the material world, from and into material bodies—from the present "birth" of a priest, who must try to curb a material, Ruha-ruled life.

The long prayer 75 celebrates Life as it manifests itself in the lower worlds.[26] *Exalted Kingship* briefly states the recital's effect as follows: "Ruha and the Seven run away from his [the novice's] presence and take to the depths."[27] The prayer's contents support this interpretation, but the prayer is also one of the few instances in which Mandaean liturgy gives voice to Ruha's pitiful complaint:

> Spirit (Ruha) lifted up her voice
> She cried aloud and said, "My Father, My Father
> Why didst thou create me? My God, My God,
> My Allah, why hast thou set me afar off
> And cut me off and left me in the depths of the earth
> And in the nether glooms of darkness
> So that I have no strength to rise up thither?"[28]

This segment of the prayer portrays Ruha in need of salvation, a topic not in *Exalted Kingship*'s interest. For in the present context of priest initiation only the element ruha can be saved, not the mythological figure Ruha, whom *Exalted Kingship* summarily relegates to the depths.

The myrtle in the candidate's hand wakes up during his recitation of the myrtle prayer, number 79. Now the plant begins to anticipate its future use, when the same prayer will be recited during the new priest's baptism of his teacher.[29] Another kind of plant imagery emerges in prayer 83, which begins, "How lovely are the plants which the jordan hath planted / And raised up!"[30] "Plants" (*šitlia*) is a common metaphor for people, Mandaeans. Turning against Ruha, *Exalted Kingship* interprets the effect of prayer 83 by insisting that she sowed the seed, but that the resulting fruit was not at all what she planned, for the fruit "went and became the portion of others."[31] Here is a connection with prayer 68, in which the souls stated that their nurturing mother was Ruha, from whom they are now emancipated. Despite the polemics, it seems daring to let the offended mother be heard on her own terms, as *Exalted Kingship* does.

In explicit, polemical contrast to the Jewish Sabbath (šapta), Habšaba, the Mandaean, personified female Sunday, is evoked twice in the prayers toward the end of the recital, in prayers 81 and 95. According to *Exalted Kingship*, Sunday blesses the candidate in response to his recitals of both prayers. In the latter one, Sunday promises the soul that a guardian shall conceal it from the tollhouse interrogators when the ascending soul is "delivered from evil deeds."[32] Just a bit earlier, in line 209, the soul reacted to the novice's recital of prayer 94 with happiness at being split away from the "stinking body."

In response to prayer 96, the soul boasts to the spirit that it, the soul, is now provided with "pure fruit and sublime blossom."[33] The two-line prayer 97 reads, "He rose and took me with him / And did not leave me in the perishable dwelling."[34] This can be interpreted in two ways, depending on whether one reads "he" as the savior or as the soul. Either the soul has been taken away by the savior, or the spirit has been saved *by* and *with* the soul. The prayer probably tends toward the first interpretation. But *Exalted Kingship* does not consider the matter settled, for it lets the spirit react to the recital by imploring the soul, "By your life, by your life, soul! When you ascend to the House of Life, take me with you! If I inflicted persecution on you, do remember me in kindness, for I did not know you and did not understand you."[35] The text still understands the spirit's salvation to be pending.

The final prayer in this ritual round is prayer 103, which states that darkness is pushed back and Light established in its place. In response to this recital, the earth's foundations shake and the monster-dragon ʿUr (Ruha's nonplanetary son) "moans like a dove."[36] For the time being, then, the dark forces are kept in check. But the ritual is only in its second day; sixty-six days remain, and much can go wrong.

What Does It All Mean?

The preceding section has shown examples of how words produce actions according to a pattern roughly like this: "When you say word/sentence A in prayer B, the result is C with respect to D." *Exalted Kingship* demonstrates a strikingly wide range of what I call "activated fields" responding to the novice's recital. These fields include the candidate's own soul, spirit and body; his teacher; ritual implements or formulas to be used later on in the initiation; Lightworld emblems; Ruha and the evil forces. Energies and entities are moved around, strengthened, weakened, or otherwise changed. Future and past events come into play, and the novice's transition from lay level to priesthood affects and effects forces on the most minute and the most cosmic of scales.

Two points deserve emphasis. First, the activated fields include past, present, and future ones, which makes for a dizzying philosophy of time in *Exalted Kingship*. It is worth noting when and how a specific time segment is invoked, for there is a modicum of optimism regarding errors committed in the present (e.g., regarding prayers 52 and 53), but dire warnings emerge against future mistakes. One might call this a "so far, so good" attitude.

Second, lines 7–255 treat a segment of prayers recited by heart, without any of the accompanying actions or created environments normally associated with the prayers. The novice handles no priestly implements, is not immersed in water, eats nothing, is not being prayed over by someone else, and so on. The novice's superiors monitor his words—but the postulant himself performs no actions aside from speaking. His utterances are invested with great power and consequences. The supremacy of the word in this ritual segment testifies to a necessary, early round in the edifice of priest-building.

By sheer words the novice creates parts of the person he is about to become. It is not a matter of thrusting himself back into the ideal condition of the ʿutras at the time of the world creation. Neither is he projecting himself forward onto ʿutra status entirely outside of the earthly world. Slowly and methodically, he becomes both an ʿutra and a priest, set squarely in this world as a servant to his community. But specifically when he will officiate at rituals, he belongs to the Lightworld. As a human being, he is subject to Ruha's attacks, but as a priest, his own spirit, ruha, seems to have been joined to his soul in a way that otherwise holds only for dead Mandaeans whose masiqta has been successfully performed. "Father" and "Mother" aspect in the novice are both active, but the former dominates.

A Mandaean priest continually shifts roles, alternating between opposite slots where "human" marks one end, "divine" the other. But "divine" and "human" would hardly be relevant terms in Mandaeism, I think, because a priest is an ʿutra on earth, and a human being made priest can leap above the earth into Lightworld geography. As an objectified status, the priestly office is unthinkable without the prescribed dynamic enterings into and exits out of ʿutra-hood. When he consecrates himself and his insignia for specific rituals, the priest activates his ʿutra status. In the opposed move, he exits from that level by deconsecrating himself and his accoutrements. Only priests can "enter" and "exit" in this way.[37]

The various "markers" for priests entering or exiting ʿutra-hood are a so far unstudied area in the interpretation of Mandaean rituals. But prayers, formulas, gestures, and the eating of certain foods seem to be primary signals for being "on the job" or "taking a break." Watching part of a video of a Mandaean priest initiation that took place in Khuzistan, Iran, in 1991, I was struck by the rhythm in segments of the ritual. At times, the priests took a break, laughed, relaxed, and talked with spectators who entered the ritual space. After eating particular foods and at gestures such as honoring their crowns, the priests went back to work. Spectators knew when the priests were on or off the job, that is, when it was appropriate for them to approach the priests or to withdraw to the edges of the arena, respectfully resuming their role as witnesses to the priestly activities.

The conditions for making and marking ritual space and time can be glimpsed in the text's lines 7–225. The novice begins to learn how to create himself and his own working conditions and to be alert to his own, new self as it evolves. What he does at the moment has repercussions for the future. When *Exalted Kingship* focuses on certain future parts of the ritual, for instance, the awakening of a ritual item or prayer for use later on, the priest learns to look ahead, to make the relevant associations between what happens in the present with another creative round further on. A tool or an association that is needed days hence must be kept in mind now; otherwise, the work space may be insufficiently prepared.

No ritual context is a "given"—performers create it.[38] The full-fledged priests construct a temporal and spatial "laboratory" for priest-making, while the novice is responsible for his part of self-work. The relative passivity of the officials is worth noting. In the segment under treatment, the novice starts to create himself, for it is *his* spoken prayers that create and affect the elements in the laboratory. Speech arises in the same body as that affected by the speech. Assuming that the power inheres in neither novice nor words as such, but in the dynamic between them, one may see the novice's knowledgeable activation of the words as resulting in the desired creation.

The priests watch and listen. One might have expected a more stereotypical scene with a priest of superior rank uttering prayers over a passive, perhaps kneeling or prostrate candidate. Not so here. The novice is creating himself, guarded by his teacher and other priests, plus the two laymen. The latter know that the proceedings are profoundly beyond their capacity and ken; they act simply as witnesses. But the required presence of laymen is important, for it signifies nothing less than the abiding existence of "the Left," the flank associated with Ruha. It is precisely *her* influence that the novice is trying to escape. Still, the two men's attendance reminds the novice of his human standing, that his spirit will live with his soul in his body, that his constituency is the laypeople, "the Left."

If rituals take control by cutting what is united and, conversely, by binding together what is severed, and if ritual practice aims to facilitate passages and/or authorize encounters between opposed orders,[39] let me conclude this chapter by loosely tying these ideas to the priest initiation. A consistent theme regarding the effects of the treated recitals is the banishment of the mythological Ruha to the depths, while her elemental spirit counterpart in the novice's body must be joined with, yet subordinated, to his soul. Here is an implicit mapping of a macrocosm, for Ruha needs to be enclosed, if possible, in a territory safely removed from the Lightworld. The analogue in the human body, the microcosm, is ruha, whose existence is both too close for comfort and necessary, and who may be manipulated and controlled in the body. She will live there, and the priest's continuous task is to police her influence over him. It is vitally important to acquire control over the body-residing ruha because she not only is the soul's companion but also at the end of the body's life must merge with the soul.

Matters seem a bit different with respect to the quite autonomous mythological Ruha, who may not submit to being "geographically" hemmed in by means of sheer words. In no part of *Exalted Kingship* do any material items control Ruha—in contrast to the spirit element ruha. Perhaps one might say that the microcosmic ruha falls within practical, ritual reach, while her mythological, macrocosmic counterpart remains at large as long as the material world stands.

The priest initiation can be seen as a strategic "inoculation" against the vicissitudes of earthly/bodily life. Priestly spirit and soul are joined in a way that for laypeople requires a real, bodily death. In a sense, priests have reaped the rewards of bodily death while they exist on earth. The switch from "Mother'"to "Father" domination works in an analogous manner, for both domains are effective in the novice's body, but the "Father" side predominates. The ritual makes possible the passage from one to the other and enables the developing/developed priest to handle the opposing forces within himself. Only the dead are fully citizens of the "Father" side. When the novice's new body starts to emerge like a plant out of his old body during prayer 14, that body does not really die, but continues, subdued. Collectively and symbolically, this body is also present in the laypeople.

This chapter has shown how words create realities. Sitting in the škinta with watchful priests, the novice inhabits a ritual space, one that makes his words effective. His status approximates that of an ʿutra-in-the-making. And ʿutras/priests are capable of creating realities on a vastly different scale than the merely human laypeople can. The next chapter will also deal with creative words, but it centers more on play and puns. When words are allowed to take charge and be creative on their own, Mandaeism comes close to accepting a potentially dangerous autonomy of letters, sounds, and words. The question is to what extent human or ʿutra agency may be able to rein in that power.

13

Mandaean Language Games and Obstacles

A B G D H U Z Ḫ Ṭ I K L M N S ʿ P Ṣ Q R Š T Ḏ A

This is the Mandaean alphabet, the *abagada*, consisting of twenty-four letters and so named because of its first four letters. One of them is not a real letter, for the Ḏ, the relative particle "of," is added on as the penultimate letter of the alphabet. The first letter, A, is repeated at the very end of the abagada in order to make the auspicious number, twenty-four.[1] The abagada comes from the female, primordial Wellspring, the *aina* (often paired with its corresponding male principal, the Datepalm). Created prior to the universe and human beings, the letters are the Wellspring's children. One may say that no universe could have been made prior to the letters, because neither speech nor writing were possible until the abagada came into being.

Ayar (Ether), cosmic breath, speaks in the abagada, but he himself did not emanate from it.[2] Imitating Ether, human beings utter the letters and, in combining them, create their lives. But the Mandaeans accord a somewhat disturbing autonomy to the abagada, and it is a question how much power human beings have in their use of it. Who is in charge, the letters or the people? To explore this problem, this chapter will focus on errors, subversive word games, jokes, double entendres, and polemics; in short, they are the kinds of language games that people play on the alphabet—or that it plays on them. If we assume that Mandaeism sides with the letters, and therefore in a sense against itself, the religion is playing a joke on itself.

The Letters

According to *1012*, Book I, II,[3] the B emanates from the A,[4] and the B then turns to the A and praises it. The G, coming into existence next, turns to its predecessor, B, and praises it, and so on through the alphabet. "Each king (*malka*) praised and worshipped him who was anterior to himself, until a structure was built up, composed of twenty-four kings who held themselves together so that their edifice might not be destroyed."[5] Notice here the concern for the completeness of the alphabet, the emphasis on harmony and co-work.

Because Mandaeism is, after all, a form of Gnosticism, we should already be prepared for signs of disharmony, for things going awry. Indeed, the abagada is threatened because "the construction became swollen with pride and no consolidation took place within that Wellspring, and it became deprived, fell, and was abortive."[6] This information recalls a central creation myth in which the world creator Ptahil stands in the primeval waters and speaks what he thinks are creative words (he is imitating Yahweh in the Bible's Old Testament).[7] But no solidification of the waters occurs, for Ptahil has not been sufficiently instructed by his father/predecessor in how to create the world. He becomes despondent and has to give up his attempt, at least for the time being. Ptahil is not accused of pride—the sin of the letters in *1012*—but merely of being ignorant. His father, Abatur, has failed to instruct his son. Comparing this story with the myth about the letters, we see a common theme: something is amiss in the relationship between the actors. The lesson seems to be that incorrect use of language produces no world, and, in Ptahil's and Abatur's case, the predecessor must instruct the next creator.

According to *1012*, no solidarity could take place between the letters when pride and individualism entered the picture, sabotaging the collective. *1012* says that the L marks the middle of the abagada, and that twelve letters now assemble on the right, twelve on the left, the groups facing one another like hostile armies.[8] Abhorring this stalemate, the text tries to determine exactly *where* in the succession of emanations things went awry. It assumes that when they reached H̲, the letters expressed themselves defectively, but they encouraged themselves, saying:

> If we separate ourselves and place ourselves at a distance from one another, the building will not hold together. (But) if we approach one another and merge together we shall construct the building soundly and lay it in an orderly fashion . . . [If] we do not join with one another, the Right will be useless, the Left ruined, and the mouth (mouthing?) of every one of the mysteries will be spoiled.[9]

That the H̲, appearing one-third into the abagada, marks the spot where defectiveness came about is a significant piece of information. For the H̲ links up with the Mandaean anthropological theory regarding body, spirit, and soul. The spirit as the trouble spot in the human being parallels the status of the H̲, for *Exalted Kingship*, in its dissertation on the alphabet, states that the H̲ signifies the spirit, while the two other nonletters, the ʿ (*ayin*) and the d̲, symbolize body and soul, respectively.[10] Therefore, in the layout of both the alphabet and the human being, structure and cohesiveness are emphasized, but so are difference and discord. No human being can exist without the interaction of its three components—body, spirit, and soul—just as no language can arise from an alphabet of staunchly individualistic letters.

In *1012*, the letters encouraged themselves, calling for co-operation. "The mouth of every one of the mysteries will be spoiled"[11] if discord continued. "Mysteries," razas, among many other things, mean "rituals" or "sacraments."[12] If no work can be done without collective effort, creative words are of no account, and, worse than nonsense, result in the ruin of language. To counter such threats, the letters take each other's hands. In what follows, *1012* shows a very characteristic interest not only in the pragmatics of language building but also in the pragmatic language of construction. Real construction is intended—in this case, masonry. Along with other kinds of construction and artisan work, masonry for centuries remained one of the traditional occupations of Mandaeans.

At the spot where the letters grasp one another's hands, *1012* gives a simple drawing of a rectangle.[13] This is building material, a brick (*libna*). The stunningly concrete image may seem strange in an utterly esoteric dissertation on the alphabet, but it demonstrates very well the Mandaean love of practical thinking and down-to-earth metaphors. The letters grab each other's hands at the corners of each brick. So, building language and reality is like building a house, for the letters must join in the correct relation to one another, corners to corners. Otherwise, house/language/world will fall down.

The letter L gives the first illustration, says *1012*, for the Š watches the L working and asks, "This that thou makest, what is its name?" The L answers—as we might expect—"libna," L for libna![14] *1012* says that all buildings have four corners, and all things are constructed out of four mysteries: cosmic Father and Mother, soul and spirit. Everything depends on these four: all creations, all natural phenomena, and all Mandaean rituals and prayers. "[A]nything which is not constructed of four mysteries will not rise" [i.e., to the Lightworld], but will be spoilt and unworthy."[15]

Correct Speech

How does this "anthropomorphic" alphabet philosophy work in practice? If the abagada, both collectively and in terms of its individual letters, is relatively autonomous, what are the implications for language use? Which kinds of tricks does language play on performers—or do they, the performers, play on it? What sorts of strategies are at work? Who uses the abagada, rightly or wrongly? It is worth looking at puns, polemics, double (even triple) entendres, errors in language and ritual, and silences.

Exalted Kingship contains a surprising admission of error by the Lord of Greatness, a primordial creator and Lightbeing. At a crucial point in his creating activities, he spoke—or thought of—a word that carries at least two meanings. The Lord committed this error when he created the male human being. He concedes:

> I clothed the body with a suitable armor and I performed the marriage ceremony and the mysteries slept together. And from that moment it was called "sin," because I made a mistake and was doubly foolish and divided it. Behold the date-pit of a date!—its seed which issues from its loins! Its name is seedling-palm and it cleaves the ground! Behold the human being—his seed stands in the middle of his body, its name is seedling-palm, and they call it virility because it brings virility to the body! The seedling-palm is the edifice and the seal of the king.[16]

The Lord ends his speech by extolling marriage. Still, he did make a mistake by using the word *hṭit*, which means "suitable" and "sin" (and, also, "wheat") as he created the male. As a result, ambiguity is attached to the male organ for ever after, and what has been said and done cannot be erased. The Lord's employment of that freighted word, "hṭit," continues to play its joke on human beings, sexuality being both suitable and sinful. Trying to rescue the situation by stressing the suitability and necessity of marriage, the Lord must deflect attention away from his error by saying, in effect, that

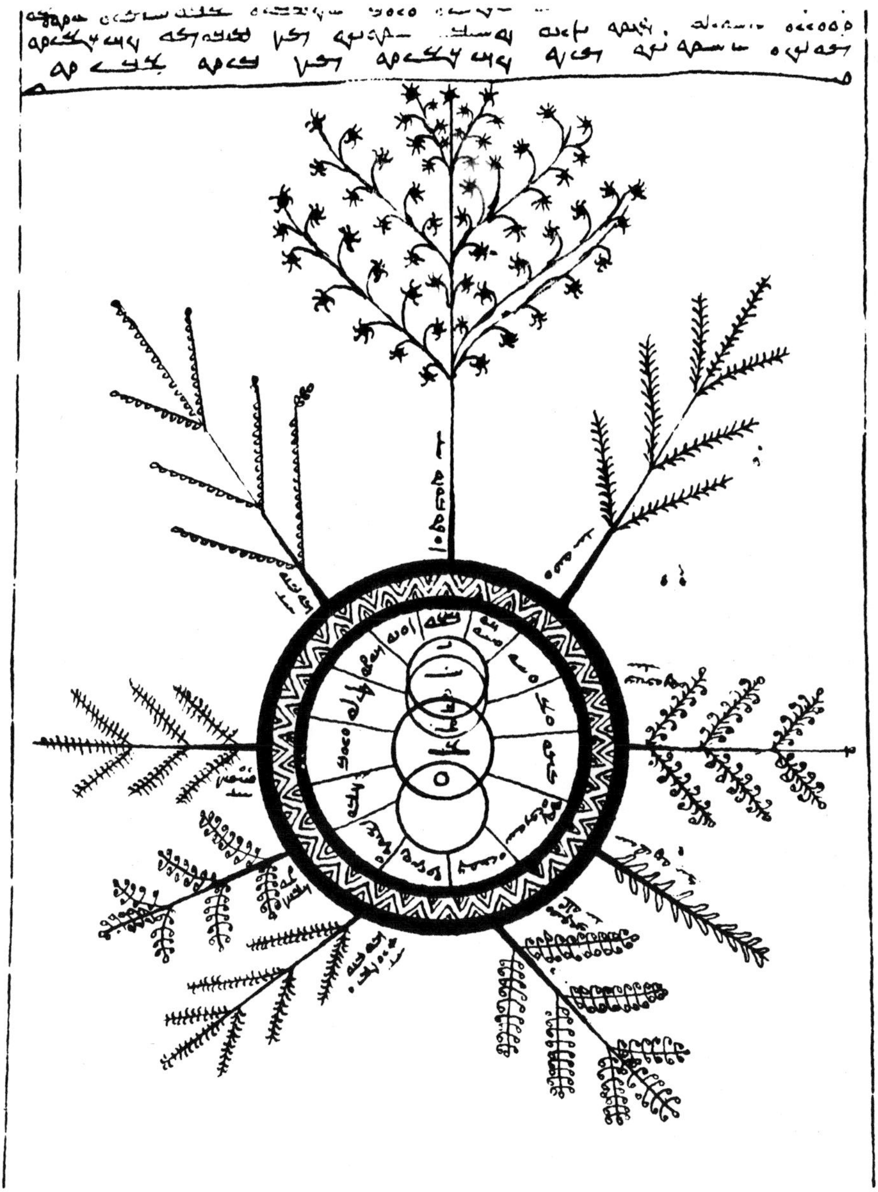

The Wellspring, the origin of the Mandaean alphabet. The nine trees (all identified) emerge from the Wellspring. The four overlapping circles carry the six letters *a b g d h u*. These are the first six letters of the Mandaic alphabet. The fourteen sections of the Wellspring have these words: teacher, crown, wreath, ether, fire, garment, stole, tunic, girdle, mother, father, brother, sister. From Buckley, *Exalted Kingship*. Used by permission.

male sexuality is good in certain respects. Because Mandaeans are antiascetic and pro-marriage, his reassurance makes good sense. Still, the word *ḥṭit* played a game on the Lord, and if he had paid closer attention and not used that word, it would not have been awakened to grasp its own power.

The idea that words cannot be undone appears in the rules for copying Mandaean manuscripts. Those who peruse such original texts will find that words wrongly copied, letters gone astray, or whole sentences written in the wrong place are rarely erased. The common way of indicating errors in manuscripts is to place a line of dots under the affected letters. This suggests a profound understanding of the impossibility of undoing errors, for what was written must remain so, even if it is wrong. Like male sexuality, as we saw in *Exalted Kingship*, errors and ambiguities are here to stay.

However, some acts and words can be corrected, but they require meticulous work, sometimes of staggering proportions. Sections of *1012*, especially, and to a lesser extent of *Exalted Kingship*, pay detailed attention to words or gestures that are performed wrongly or that are out of place in rituals.[17] Pages of instructions are devoted to the rectification of a variety of mishaps, such as if the officiating priest during a baptism or a death mass were to make an error in a prayer, or to utter a prayer at the wrong moment, or to forget a specific ritual gesture. These types of listed errors reflect experienced realities and are neither merely hypothetical nor figments of a quarrelsome imagination.

Originally, prayers and rituals were created in the Lightworld by the beings there, which were sent down to earth in order to be returned, conveyed upward by human performers. Wrong words and acts are not accepted by the Lightworld, which vigilantly watches every ritual ascending from the earth. What can a priest caught in error do to rectify his mistake? The previously mentioned parts of *1012* and *Exalted Kingship* contain what appear to be manuals on these matters. For example, if a priest omits prayers 31, 57, 59, or 60 in a baptism ritual, that baptism is void. The priest must stop what he is doing and go back to prayer 18 to put things right again,[18] for that is the prayer that opens the river, making it ready for baptism.

If, during a masiqta, the priest forgets to sign any of the fifty-nine faṭiras in the first sequence of the ritual during the recital of prayer 52, there will be deafness in the right ear of the priest and of the soul of the dead person.[19] This calamity can be remedied only by stopping the proceedings, where the priest himself undergoes baptism by seven priests for his own cleansing, which renews his fitness for office. Only after this long hiatus—a stopping of time, a parenthesis—is the deafness lifted from both priest and soul, and the priest may start up the ritual where he left off.

Should the priest, in the first round of the masiqta, mistakenly sign the sixtieth faṭira at prayer 52, "he is like unto a datepalm which fire hath consumed; the right eye of the priest and the left eye of the soul will have incurred injury thereby and that priest is polluted."[20] And, if he forgets to recite prayer 53, removes his pandama, or detaches the klila from the pihta at the wrong moment, "all rites (*celebrated*) for that soul are blackened, and blemish hath been caused to its right hand."[21] These kinds of errors necessitate 360 baptisms of the offending priest, a time-consuming remedy speeded up by the presence of eight fellow priests who must gather to spring immediately into action, like workers by a conveyor belt laboring to purify their colleague.

Natural mishaps, such as a tooth that suddenly falls out of a priest's mouth during ritual proceedings, are not serious. "Trouble not thyself about that tooth; it is, as it were, a letter that droppeth off the tongue," reassures *1012*.[22] The tooth is, in fact, like a finished letter, in a finished word, an item that has served its natural purpose and has arrived at its natural end. Accidentally severed fingers or toes are another matter, barring a priest from office for life.

The interpretations and rectifications of errors are based on real experiences. Some mistakes can be made right, others not. Rituals aim to perform satisfying, correct work. Spacing and timing, with their rhythms, starts, stops, and resting periods, are vitally important and modeled on practical activities. Ritual work builds imagined houses and universes. Speech and gestures function as the building blocks, comparable to building materials, for more concrete habitations. In chapter 8, I noted that prayers, especially rahmas, are considered as *built*, not recited or uttered. As in the abagada speculations, the use of construction language shows the religion's comfort with concrete imagery.

At the end of *Exalted Kingship*, the text states why, at the conclusion of the priest initiation, the novice priest must celebrate a death mass for his rba:

> For the novice is a builder who constructs a beautiful palace; if he did not put a brick in its (proper) place, all that he built is spoilt. If he does not read the *masiqta* for his teacher, that building and palace is not beautiful. For the *masiqta* is the roof of that palace, and all the *rahmas* hold together the garment, so that Pure Ether takes them before the Lofty King.[23]

The masiqta—in this case for his teacher, who is still alive—marks not only the new priest's "test case" but also the completion of his own initiation. Now the new priest takes the lead as official, and his teacher submits to the position of "object." The role switch is complete, because the teacher conveyed his novice from lay status, which is characterized by babbling speech, to the fully grown, eloquent priestly state. In the death mass the teacher remains silent, playing dead, while the new, fully hatched priest speaks creative, transforming words over his teacher. Earlier in the ritual, identification between the two actors was stressed by the use of the favorite Mandaean idiom "garment." "Both stand in a single garment just as spirit and soul (*are both covered by a body*)," says *1012*.[24]

Should the rba die during the škinta period, his brother must step in and complete the priest initiation. If there is no brother, one of the rba's former pupils may substitute. Should the postulant die during the seven days, the same rule holds, but with a switch: the rba's brother or former pupil will now take the place of the dead novice. At the very end of the priest initiation, however, both rba and initiand substitute must undergo the "Great Baptism"—360 baptisms—to rectify the impurity incurred.[25]

Drower gives a list of the different kinds of masiqtas for accidental deaths.[26] How to deal with such deaths is a subscience unto itself and shall not be treated here. But it seems that "inner zharas," that is, whispered name insertions, are required in masiqtas for those who die under impure circumstances.[27] In all instances of accidental deaths and in the uses of substitutes, the logic seems to be that work takes precedence over actors.

A man impersonating a dead coreligionist is silent, projecting himself toward the end of his life, in a sense, as he envisions his own future self. Impersonators of the dead do not speak, and the speech of those in transitional states is carefully guided. A Mandaean infant dying during or before its own baptism at the age of forty-five days is substituted by a baby-sized bread dough.[28] The dough, of course, ensures total silence. Baptism interrupted by death is open-ended and therefore intolerable, like a half-built house. The ritual must take its course, with actors and gestures, but who the speaker is—or who keeps silent—is subject to rules.

Excessive speech can be disconcerting, too, as shown in the haunting story of Dinanukht in *GR* 6 (see chapter 4). Dinanukht (from the Persian: "the one who speaks in accordance with the religion") is the hybrid half man, half book who sits by the waters, reading in himself. Another half man, half book, Diṣai, comes along and speaks disturbing words: "There is death, there is life, there is darkness, there is light; there is error, there is truth."[29] Dinanukht thinks Diṣai is too loquacious and tries to burn and drown him, but to no avail. Exhausted, Dinanukht falls into a trance, and Ruha appears to him, declaring herself to be the dichotomies (and others, too) stated by Diṣai, thus proving his message. Dinanukht goes on a tour of the heavenly worlds, sees and hears marvelous things, including the dichotomies already encountered twice. He wants to stay on in the upper worlds, but his wish is not granted, for he must return to earth and preach his revelation. He tries to convince his listeners, but his words are so strange that he is considered quite mad.

This story can be seen as Mandaeism's own cautionary tale to itself, for Gnostics overly interested in esoteric knowledge may find what they cannot handle. Such self-critical messages are not unusual in religious traditions. One could press the issue here and investigate further how a religion like Mandaeism plays jokes or tricks on itself. We have seen an example in the hṭit incident. Also, in sections of *1012* and of *Exalted Kingship* where an inquirer presents a high-ranking ʿutra with a long list of questions about ritual errors and their rectifications and about specific Lightworld secrets, the questioner often begs that the answers be furnished "without priestly circumlocutions." This is a form of tongue-in-cheek self-criticism, an admission that obscurantism often plays a role in lofty discourses, that too many words are often simply just that: too much.

A different form of critique, directed away from Mandaeism itself, is polemics, concerned with those "others" who are too similar to the Mandaeans, too close for comfort. Mandaean polemics might admit that they themselves once were, but no longer are, those others, though Mandaeans may still fear that they resemble their neighbors too much. Those too close for comfort include the Jews, who can be taunted because the Mandaeans are no longer Jews. But the relationship remains close, and the proximity breeds polemical battles. We have seen, elsewhere, the relished pun on the word for Jews (iahuṭaiia) by the word meaning "miscarriage:" iahṭa.

Mandaeism's relationship to Christianity is more like sibling rivalry than an intergenerational conflict. Jesus comes to John the Baptist at the river Jordan, demanding baptism, according to *John*. [30] John the Baptist suspects Jesus, a "fallen" Mandaean, of impure motives. Disturbed by what he perceives to be Jesus' hypocrisy, John hesitates and asks the Lightworld for advice, but the Lightworld commands John to perform the baptism. Evil omens occur during it, for the water turns into many colors, and Ruha appears as a dove making the sign of the cross over the river.

When the baptism is completed, it looks like Mandaeism has suffered a defeat. But the text plays its cards close to the chest until the end, for only then does the baptism turn out to have been counterfeit! It was not the Mandaean baptism at all but the Christian one. Surreptitiously, Jesus has been treated to his own baptism, leaving the Mandaean ritual unscathed. At the last minute, the Lightworld magically switched the rituals and turned the tables, and Jesus got what he deserved.

Such playing with polemical fire can only work when a religion is secure enough in its own position and victory is guaranteed. Also in *John*, Jesus and the ʿutra Anuš (who is a competitor to Jesus) engage in arguments and bickering.[31] Anuš appears in Jerusalem, heals the sick, gives the blind sight, and so forth. He even claims that he will destroy his (own?) temple and rebuild it.[32] Jesus occupies a very subordinate position, as he humbly asks about Anuš's identity and testifies to Anuš's miracles—which, from a Christian perspective of course are Jesus' own. But when Jesus speaks, he twists his tongue, changing the color and tone of his speech. He literally utters contorted, incorrect words, which demonstrate his affinity with the Jews, who are devious babblers incapable of straightforward speech. Jesus asks Anuš for Mandaean salvation, but we do not learn whether Anuš agrees to this request. *John*'s story might demonstrate Mandaean arrogance vis-à-vis Christianity. But it is a matter of *who* speaks, *whose* words are effective, and perhaps less a question of origins, ownership, and legitimacy.

A religion can afford to challenge itself if the risks are not so high as to be unmanageable. Again, it is a question of *whose* voice predominates. Chapter 12 already pointed out that at a particular spot in the priest initiation, prayer 1, in *Exalted Kingship*'s interpretation, stirs up Ruha at the mere mention of the primordial black waters and the evil forces. The power of association alone suffices. Also, in chapter 5, I noted how Mandaean priests have recited prayers 149 and 159 every Friday and every Saturday morning for about 1,800 years now, prayers that conjure up and mock the Jewish Sabbath. Every week, the threat of the Jewishness of those days rears up, but just as inexorably, Mandaeism wins as Sunday, Habšabba, comes around. For the moment, the danger has passed, although it is sure to return next week.

The Punning Goes On

There is no end to the combinations of hand-holding among the letters of the abagada. Once the bricks have been made, all kinds of language houses may be constructed. Some of the most intriguing ones result in seemingly unintended habitations, as in the hṭit incident, which demonstrates the autonomy of the letters, not of the users of language. But the unplanned can also result in errors uncontainable as puns, and such mistakes must be redressed, when possible. Erring, unwary performers may wreak havoc not only on themselves but also on those for whom they perform rituals. In contrast, a more self-assured, combative mood invites polemics and internal critique. Self-directed jokes show the extent of Mandaeism's secure identity and generous psycho-economy, demonstrating that the religion can afford internally directed humor.

One pointed example comes from the present day, not from an esoteric text, and illustrates the powers of Mandaean evocation, subversion, and control. Mandaeans run a disco club named Ginza in Madrid, Spain. To most people, this is the name of the entertainment district in Tokyo, Japan. But Mandaeans know—and the reader, now, does too—that this is a true Gnostic pun, for the name really refers to the Mandaean holy scripture, the *Ginza* (treasure).

In Mandaean manuscripts, their colophons, that is, the lists of names of copyists at the end of each document, often include a special curse on the Arabs. A copyist of a text ends his work with a set formula, which includes a precise date on which the copying task was completed. Right after giving the date according to the Arab calendar, the copyist adds the formula "according to the computation of the Arabs—may the world founder upon them!" This pun and curse take advantage of the word *arbaiia* (Arabs) and its similarity to the verb "to fall," verbal root: *ARB*.[33] Sometimes the formula is missing in a manuscript, an omission that may indicate times of persecution, times when it is more prudent not to engage in polemics of this kind. How unlikely is it that a Mandaean document, in Mandaean script, would fall into the hands of a comprehending Muslim?

In the last chapter, I shall deal with some aspects of the colophons, including the postscripts, which are called *tariks*.[34] Colophons form family trees because they list names and thereby show the vital threads of scribal lineages through the centuries. They are like woven lengths of fabric, offering yet another facet of the central concept of laufa. The names of a great number of copyist priests, the colophons present nothing less than an unbroken Mandaean history.

14

Thousands of Names, Hundreds of Lineages

History and Tribulations

Many years after I had met Sheikh Abdullah Khaffagi in Ahwaz, I started studying Mandaean colophons (tariks) and found that he was the sixteenth in an unbroken lineage of priests. Calculating one generation to equal approximately thirty years, one may place the first priest in his lineage to a time around the year 1300. The manuscript-copying activities of Sheikh Abdullah's grandfather Ram Zihrun, son of Sam Bihram, are well attested and can be traced to 1802 and 1843, among other years. Since the late 1980s, I have been unraveling skeins of the history of the transmission of Mandaean documents, seeking a clearer view of Mandaean history. In order to systematize this kind of study, I continually add to a card catalog containing thousands of names and hundreds of lineages. But mainly, I create long charts of "family trees" of the names in priestly copyist lineages. These sheets of paper stand rolled up in a corner of my study space, and they are easy to spread out across a floor surface or a large table. It is often necessary to compare a sequence of lineages with that of another scroll. A computer screen would not be large enough for such a task, but a wide film screen would do.

Except for certain exorcisms and talismans, nearly every Mandaean original textual document contains one or more tariks. After completing a copying task, the scribe will write out the traditional formula in which he stresses his own inferiority and humility in comparison to his priest colleagues. He gives his own name, specifies where and when he completed the copying task, and offers information about Muslim rulers. Sometimes a scribe may add descriptions about the state of affairs in the Mandaean communities and in the province where he lives. There may also be heartrending words about persecutions and sufferings. The curse on the Arabs (as seen in chapter 13) is usually included, and formulaic petitions to the Lightworld for protection are always present.

It is a meritorious task to copy a manuscript. A priest may do it for his own benefit as an aid toward the forgiveness of his sins, or he may be hired to do the work for the good of someone else. If he copies for a member of his own immediate family, he is in all likelihood not paid. Whenever the text calls for a name insertion (zhara), the copyist writes the name of the person for whom the manuscript is copied. A priest may spend a considerable amount of time on a copying task, taking care to avoid errors, to add or subtract nothing, and to keep his penmanship up to standards. Some manuscripts are astoundingly beautiful, written in clear, unblemished script—tiny or large, according to the size of the paper. Lines must be kept straight, margins even. Should errors occur, the affected letters or words are dotted underneath (as seen in chapter 13), while forgotten words or sentences may be added between the lines or creep out into and along the margin, despite the standard of keeping even margins. The most common form of a Mandaean text is the scroll (*šapta*), but a codex format occurs in certain texts.

The Portuguese began to bring back Mandaean manuscripts to Europe in the seventeenth century. From the 1930s on, Lady Drower bought some fifty-odd texts that became the Drower Collection in the Bodleian Library at Oxford University. Other Mandaean manuscripts rest, in the main, completely undisturbed in European university collections or other research libraries. Inscribed pottery bowls and talismans written on lead strips also exist in research collections or in private ownership.[1] Mostly, Mandaeans resist selling their texts to outsiders, and the great majority of documents remain in Iraq and Iran, in Mandaean hands, many of them texts whose titles and contents are unknown to us. This is as it should be, I feel, for nowadays there are very few researchers on Mandaeism to work on what is already available in the West.

In 1889–91, J. de Morgan went to Persia and acquired a few Mandaean texts.[2] He encountered great difficulties in doing so and was assured that this was illegal, to the point of threat of death for his informers, middlemen, and sellers. Atrocious persecutions had occurred in Persia in 1782. Less than a hundred years later, there was, as already noted, a massacre in Šuštar.[3] In 1782, de Morgan is told, Persian authorities tried to lay violent hands on any Mandaean manuscript, and recalcitrant Mandaeans were arrested, tortured, and killed (eyes burned with red-hot irons, body parts cut off, decapitation and impalement being among the usual assortment of atrocities). A ganzibra named Adam, having lost his right hand to torture, fled to Turkey. He had tucked away a copy of the response prayers (the ʿnianas)[4] and managed to make his own copy of these prayers with his left hand. This manuscript, which forms the basis for one of de Morgan's published manuscripts, found its way to Amara, in Iraq. De Morgan did not know Mandaic and had no idea precisely which text he had on his hands. The incomplete and less than perfect document (perhaps due to the difficulties of the one-handed copyist) derives from 1833 (A.H. 1249) by the scribe Yahia Yuhana, son of Sam.

This date, 1833, is only two years after the calamitous *muṭana* (cholera) of 1831. Polluted river water kills the whole priesthood, and a very few yalufas and sons of priests—no more than three or four men—create new priests from their own ranks. Because no priests had survived, these few men know that they cannot initiate priests in the correct way. Therefore, they suffer enormous pangs of conscience. Still, if they do not act, Mandaeism will perish.[5]

On this background, one may appreciate the usual Mandaic formula invoked by Yahia Yuhana, son of Sam, who, while copying prayer 5 in the *Prayerbook*, veers off from his text and exclaims:

> Turn away and expel from me—Yahia Yuhana, son of Maliha,[6] and from these souls who went down to the yardna and were baptised—from fright and fear and trembling and demons

and evil spirits and devils and incubi and spirits and amulet spirits and female demons and false gods and angels and temple spirits and shrine goblins.[7]

Later in his copying work, Yahia Yuhana yearns plaintively for Manda d̲-Hiia, who, he says, has been driven off. He ends with the common formula, "Everything is fleeting and lacking, except for prayer and praise! Life is victorious over all (created) works!"[8]

During those same traumatic years another scribe, one of the yalufas who rescues the Mandaean religion, is busily at work: he is Yahia Bihram, son of Adam Yuhana. Almost fifty years earlier, in the terrible year 1782 -the time of the Persian persecutions -Yahia Bihram's father, Adam Yuhana, son of Sam, copies *Pašar Haršia* (*The Exorcism of Wizards*).[9] But this does not repel or prevent the persecutions in Persia that year. Much later, Adam Yuhana succumbs to the cholera. Yahia Bihram himself copies a number of texts in the aftermath of the epidemic, and he writes wrenching words about the attempts to rescue the remnants of the Mandaean community and to create priests from the ranks of the yalufas—to which he himself belongs.

In the tiniest script I have yet seen in any Mandaean manuscript, Yahia Bihram in 1833 copies *The Scroll of Parwanaia*, the text for the five-day Panja festival. Much later, in 1864, when he is about fifty-four years old,[10] Yahia Bihram copies *Šarh d̲-Maṣbuta Rabia*, a scroll describing the ritual of 360 baptisms for a polluted priest.[11] In the postscript to his tarik, Yahia Bihram writes that long ago, before the cholera, he and his father, Adam Yuhana, traveled together to Baghdad (Babil) "to remove the *Ginza* from the Muslims of error."[12] Evidently, local authorities had confiscated the *Ginza*, but we do not learn whether Yahia Bihram and his father succeed in retrieving the holy book.

Yahia Bihram copies many other texts, such as *A Phylactery for Rue* and *The Scroll of the Great Overthrower*. Together with another scribe he is the copyist of *Exorcism of "I Sought to Lift My Eyes."*[13] In the postscript to *The Poor Priest's Treasury*, from 1853, Yahia Bihram tells of starvation, persecutions, and killings. He takes his donkey and flees from Iran with his two wives and six children. One of the children seems to have been born during the flight, and Yahia Bihram is robbed of all his belongings.[14]

"Cleanse us from the sons of Krun!"[15] he implores Manda d̲-Hiia, and continues, " May Hibil Ziwa and his brothers help us and our root [i.e., 'our tribe']! Rescue us into the world of the Great Alien Life! Oh, our brothers who are coming after us, seek not the blow of the Khalif on us, [the blow] of the sons of the Seven [i.e. the planets] and the Twelve [i.e. the zodiac spirits]!"[16] At the very end, Yahia Bihram does not add the usual curse on the Arabs, perhaps because times are too dangerous for that.

Peaceful periods are rarely documented in Mandaean tariks, but they do exist. The first European edition of the *Ginza*, by H. Petermann in 1867,[17] depends on the four *Ginza* manuscripts in Bibliothèque Nationale in Paris. Unlike Lidzbarski later on, Petermann wrote out all the colophons in Mandaic. Because there are seven colophons in each *Ginza* and we, in this case, have four manuscripts (dubbed A, B, C, and D), twenty-eight colophons in all can be studied and correlated with each another.[18]

The scribe of manuscript A is Ram Baktiar, son of Bihram Šadan, who copies the *Ginza* in the year 1560 C.E. (A.H. 968) in the village of Maqdam, which belongs to the greater town of Huwaiza, in Khuzistan. After *GR* 18, which marks the end of *GR*, Ram Baktiar adds a voluminous tarik, in fact, among the longest I have seen in any manuscript. It is unusual, in part because of its optimistic tone. Ram Baktiar asks "the Precious Light" to bless the local ruler, Sultan Sušad, for "we had access to him and support and respect, and we had a permitted religion, and we dwelt (there), and he did not overpower us."[19]

There seems to have been no curfew for the Mandaeans. The governor Salman (Sayyid Sajjad)—likened to his namesake, Solomon, son of David—is credited with having chased away certain rebels who threaten the stability of the region and, implicitly, the Mandaeans. Extremist Shiʿites, the Mushaʿshaʿ dynasty, rule in Khuzistan at that time and permit the Mandaeans to prosper.[20] They and their priestly leaders are allowed to instruct their children in the religion, and they even hope to build a mandi soon.

This idyllic picture is shattered in manuscript B, seventy-two years after Ram Baktiar's activities, when Baktiar Bulbul (nightingale), son of Ram Ziwa, finishes his copying in Maqdam (though the task was begun in the harbor city of Basra). Saʿdan, son of Baktiar, is the man for whose salvific benefit Baktiar Bulbul copies the *Ginza*. The scribe at some point asks Manda d̠-Hiia to forgive Saʿdan his sins—a set formula in texts. However, right after this expressed hope, Baktiar Bulbul mentions the Sultan of Basra and tersely adds, "May his sins not be forgiven!"

Connections

On August 19, 1988, the very day that the war ends between Iraq and Iran, I ring a buzzer and am admitted into the goldsmith shop of Mr. Neshet Hermes in what is then West Berlin. I have not met him before, and he does not know of me, but he is the uncle of my friend Issam Hermiz. I have come from England, where I have sorted through cartons of correspondence and papers of Lady Drower. Lady Drower's daughter, Mrs. Margaret ("Peggy") Hackforth-Jones—a woman then in her seventies and a former Near Eastern archaeologist—had asked me to do so. Peggy has given me an old postcard depicting her mother's primary informant in Iraq, the famous goldsmith Hirmiz bar Anhar, and two of his seven sons at work in the father's shop. I say that I will give the postcard to one of the seven sons, Mr. Hermes in Berlin, Maybe he is in the photo (he turns out not to be).

Admitting me into his store, Mr. Hermes peers at me, thinking me a regular customer, and inquires, "Und die junge Dame . . . ?" I smile and say that I have greetings to him from his nephew, Issam, and I tell him who I am. As I put the postcard down on the glass counter, Mr. Hermes exclaims, "Yi-yi-yi-yi-yiiii!" and then throws up his hands and laughs. He disappears into the back room and returns with the exact same picture, but in a much larger print.[21] As I give him the postcard, he says he will send it to Baghdad, so it can go home again. As far as I know, the return is made, but Mr. Hermes's own Baghdad house, recently bought with an eye to retirement there, is bombed in the subsequent war, the Gulf War. Where Mr. Hermes is now I do not know.

The old goldsmith in Baghdad during Lady Drower's time in Iraq, Hirmiz bar Anhar, is a layman of great knowledge and spirit. Another one of Lady Drower's main helpers in Iraq is the priest Sheikh Negm. He plays the role of middleman in Lady Drower's negotiations to purchase Mandaean texts, and the two remain close friends for many years. Without Sheikh Negm, the Drower Collection in the Bodleian Library would not exist.

During the 1930s, especially, correspondence between Lady Drower and the priest reflects the ups and downs of a friendship tested by difficult business transactions. Using local scribes with a reasonable knowledge of English to write his letters for him, Sheikh Negm keeps Lady Drower informed of texts that may be purchased (mainly from Persia), of prices, and of the conditions of the texts. Money must be relayed between England and Iraq, books and scrolls copied and sent, but then the Second World War intervenes. Sometimes Sheikh Negm sends a package of dates to England. Lady Drower gives money gifts to the sheikh and his community in Liṭlaṭa for the rest of her life.[22]

Sheikh Negm's grandfather is initiated into priesthood by the grandfather of Sheikh Abdullah Khaffagi, the old priest I meet in Ahwaz in 1973. The two men, Sheikh Negm and Sheikh Abdullah, are cousins, and the latter initiates the former into priesthood, says Macuch.[23] While there is nothing unorthodox about this, it may be more common to be initiated by a priest in the older generation, often a father or an uncle. Sheikh Negm's and Sheikh Abdullah's fathers are brothers, sons of Ram Zihrun, the priest mentioned at the beginning of this chapter. Together with his cousin and brother-in-law, Yahia Bihram, Ram Zihrun becomes a priest in the aftermath of the 1831 cholera.[24]

Ram Zihrun copies the *Ginza* that Sheikh Negm procures more than a hundred years later for Lady Drower, in 1936. This book (DC 22) dates to the year of the cholera. Anyone leafing through this beautifully written, large codex in the Bodleian Library may still find the two flies squashed between two pages, just before the beginning of *GL*. I imagine the book accidentally snapping shut during a ritual many years ago, the flies ever since an inextricable part of the tome. Unlike the insects, the dry snakeskin that used to lie hidden elsewhere in the volume has disappeared.

A Colophon

So far in my colophon studies, I have correlated eleven different *GL* colophons, and they all cohere at the end,[25] going back beyond the man who is usually thought to be the most ancient scribe: Zazai of Gawazta, who is datable to around the year 270.[26] Four *Prayerbook* colophons go back to him,[27] So do a manuscript of *1012*, *Exalted Kingship*, and *Šarh d-Qabin*. Aside from the *GL* colophon, which extends beyond Zazai and which lists clearly human (not Lightworld) scribal predecessors, other colophons provide names of ʿutras as scribal ancestors. Such Lightworld scribes function to secure the Lightworld provenance of the text but provide no historical names beyond Zazai.

However, *GL*'s most ancient names appear to be human ones. Zazai himself is not indicated as one of the scribes, though his pupil, Ṭabia (gazelle), appears as the son, that is, initiate, of Zazai. To give the reader an impression of an entire colophon, I provide my translation of the *GL* colophon from MS. A (from the year 1560) in Petermann's *Ginza*.[28]

> These are the teachings on the souls that I copied for myself—I am poor and a child, small among my brethren tarmidas and a slave of naṣuraiia. I am Ram Baktiar, son of R. Bihram Šadan, son of Yahia Maimun, son of Adam, son of Yahia, son of Ram, son of Baktiar, son of Zihrun, son of R.[29] Adam, son of R. Sam Yuhana, son of R. Sam, family name Quṭana.

(The book) which I copied for myself from the book of our head, a learned (man), son of a steadfast root, son of an elevated family; he is a precious craftsman, son of a precious craftsman,
Manṣur ʿUbadia, by the name Anuš, son of Zihrun, son of Zakia, son of Manṣur, son of Praš, son of Yahia, son of Naṣir, son of R. Yahia, son of Anuš, son of Danqa,[30] father's family name,[31] and mother's family name:[32] the sons of Šapaia,
(the book) that I copied—a slave and a child, small among my brethren—I am Ram Baktiar, son of R. Bihram Šadan, son of Yahia Maimun, son of Adam, son of Yahia, son of Ram, son of Baktiar, son of Zihrun, son of R. Adam, son of R. Sam Yuhana, son ["son" is repeated] of R. Sam, family name Quṭana, which I[33] copied the book of Yahia Bayan, son of Sam, son of Bihram, family name Diqnana,
(the book) that he copied (from) the lofty and precious R.—blessed be he in naṣiruta!—Yahia Sam, son of Zihrun Hibil, son of Anuš Adam, son of Zakia Bulbul, son of Bihdad ʿAziz, family name Furaihia;
which he copied from the book of the lofty and learned Dihdar Mhatam Bulbul, son of Sam Bihram, son of R. Mhatam, family name ʿAsikir. And he is the father of the wife of the master of this book;
which he copied again (from) R. Yahia Sam, son of Zihrun Hibil, son of Anuš Bihdad, ʿAziz,
from the book of R. Adam Yuhana, son of Yahia Šuʿailia, of the sons of ʿArip, which he copied (from) our teacher Sarwan Bulbul, son of Adam Bayan, son of Šadan Zarzuia,
which he copied from the book that he copied for his older brother, R. Yuhana, son of Adam Bayan,[34] son of Šadan Zarzuia,
from the book that he copied for himself from the book of Mhatam Zihrun, son of Bahran Mušarah,
which he copied (from) R. Bayan, son of Adam Šupartaiia,
from the book of Adam, son of Bayan,
which he copied for Bahran, son of Yuhana Zakia, son of Bungir,
from the book of Bihdad, son of Yuhana Zakia, son of Sam Maʿuan,
which he copied from the book of Hibil, son of Bihram Šitil,
which he copied from the book of Baktiar Abulʿiz, son of Šitluia Gadana,
which he copied (from) our head Anuš Maʿilia, son of Anuš Bihdad,
from the book of Sam Hibil, son of Šitluia,
which he copied (from) R. Bihram Hibil, son of Mhatam Hibil Yuhana,
from the book of Hibil Yuhana, son of Zakia,
from the book that he copied (from) Yahia Zakia, son of Brik Yawar,
who copied it (from) Adam, son of Yahia Papia, and Adam copied it
(from) Bayan Šaiar, son of Zihrun
from the book of BrHiia Gadana, and BrHiia copied it
(from) Šaiar and Sam Ziwa, son(s) of Bayan Hibil,
from the book of Zakria, son of Hibil, and Zakria copied it
(from) Zihrun, son of Ram Ziwa,
from the book of Nṣab, son of Maškna, son of Yuhana, and Nṣab, son of Maškna, son of Yuhana
[who] copied from the book of Bayan Hibil, son of Šadan, and Banan Bihram, the sons of Brik Yawar, and Bayan Hibil and his brother copied[35]
(from) ʿQaiam, son of Zindana,[36]
from a scroll (šapta) of Miriai, daughter of Simat,[37] and Miriai wrote it
(from) Sam, son of Sakara, son of Zakia,
from his own scroll that he copied from a scroll of Ruzba, son of Hawa,[38] that was among

the books
of Sam, son of Zakia, and Ruzba [who] copied it
(from) Ram, son of Bihram,
from the scroll of Brik Manda Šitil, son of Sku Hiia, and Brik Manda copied
from a scroll of Anuš Šabur, son of Šiglai,
from the scroll of Nṣab, son of Maškna, son of BrHiia,
from the scroll of Ṭabia, son of Zazai,
(from) an old book [*ktaba*] that was in the naṣiruta of Nṣab, son of Maškna,
from Yuzaṭaq, son of Sasa;
again, from the scroll of the father (of) Šlama, daughter of Qidra.
And they were in the spirit of Life for the believers who came forth from our building and mine, Ram Baktiar, son of Hawa Mudalal,[39] and for my father Bihram Šadan, son of Šadia Kisna; for my mother Hawa Mudalal, daughter of Anhar; and for my wife Šadia Mamania, daughter of Hawa, and for my children Hawa Bana and Bihram Šitil and Zakia Šitil and Zihrun Baktiar and Adam, children of Šadia Mamania.
And Life persists that does not come to nought; and radiance, light and glory that do not depart and do not end!
The End.

As noted earlier, I place Šlama in the second century.[40] Her predecessor-initiator, Qidra (cooking pot), is a woman. There are, in fact, a great number of female names in many Mandaean colophons. As copyists, women are not only owners of books and of libraries but also priests.[41]

In the quoted *GL* colophon, a number of illustrious Mandaeans appear. I will single out just a few. First, there is Anuš, son of Danqa, who set out at the head of a delegation of Mandaeans to the Muslim rulers to obtain protection as "people of the Book" in the mid-seventh century. Second, Anuš Mai'lia, son of Anuš Bihdad, is an ubiquitous copyist and one of the great leaders mentioned by name and blessed in prayer 170, in the *Prayerbook*. This prayer is Ṭabahatan (Our Ancestors).[42] Third, Bayan Hibil, the initiator of Šaiar and Sam Ziwa and at least two additional initiates, is another prolific copyist. An important coordinator of texts, Bayan Hibil lived in early Islamic times and strove to establish coherent, orthodox copies of prayers. Regarding his work, Bayan Hibil says that he has traveled on foot to many Mandaean communities to compare liturgies. He compiles a canonical version, so to speak, and instructs his fellow religionists to be faithful to this canon.[43]

Life Is Victorious

In 1936, during the time of the British mandate in Iraq, two talismans (*qmahas*)—DC 26—are copied for Lady Drower's daughter, Peggy (the later Mrs. Hackforth-Jones). Her ritual name is given as Marganita pt Klila (Pearl, daugher of Wreath), which is a rendition of the two women's names: for Margaret, of which Peggy is a diminutive, means "pearl," and Lady Drower's second first name, Stefana, is "wreath" in Greek. The copyist of the qmaha identifies the rulership in this manner, "in the governance of the Arabs and the *Nglizia* [i.e. the English]. " The two rulers are king Aduar (Edward), son of king Šurš (George), and the Iraqi king Gazia, son of king Faiṣil.

Mandaean texts not only travel to Europe from the seventeenth century on but also, in more recent years, move with Mandaeans in emigration. The laufa now reaches from the present Mandaeans to the ancients, and it circles the globe, too, with time and space held by the threads of texts and people. In June 1999, the first international conference on the Mandaeans is held at Harvard University, attended by scholars and Mandaeans from all over the world. Scholarly papers, a cultural evening, and a maṣbuta in the Charles River contribute to making this a very special event. The scholarly organization ARAM, devoted to Syro-Mesopotamian studies, sponsors the conference,[44] and other, similar events are planned for the future. The next one is in Oxford, England, July 2002.

Frouzanda Mahrad

I was sitting in the lobby
of the Shaateh Hotel, Libya
when she passed by
in a long dress
hair bound in a kerchief
carrying two bundles in her hands
as if she had just arrived from a journey

At her side
two young men
—two moons or two angels.
I guessed they were her sons.

I knew this woman.
I knew the luster in those eyes
I started to call her—
I forgot her name.
My face smiled at her.
She noticed me
Her gaze penetrated mine—
She also was trying to remember.

She did not stop
did not let on to her sons
but kept walking across the lobby
as I continued to struggle with my memory.
She disappeared
but everything about her came back—
except her name.
My college classmate in Baghdad.
Daughter of a diplomatic offficial
in the Iranian embassy.
She spoke Arabic like we did
But she failed in the first year

and dropped out of a class
made up mostly of poets

I remembered her witty comments
and her strange behavior.
Once she jumped on a freight train
that was going from the college to Bab al-Muatham.[1]
Once the English teacher entered
while some students were drawing
ugly figures on the blackboard.
He shouted angrily
what are you doing?
Quietly she answered
they are drawing themselves.

Once she had a fit of epilepsy in the class
and started writhing on the floor.
I held her and smoothed her clothes.
She rested against my breast
between my arms.
And the first thing she said was
how kind you are!

Everything about her was strange
Even her name which I had forgotten
I remembered everything about her—
except her name.
How difficult it was to recall
after more than thirty years.
Suddenly it came to me.

Frouzanda Mahrad.
I even remembered her sister's name:
Drakshanda Mahrad.
I repeated this impossible name
so I would not lose it again
Frouzanda, Frouzanda, Frouzanda
but she had already disappeared
down the long corridors of the hotel.
I considered asking the desk
for her room number
Then I backed down
and asked myself
after greeting her
what would we talk about after thirty years?
About work?
When both of us were retired?
About our marriages?
When we were at that age
where we were either widowed or divorced?
There remained one other question:
our sons.

What would she say to me?
Or I to her?
Would she say she had come to Libya
so her sons could train for combat?[2]
Would I say that my son
is a soldier in the Iraqi army
on the Mesan front?
Then we would be quiet.
Silence and glances would be our talk.
Who would kill first?
Would my son kill hers
or hers mine?

Two mothers prepared for bereavement
meeting on the razor's edge.

Frouzanda would remember me
no doubt
after a while
as I had remembered her.
Her companion, the beautiful poet.
The kind person who had embraced her daily.
Perhaps she would even see my face
soiled with battle dust.
And on the loving breast
Piercing claws
clinging war medals.

The same loving breast
that had nursed the soldier
alert on the battlefield
threatening the life of her sons
defending himself and his land
exactly as her sons were doing.

I hoped she had not recognized me.
Perhaps she had not remembered.

Fortunately
I did not encounter her again.
What a blessing forgetfulness is!

Why should we hate the people we once loved
because of a war that mars even our memories?

By Lamea Abbas Amara
Translated by Mike Maggio

Glossary

Words are given in alphabetical order, according to the Mandaic alphabet (see chapter 11). Non-Mandaic words are specified as such. Note that P and F are identical in Semitic, and so are I and Y; E does not exist, but the letter ʿayin, ʿ, approximates an E in pronounciation.

Abagada: alphabet
Abahatan/Ṭabahatan: the Parents; of the Parents (a prayer, a formula, or a type of masiqta)
Abaya: cloak
Ahl al-kitab (Arabic): People of the Book
Azga: vault
Aina: wellspring; eye
Alma: world
Alma ḏ-nhura: Lightworld
Alf: thousand
Andiruna: temporary hut
Asa: myrtle
Arab/arbaiia: Arab(s)

Ba: dove; spirit
Burzinqa: turban
Bit ama: Mandaean house of worship
Br: son

Ganzibra: "treasurer"; high priest staus
Gimra: jewel
Ginza: treasure; main Mandaean sacred scripture

Dahilek (Arabic): "under your protection"
Daša: pocket on sacred dress

Dukhrana: memorial meal for the dead; prayer for the dead
Dehwa Rabba: Great New Year's feast
Diwan: illustrated scroll
Diwaniyya (Arabic): sitting room where one receives guests
Dhimmi (Arabic): recognized minority people under taxable protection by Islam
Dmuta: Lightworld image
Drabša: white silk banner
Draša: type of prayer

Habšaba: Sunday
Hala: hallah (Jewish bread)
Halal (Arabic): pure, clean
Hallali: pure (lay)men in a ritual context
Hamra: water with macerated raisins
Haršia: wizards
Haṭamta: sealing prayer
halalta: rinsing water
Hṭit: sin; suitable; wheat
Hieros gamos (Greek): sacred marriage
Hilbuna: egg
Himiana: ritual belt
Hšuka: darkness

Zardusht (Arabic): Zoroastrian
Zhara: name insertion
Zidqa brikha: blessed oblation
Ziwa: radiance
Zirqa: unknown word (perhaps error for "zidqa)

Ṭab: good
Ṭabahatan/d̲-abahatan: "of our ancestors," a prayer or a masiqta
Ṭamaša: ablution, washing
Ṭariana: ritual tray
Ṭuṭifta: Jewish headgear (tefillim?)

Ia: oh!
Iahṭa/iahuṭaiia: abortion or miscarriage; Jews
Yalufa: learned layman
Yardna: running water; Jordan

Kana: cosmic container
Kanzala: priestly stole when held under the chin (see naṣifa)
Kasia: hidden; mystical
Kurasa: loose-leaved manuscript
Kušṭa: truth; sacred hand clasp
Kinta: instrument for incense

Kiniana: clan name (father's name)
Klila: myrtle wreath
Ktaba: book
K<u>d</u> azil: "when he came": a category of prayers

Laufa: connection between earth and Lightworld
Laqab: clan name (mother's name)
Lbuša: dress; clothing
Lofani: meal connecting the living and the dead
Libna: brick

Ma <u>d-bh</u>: "that which is with her," a circumlocution for the spirit
Maţarta: toll station or purification level on the way to the Lightworld
Malwašia: stars; pertaining to the stars
Malka: king
Malkuta: kingship
Mambuha: water drunk in ritual
Mana: vessel; power
Manda: knowledge; gnosis
Mandaiuta: lay status
Mandai/mandaiia: Mandaean(s)
Mandi: cult building
Maşbuta: baptism
Mara <u>d</u>-rabuta: Lord of Greatness (a mythological figure)
Margna: priestly staff
Masiqta: death mass
Maškna: (same as mandi); polemically: Jewish house of worship
Mbaţţal: astrologically inauspicious
Muţana: cholera epidemic
Mina: black dye used in jewelry
Morga: (Arabic?) a meat and vegetable stew
Mişra: ritual boundary
Miša: oil
Mqadšia: Jewish temple
Mqaimitun: a prayer formula: "be raised up"
Mrara: bitterness
Mšunia Kušţa: the world of ideal counterparts; a paradisial world
Mšiha: messiah

Nadhif (Arabic): pure, clearn
Nahra: channel, river
Natri: watchers
Naşuraiia: the priestly class, the learned ones
Naşifa: priestly stole
Naşiruta: priestly wisdom
Nglizia (Arabic): English

Nhura: light
Niṭupta: cloud, wife
Nišimta/nišma: soul

Sheikh: leader, priest
Surah (Arabic): chapter or section of the Qur'an
Sindirka: date(palm)
Sidra: book
Skandola: seal on iron knife
Sfar: book

ʿustad: craftsman
ʿuṣṭuna: Lightworld body
ʿuraita: Torah
ʿutra: Lightworld figure
ʿlaia/ʿlaita: elevated, exalted
ʿngirta: "letter" prayer
ʿniana: "response"prayer

Pagra: body
Pandama: mouth cover
Panja/Parwanaiia: the five-day intercalary feast
Faṭira: half-baked biscuit
Pašar: exorcism
Fateha (Arabic): "opening," a mourning ritual for the dead
Fatwa: legal opinion
Fidwa: ransom
Pihta: piece of dough
Pt: daughter

Ṣa: rolled-up piece of flat bread
Ṣauta: companion/companionship

Qabin: wedding ritual
Qanina: water bottle
Qudša: holy
Qulasta: collection
Qina: arrangement of faṭiras
Qmaha: exorcism

Rabuta: greatness
Raza: secret, hidden, symbol
Rahma: "devotion" prayer
Rasta: ritual dress
Raṭna: spoken Mandaic
Rba: teacher

Ruha: spirit
Ruman (Arabic): pomegranate
Riha: incense
Riš ama: head of the people, highest priestly rank

Šapta: scroll
Šarh: commentary, explanation
Šganda/ašganda: ritual helper
Šualia: pupil, questions
Širiata: "loosening" prayer
Šitlia: plants
Škinta: cult hut

Taga: crown
Tannur: baking oven
Tafsir: explanation
Tarik: colophon, postscript
Tarmida: lower level priest
Tibil: the earthly world

Notes

Preface

1. Sheikh Abduallah was Professor Macuch's primary informant on spoken Mandaic, an invaluable source for the study of modern Mandaic.

Chapter 1

1. "Jordan."
2. E.g., Rudolf Macuch, "Gnostische Ethik und die Anfänge der Mandäer," in *Christentum am Roten Meer*, vol. 2, ed. Franz Altheim and Ruth Stiehl (Berlin: de Gruyter, 1973), 258.
3. Kurt Rudolph, "Die Mandäer heute: Ein Zwischenbilanz ihrer Erforschung und ihres Wandels in der Gegenwart," *Zeitschrift für Religionsgeschichte* 94, no. 2 (1994): 166–72. Rudolph offers a short statement of current views.
4. Torgny Säve-Söderbergh, *Studies in the Coptic-Manichaean Psalm-Book* (Uppsala: Almqvist and Wiksell, 1949), 137-62. See also Carsten Colpe, "Die Thomaspsalmen als chronologischer Fixpunkt in der Geschichte der orientalischen Gnosis," *Jahrbuch für Antike und Chirstentum* 7 (1964): 77-93.
5. Kurt Rudolph, "Coptica–Mandaica: Zu einigen Übereinstimmungen zwischen koptisch-gnostischen und mandäischen Texten," in *Essays on the Nag Hammadi Texts in Honor of Pahor Labib*, ed. M. Krause (Leiden: Brill, 1975), 191-216.
6. E. S. Drower. *Haran Gawaita* and *The Baptism of Hihl Ziwa*. Studi e Testi 176 (Vatican City: Biblioteca Apostolica Vaticana, 1953), 3.
7. See Macuch's "Gnostische Ethik," which constitutes an extended, critical book review of Edwin Yamauchi's *Gnostic Ethics and Mandaean Origins*, Harvard Theological Studies 26 (Cambridge, Mass.: Harvard University Press, 1970). Unfortunately, some scholars still perpetuate the idea of a late origin of the Mandaeans. One example is Michael G. Morony's *Iraq after the Muslim Conquest* (Princeton, N.J.: Princeton University Press, 1984), 410. Here, the scholar states that the Mandaeans originate in lower Iraq in the seventh century, and it is telling that his footnotes make no reference to the dating debates involving Macuch, Rudolph, and Yamauchi.
8. Mark Lidzbarski, *Ginza: Der Schatz oder das grosse Buch der Mandäer* (Göttingen: Vandenhoeck and Ruprecht, 1925).
9. See the reference to Säve-Söderbergh, note 4.
10. See Macuch, "Anfänge der Mandäer," 139–40.

11. E. S. Drower, *The Canonical Prayerbook of the Mandaeans* (Leiden: Brill, 1959). For details, see my "The Colophons in The Canonical Prayerbook of the Mandaeans," *Journal of Near Eastern Studies* 51, no. 1 (1992): 40.

12. Two recent books are Sinaşi Gündüz, *The Knowledge of Life: The Origins and Early History of the Mandaeans and Their Relationship to the Sabeans of the Qur'an and to the Harranians*, Journal of Semitic Studies, Supplement 3 (Oxford: Oxford University Press for the University of Manchester, 1994); and Tamara M. Green, *The City of the Moon God: Religious Traditions of Harran*, Religions in the Graeco-Roman World, vol. 114 (Leiden: Brill, 1992).

13. Bat Ye'or, *The Dhimmi: Jews and Christians under Islam.* (Rutherford, N.J.: Fairleigh Dickinson University Press, 1985), 192.

14. Yaqut al-Hamawi al-Rumi, *Mu'ajjam al-Buldan*, vol. 6 (Cairo), 76. This reference is found in Ethel S. Drower, *The Thousand and Twelve Questions: A Mandaean Text (Alf Trisar Šuialia)*, (Berlin: Akademie Verlag, 1960), 4. For an amplification, see Gündüz's *The Knowledge of Life*, 57 n. 13.

15. Edmondo Lupieri, *The Mandaeans: The Last Gnostics* (Grand Rapids, Mich.: Eerdmans, 2002), translated by Charles Hindley (Italian original, 1993), 61–122. For Mandaeans being subject to the Jesuit mission in Hormuz and in Goa at mid-sixteenth century, see J. H. Crehan's "The Mandaeans and Christian Infiltration," *Journal of Theological Studies* 19 (1968): 623–26, though the author's conclusions about Mandaean-Christian historical influences should be taken with more than a grain of salt.

16. The "host" document, *The Exorcism of Wizards*, belongs in the repository of Mandaean texts known as the Drower Collection (DC) in the Bodleian Library, Oxford. The document is DC 12, and the old, narrower tarik is glued onto its end.

17. See my "A Study of the Two Liturgical Collections in J. de Morgan's *Textes Mandaïtes*," *Le Muséon* 104, vol. 1–2 (1991): 192–93.

18. See chapter 14. The topic of the cholera and the life of Yahia Bihram are developed in my ongoing works on Mandaean colophons.

19. The last, firm copyist activity date I have for Yahia Bihram is 1867. Lupieri's *The Mandaeans* (117–118, nn. 121–28), depends on information in *The Baptism of Hibil Ziwa* and in M. N. Siouffi's *Études sur la religion des Soubbas ou Sabéens, leur dogmes, leur moeurs* (Paris: Imprimerie Nationale, 1880). Here we learn that Yahia is still alive in 1870.

20. See chapter 6 for my visit with the Mandaeans in Iran in 1996.

21. See the two works by Rudolf Macuch, *Neumandäische Texte in Dialekt von Ahvaz* (with Guido Dankwart), Semitica Viva 12 (Wiesbaden: Harrassowitz, 1993); and *Neumandäische Chrestomatie mit grammatischer Skizze, kommentierter Übersetzung und Glossar* (with Klaus Boekels), Porta Linguarum Orientalium 18 (Wiesbaden: Harrassowitz, 1989).

22. For his discovery, in 1953, of the still spoken Mandaic in southwest Iran, see Macuch's description in his *Neumandäische Chrestomatie*, 7–8.

23. For a good sample of Mandaean creation mythologies translated into English, see Werner Foerster, *Gnosis: A Selection of Gnostic Texts*, vol. 2, *Coptic and Mandaic Sources*, ed. R. McL. Wilson (Oxford: Clarendon Press, 1974). The selection of Mandaean creation mythologies begins on 148.

24. See, however, the more nuanced picture presented by the majority of essays in Karen King, ed., *Images of the Feminine in Gnosticism*, Studies in Antiquity and Christianity (Philadelphia: Fortress Press, 1988).

25. Chapter 4 contains a synopsis of this myth.

26. The tree is depicted in an illustrated scroll, Ethel S. Drower, *Diwan Abatur or Progress through the Purgatories*, Studi e Testi 151 (Vatican City: Biblioteca Apostolica Vaticana, 1950).

27. Different kinds of death masses are required for "unclean" deaths, such as death after childbirth, without proper baptism, by a fall from a tree or an attack by wild animals, and so

forth. Mandaeans have been known to kidnap their dying kin from hospitals, impure locales par excellence.

28. Some of the proceedings necessary to rectify errors in rituals will be shown in chapter 13.

29. Chapter 14 will give a very compressed description of Mandaean copyist activities through the ages.

30. The book weighs 3¾ pounds. An international committee, based in Australia, has quite recently been formed to produce the first English *Ginza* translation.

31. See Macuch, "Anfänge der Mandäer," 186; and the diverging opinion of Kurt Rudolph in his chapter, "Die mandäische Literatur," in *Zur Sprache und Literatur der Mandäer*, ed. Rudolf Macuch, Studia Mandaica, vol. 1 (Berlin: de Gruyter, 1976), 157.

32. Heinrich Petermann, *Sidra Rabba: Thesaurus sive Liber magnus vulgo "Liber Adami" appellatus opus Mandaeorum summi ponderis* (Lipsiae: Weigel, 1867).

33. Theories on the age of the various *Ginza* tractates—and of many other Mandaean documents—belong to a separate study of mine still in progress and cannot be treated in detail here. For brief statements of my research on this topic so far, see chapter 14.

34. This observation was first made by Richard Reitzenstein in his *Das mandäische Buch des Herrn der Grösse und die Evangelienüberlieferung* (Heidelberg: Sitzungsberichte der Heidelberger Akademie der Wissenschaften, 1919).

35. This is the meaning of his name in Iranian; see Lidzbarski, *Ginza*, 205.

36. For treatment of the first part of this tractate, see my "Two Female Gnostic Revealers," *History of Religions* 19, no. 3 (1980): 259–69. See also my "A Rehabilitation of Spirit Ruha in Mandaean Religion," *History of Religions* 22, no. 1 (1982): 73–74. (The same material appears in chapter 4.)

37. Lidzbarski, *Ginza*, 235.

38. A Mandaean, Mr. Dakhil A. Shooshtary, helped by the designer and producer Michael I. Kaplow, publishes the "Mandaee Calendar" every year. In the traditional Mandaean home countries, similar calendars are of course also produced.

39. "Vessel" or "garment" (see E. S. Drower and Rudolf Macuch, *A Mandaic Dictionary* [Oxford: Clarendon Press, 1963], 246b–247a, for the multiple meanings of this central Mandaean term).

40. Mark Lidzbarski, *Mandäische Liturgien*, Abhandlungen des Königlichen Gesellschaft der Wissenschaften zu Göttingen, phil.-hist. Klasse, N.F., vol. 17, 1 (Berlin: Weidmannsche Buchhandlung, 1920; reprint, Hildesheim: Olms, 1962); Drower, *Prayerbook*.

41. Drower, *Prayerbook*, 15.

42. I use the terms *prayer* and *hymn* more or less interchangeably, although Mandaean prayers are not, strictly speaking, sung, but recited (sometimes very rapidly) in a form in between speech and song.

43. This prayer has proved useful for my colophon research (in progress) in order to reconstruct strands of Mandaean history.

44. Information on esoteric uses of the Mandaic alphabet is found in chapter 13 (see also chapter 11).

45. See chapter 9.

46. See chapter 12 for illuminating examples of internal-referential patterns in Mandaean esoteric commentary literature.

47. M. Lidzbarski, *Das Johannesbuch der Mandäer* (Giessen: Töpelmann, 1915; reprint, Berlin: Töpelmann, 1966).

48. It is possible that this formula consciously contrasts John's baptizing at night with the tradition that John baptized during the day, that he was a so-called hemero-baptist. Consult Kurt Rudolph's "Antike Baptisten: Zu den Überlieferungen über frühjüdische und -christliche Taufsekten," *Sitzungsberichte der Sächsischen Akademie der Wissenschaften zu Leipzig*, philosophisch-

historische Klasse, vol. 121, no. 4 (Berlin: Akademie, 1981), 1-37, 8, and the chart between 16 and 17.

49. See my study, which includes a new translation of this text, "Professional Fatigue: 'Hibil's Lament' in the Mandaean *Book of John*," *Le Muséon* 110, Fasc. 3-4 (1997): 367–81. (Parts of my translation contain errors that occurred in the transition from disc-and-paper copy to print.)

50. See chapter 5 for Miriai.

51. Parts of this material are treated in chapter 13.

52. Drower, *1012*, 289 (434).

53. Ibid.

54. To my knowledge, no art historian has ever tackled the issue of the Mandaean set style of drawing in scrolls. The style of drawing in Mandaean bowls has been treated by Erica C. D. Hunter.

55. The esoteric interpretation schemes of this text are treated in chapter 12. For a full treatment of the text, see my *The Scroll of Exalted Kingship: Diwan malkuta ʿlaita*. American Oriental Society Translation Series 3 (New Haven, Conn.: American Oriental Society, 1993).

56. See Macuch's theory (note 2).

57. Ethel S. Drower, *The Book of the Zodiac: Sfar Malwašia* (London: Murray, 1949). Consult Appendix II, 205-16.

58. But see Francesca Rochberg, "The Babylonian Origins of the Mandaean Book of the Zodiac," ARAM, 11-12 (1999-2000). ARAM Thirteenth International Conference. The Mandaeans: 13-15 June 1999. Harvard University (237–247).

59. E. S. Drower, *Šarh ḏ-Qabin ḏ-Šišlam Rba: Explanatory Commentary on the Marriage-Ceremony of the Great Šišlam* (Rome: Pontificio Istituto Biblico, 1950). This figure is the priestly prototype par excellence.

60. Ten inches is the width of the facsimile scroll.

61. Kurt Rudolph, *Der Mandäische 'Diwan der Flüsse,'* Abhandlungen der Sächsischen Akademie der Wissenschaften zu Leipzig, philosophisch-historische Klasse, vol. 70, no. 1 (Berlin: Akademie, 1982).

62. Rudolph, "Die mandäische Literatur," 166 n. 39; see also Rudolph's *Der Mandäische 'Diwan der Flüsse,'* 9, n. 10.

63. A good overview on the research of this literature can be found in Gündüz, *The Knowledge of Life*, 60–61. See also K. Rudolph, "Die Mandäismus in der neueren Gnosisforschung," in *Gnosis: Festschrift für Hans Jonas*, ed. B. Aland (Göttingen: Vandenhoeck and Ruprecht, 1978), 253–55. On its last three pages, this article contains an instructive schematic list giving an overview of Mandaean history and the history of research on the religion.

64. See Gündüz, *The Knowledge of Life*, 60–61.

65. A photo of this bowl is part of Lady Drower's scholarly papers in my care.

66. See Erica C. D. Hunter, "Two Mandaic Incantation Bowls from the 18th Nippur Season," *Baghdader Mitteilungen* 25 (1994): 605–18. These bowls stem from the seventh century. See also E. Hunter, "Aramaic-Speaking Communities of Sasanid Mesopotamia," ARAM 7 (1995): 319–35; and consult J. B. Segal, with a contribution by Erica C. D. Hunter, *A Catalogue of Aramaic and Mandaic Incantation Bowls in the British Museum* (London: British Museum Press, 2000).

67. The document, Ms. *Asiat. Misc. C12 (R)*, was transcribed by Yahia Ram Zihrun in 1818.

68. Idenitifed as *Marsh. 691*.

69. See note 15, referring to Lupieri's work.

70. Most, but not all, texts acquired by Drower belong in DC. The above-mentioned *Exorcism of the Great Name*, for instance, is not in DC.

71. Theodor Nöldeke, *Mandäische Grammatik* (Halle: Verlag der Buchhandlung des Waisenhauses, 1875), xix, with note 1.

72. Matthias Norberg, *Codex Nasaraeus*, vols. 1–3 (London, 1815–16).

73. Petermann, *Sidra Rabba* (see note 32).

74. Heinrich Petermann, *Reisen in Orient*, vols. 1 and 2 (Leipzig: Von Veit and Co., 1865).

75. For bibliographic references to these and other early scholars, I refer the interested reader to the excellent bibliography in Rudolf Macuch, *Handbook of Classical and Modern Mandaic* (Berlin: de Gruyter, 1965), 467f. The earliest bibliography was that of Svend Aage Pallis, *Mandaean Studies* (London: Milford, 1926; reprint, Amsterdam: Philo Press, 1974).

76. The autobiography of his childhood and very early youth, *Auf Rauhen Wege, Jugenderinnerungen eines Deutschen Professors* (Giessen: Töpelmann, 1927), is a sad and moving account.

77. Rudolf Bultmann, "Die Bedeutung der neuerschlossenen mandäischen und manichäischen Quellen für das Verständnis des Johannesevangeliums," *Zeitschrift für die neutestamentliche Wissenschaft* 24 (1925): 100–146.

78. Hans Jonas, *Gnosis und spätantiker Geist*, vol. 1, part 1, *Die mythologische Gnosis* and vol. 2, part 1, *Von der Mythologie zur mythischen Philosophie* (Göttingen: Vandenhoeck and Ruprecht, 1934 and 1954; reprints 1964 and 1966). Jonas's English book *The Gnostic Religion* (Boston: Beacon Press, 1958) is a quite different work.

79. An analysis of scholarship on Gnosticism and the ties to European totalitarian ideologies of the 1920s through the 1940s remains to be written.

80. For her co-work with the Mandaean priest Sheikh Negm, see my "A Mandaean Correspondence," in *Gnosisforschung und Religionsgeschichte: Festschrift für Kurt Rudolph zum 65. Geburtstag*, ed. Holger Preissler and Hubert Seiwert (Marburg: Diagonal-Verlag, 1994), 55–60.

81. A veteran of Aramaic studies, Professor Rosenthal said this at the international conference "Who Were—or Are—the Aramaeans?" sponsored by ARAM at Harvard University, June 1996.

82. See note 39.

83. See Kurt Rudolph, *Theogonie, Kosmogonie und Anthropogonie in den mandäischen Schriften* (Göttingen: Vandenhoeck and Ruprecht, 1965), especially 339–48, and see also his chart, 78. For more recent comments, consult his "Die mandäische Literatur," 157–59.

84. K. Rudolph, *Die Mandäer*, vols. 1 and 2 (Göttingen: Vandenhoeck and Ruprecht, 1960–61). These volumes, based on Rudolph's doctoral work, deal respectively with the mythology and with the cult.

85. Kurt Rudolph, *Gnosis und spätantike Religionsgeschichte: Gesammelte Aufsätze* (Leiden: Brill, 1996).

86. See note 78.

87. For instance, the works of Hans Jonas, which became crucial for a whole generation of scholars of Gnosticism, leave out ritual. To Jonas, the Gnostics were late antiquity existentialists, on their way "from mythos to logos," uninterested in religious practice.

88. Martin Heidegger, *Sein und Zeit*, 3d ed. (Tübingen: Niemeyer, 1963). My references will be to the English translation by John Macquarrie and E. Robinson, *Being and Time* (London: SCM Press, 1962). The following analysis—which I used in my Ph.D. thesis, "Spirit Ruha in Mandaean Religion" (University of Chicago, 1978), and, with a different focus, in "Tools and Tasks: Elchasaite and Manichaean Purification Rituals," *Journal of Religion* 66, no. 4 (1986): 399–41—derives from 67–225 in *Being and Time*.

Chapter 2

1. Some years later, the living arrangements are a bit different.

2. The third sura, 22:17, mentions the Magians, too. Here all four religions are listed along with Islam in a context emphasizing judgment.

3. For the story of John baptizing Jesus, see Lidzbarski, *GR* 5, 4, 190–96; Drower, *Mandaeans*, 273–82 (see also chapter 13).

4. In this regard, one might notice Lady Drower's respect for—among other priests in Amara—Sheikh Jawdat, Lamea's grandfather. In *Mandaeans*, 54, Drower mentions nothing about the sheikh's reticence about her, but she admires "a Subbiyah mother and child that looked like a Madonna and her holy babe." These are Lamea's grandmother and aunt.

5. These traditions have been waning in recent times.

6. This second view accords with Drower's in *Mandaeans*, 85–86.

7. However, the Detroit Mandaeans now have a mandi, and they have also succeeded in bringing a priest to their community.

Chapter 3

1. A. F. J. Klijn, *Seth in Jewish, Christian, and Gnostic Literature* (Leiden: Brill, 1977), 108.

2. For instance, Birger Pearson, "The Figure of Seth in Gnostic Literature," in *The Rediscovery of Gnosticism*, vol. 2, *Proceedings of the International Conference on Gnosticism at Yale, New Haven, Conn., March 28–31, 1978*, ed. B. Layton (Leiden: Brill, 1981), 479 n. 53.

3. Drower, *Mandaeans*, 199; see also her *Prayerbook*, 106 n. 4.

4. Lidzbarski, *Ginza*, 423–29.

5. Ibid., 425, lines 1–2 (my translation of Lidzbarski's German here and in subsequent quotations from the *Ginza*).

6. The cosmic container of souls.

7. Lidzbarski, *Ginza*, 426, lines 20–24.

8. Lidzbarski, *John*, 213–17.

9. The cosmic serpent.

10. Lidzbarski, *John*, 215, lines 14–17.

11. Another ʿutra, most often equated with the "Second Life," with an interesting double character of his own, as we shall see.

12. See, for instance, "Hibil's Lament," in Lidzbarski's *John*, 196–200, and consult my analysis of this piece in "Professional Fatigue."

13. Drower, *1012*, Book I, ii, 173 (242).

14. Ibid. (243).

15. Lidzbarski, *Ginza*, 15, 6, 320, lines 9–10.

16. As far as I know, Mandaeism has no mention of the Cain and Abel story (although the name Hibil may be a faint reflection of Abel). The religion idealizes the third of Adam's sons, avoiding any hint of the biblical story of the two others.

17. Drower, *Mandaeans*, 247; see also her *Abatur*, 44.

18. See the list in Drower, *Mandaeans*, 210–11 (see my treatment of one type of the masiqta in chapter 8).

19. See Drower, *Mandaeans*, 210–11; Drower, *1012*, Book I, I, 131–32 (78). In *1012*, Book II, VI, gives the procedure for the masiqta of Šitil, starting on 230.

20. Drower, *Mandaeans*, 211.

21. Ibid., 175–76 and 46.

Chapter 4

1. Lidzbarski, *GR* 5, 1, 150–73.

2. Ibid., 157, lines 20–25.

3. Ibid., 162, lines 9–11.

4. Drower, *The Baptism of Hibil Ziwa*, 34–35.

5. Lidzbarski, *GR*, 5, 1, 167, lines 12–13.

6. Drower, *Haran Gawaita*, 34.
7. Drower, *1012*, Book I, ii, 183 (265).
8. Ibid.
9. Lidzbarski, *GR*, 5, 1, 169, lines 25–28.
10. Ibid., 170, lines 15–16, 27–29, 35–37. In *GR* 3, 82, lines 5–12, Ruha tells her son that the Lightworld is stronger than he is.
11. Drower, *Haran Gawaita*, 34 n. 4.
12. Lidzbarski, *GR* 3, 98, lines 31–32.
13. In terms of story line, *GR* 3 links up with *GR* 5, 1 here.
14. Lidzbarski, *Ginza* 3, 99, lines 26–28.
15. Ibid., 100, lines 1–7.
16. Drower, *1012*, Book I, iiib, 216.
17. Ibid., Book I, ii, 164, 218.
18. Lidzbarski, *GR* 11, 266, lines 20–22.
19. Ibid., *GL* 1, 3, 438, lines 24–35.
20. Ibid., *GL* 3, 14, 529, lines 30–31.
21. Ibid., 1, 3, 442, lines 17–19.
22. Ibid., lines 22–24.
23. Lidzbarski, *GR* 3, 130, line 14.
24. Drower, *1012*, Book I, ii, 173 (243).
25. Ibid.
26. Ibid., Book II, iv, 239, 137.
27. See my *Exalted Kingship*, 12, lines 167–76. The priesthood initiation is the subject of chapter 9.
28. The story is in Lidzbarski, *GR* 15, 11, 336–44.
29. Ibid., 342, lines 25–26.
30. Ibid., lines 35–39.
31. Lidzbarski, *GR* 16, 1, 384, lines 30–31.
32. Ibid., 385, lines 3–6, 19–24. "The second death" is a mysterious phrase often found in Mandaean texts. It may refer to the spirit losing its chance to join the soul at death, to the soul being stuck in one of the tollhouses, or, more generally, to the judgment at the end of the world.
33. Lidzbarski, *John*, 166–67.
34. Ibid., 167.
35. Drower, *Prayerbook*, no. 133, 23.
36. Lidzbarski, *John*, 15.
37. Lidzbarski, *GR* 6, 206–12. For a comparison of Ruha in this tractate with the speaker in the Nag Hammadi text "Thunder: Perfect Mind, " see my study "Two Female Gnostic Revealers," especially 259–69.
38. Lidzbarski, *GR* 6, 207, lines 32–42.
39. Ibid., lines 22–23.
40. "Blow and healing" is a Mandaean technical term for mistakes in rituals and the correction of such mistakes.
41. Recall chapter 2's story of Šitil and Adam in *GL* 1, another ascent story, in which only the son ascended fully, although at first reluctantly. Neither Šitil's nor Dinanukht's ascent is a "normal" death. Nuraita is the name of Noah's wife, and Dinanukht is a Noah/Utnapishtim figure.
42. Lidzbarski, *John*, 227–28.
43. Ibid., 228, lines 7–10. (Siniawis is one of the underworld regions.)
44. Drower, *Abatur*, 38.
45. Drower, *1012*, Book II, iiib, 211.

46. Ibid., Book I, i, 138 (107).
47. Ibid., Book II, v(b), 264–65 (307).
48. Drower, *Abatur*, 19.
49. Drower, *Prayerbook*, no. 376, 281.
50. Ibid., no. 75, 74. "My Allah" should just be translated "My God."
51. Drower, *Mandaeans*, 271.
52. Jonas, *Gnosis* I, 1, 341.

Chapter 5

1. One place is in Drower, *Haran Gawaita*, 19, where Miriam (Mariam) is the mother of the pseudo-messiah, who, Hibil Ziwa says, will appear after Muhammad. This looks like Jesus' second coming.
2. Viggo Schou-Pedersen assumes that Mandaeism was a Christian form of Gnosticism at its beginnings, *Bidrag til en analyse af de mandaeiske skrifter* (Aarhus: Universitetsforlaget, 1940), 173. See also Eric Segelberg, "Old and New Testament Figures in Mandaean Version," in *Syncretism*, ed. S. Hartman. Scripti Instituti Donneriani Aboensis, vols. 3–4 (Stockholm: Almqvist and Wiksell, 1969), 238–39.
3. Drower, *Haran Gawaita*, 3.
4. A Mandaean friend assures me that Jesus was originally a Mandaean, but he fell from his faith. Cunningly, he asked John the Baptist to baptize him first, so that his soul would be saved, despite his apostasy and his impending Christian ministry. See also Lidzbarski, *John*, for the traditions about John the Baptist and Jesus, 70, 103–9.
5. Drower, *Haran Gawaita*, 5.
6. Lidzbarski, *John*, 126–38.
7. See Drower, *Mandaeans*, 282–88, for the modern Mandaean legend of Miriai as Nebuchadnezzar's daughter. Both Miriai and her father convert to Mandaeism.
8. There may be faint references here to one of the Christian Infancy gospels, the "Protevangelium Jacobi"; see Edgar Hennecke, "The Protevangelium of James," in *The New Testament Apocrypha*, vol. 1, ed. E. Hennecke and Wilhelm Schneemelcher (Philadelphia: Westminster Press, 1959), 378–80.
9. Lidzbarski, *John*, 127.
10. Ibid., 129.
11. Hennecke and Schneemelcher, *New Testament Apocrypha*, 2:355.
12. See Drower and Macuch, *Mandaic Dictionary*, 184b.
13. The word for the food, which Lidzbarski reads as *zirqa* (in *John*, 130 n. 2 [132, line 6 in the Mandaean text]) is an otherwise undocumented noun (see *ZRQ* in Drower and Macuch, *Mandaic Dictionary*, 171b); it may very well be an error for *zidqa*, the chief oblation or offering in Mandaean rituals.
14. Encountered in chapter 4, where Ruha was identified with her.
15. For historical evidence, see my "The Evidence for Women Priests in Mandaeism," *Journal of Near Eastern Studies* 59, no. 2, 2000 (93–106).
16. This recalls the awaited *shekinah*, the kabbalistic female presence of God, or the personified, female sabbath. For echoes of information from the Christian apocryphal "Gospel of Pseudo-Matthew" regarding Jesus' mother, see, e.g., David R. Cartlidge and David L. Dungan, eds., *Documents for the Study of the Gospels* (Philadelphia: Fortress Press, 1980), 99, section 12.
17. This is my translation. It differs somewhat from Lidzbarski's, which is a bit broken (*John*, 136). See Lidzbarski's rendering of the text, ibid. 140.
18. Compare with Anuš's actions, in chapter 4, on Ruha.
19. Lidzbarski, *John*, 138.

20. Ibid. Another version of this story was told to M. N. Siouffi, *Études sur la religion des Soubbas ou Sabéens.* Here, Miriai is the daughter of the Jewish priest Eleazar. She converts to Mandaeism and receives instruction from its priests. The father tries to kill his daughter and her fellow believers, but they escape. A falcon (Anuš) appears, and Miriai wishes to follow him to the Lightworld, but she is told that her time has not yet come. In terms of gender, this legend is much tamer than the one in *John.*

21. Lidzbarski, *John,* 85–90.

22. Ibid., 85.

23. This story may be a Mandaean version of some of the information found in Hippolytos's account of the Naassenes (see A. Roberts and J. Donaldson, "The Refutation of All Heresies," in *The Ante-Nicene Fathers,* vol. 5, ed. A. Roberts and J. Donaldson [New York: Scribner's, 1926], book 5, chap. 3, 52b). "The beauteous seed of Benjamin" appears here, and there is an interesting parallel between Miriai speaking to the men, in *John,* and Mariamne as the recipient of certain of the Lord's teachings, via Jacob, in Hippolytos (ibid., chapter 2, 48a and b).

24. In the story in Drower, *Mandaeans,* Miriai and the Mandaeans depart for the hills of Media (see reference in note 7).

25. Lidzbarski, *GR* 15, 11, 341.

26. Ibid.

27. The prayers are on 129–30 and 140–41 in Drower, *Prayerbook.*

28. Ibid., 130, with the facsimile, 173.

29. Keeping in mind that Sunday is also a Christian holiday, one might wonder about the unavoidable conflicts in terms of the Mandaean choice of a holiday. Drower, *Prayerbook,* no. 113 (109–10) states that the Sunday has committed sins that need atonement. It is unclear which sins are meant, and Schou-Pedersen, pondering this, suggests that the Sunday has sinned by letting itself be worshiped by the Christians (*Bidrag,* 187).

30. Drower, *Prayerbook,* 140. As so often in descriptions of Manda d̲-Hiia and other ʿutras, this looks like an appropriation of Jesus' miracles.

31. See Friedrich Büchsel, "Mandäer und Johannesjünger," *Zeitschrift für die neutestamentliche Wissenschaft* 26 (1927): 219 n. 1.

32. See Gustav Hölscher, *Urgemeinde und Spätjudentum,* Avhandlinger utgitt av det Norske Videnskaps-Akademi i Oslo, II, historisk-filosofisk klasse 4 (Oslo: Dybvad, 1928), 24.

33. See note 11.

34. See my analysis in "Libertines or Not: Fruit, Bread, Semen and Other Body Fluids in Gnosticism," *Journal of Early Christian Studies* 2, no. 1 (1994): 15–31, for the relationships between food, sexuality, and conversion in selected Gnostic traditions.

35. For this text, see James M. Robinson, ed., *The Nag Hammadi Library in English,* rev. ed. (San Francisco: Harper and Row, 1988), 117–18, sections 22–23; and consult the analysis in chapter 3 of my *Female Fault and Fulfilment in Gnosticism* (Chapel Hill: University of North Carolina Press, 1986), 52–55.

Chapter 6

1. Mr. Askari's father, Sheikh Bandar, was a Mandaean community leader in Khorramshahr.

2. Three suras in the Qur'an deal with this issue, 2:62, 5:69, and 22:17. Only the last one mentions the Zoroastrians. Traditionally, three religious groups have enjoyed protection under Islam, and while the Jews and Christians seem to remain safely within the perimeters of protection, the situation wavers with regard to the third category, for legislation tends to allow only *one* slot for Sabeans and Zoroastrians. Evidently, both cannot be covered simultaneously.

3. See my "A Study of the Two Liturgical Collections."

4. He reigned from 1848 to 1896.

5. On the flight from Shiraz to Tehran, while I am busy writing long-neglected notes, I am surprised to find Sheikh Choheili teaching the Mandaean alphabet to the young woman in the seat next to him.

6. There are two workshops making water pumps for irrigation; a ball-bearing factory; a sheet metal cutting shop and one for smelting iron; and one making ice.

7. In Shiraz, I was taken on a long tour of local sights: the tombs of Saadi and of Hafiz. Persepolis and Naqs-i-Rustam were both majestic, magnificent.

8. For a full description of a traditional, village Mandaean wedding in Iraq, see Drower, *Mandaeans*, 59–71.

9. For details on the baptism, see chapter 7.

10. Ibid.

11. How many times had I puzzled over the injunction to place the hand in this position—and to remove it—in ritual commentaries and instructions! Now Sheikh Choheili answered this question for me.

12. Not everyone does this anymore, I am told.

13. See Drower, *Mandaeans*, chap. 8.

14. I do not succeed at this task until Mr. Shooshtary, in Mamoon's house on Long Island, patiently shows me how to do it.

15. For Saeed Moradi, see the beginning of chapter 10.

16. In M. Eliade, ed., *The Encyclopedia of Religion*, vol. 9 (New York: Macmillan, 1987),: 150–53.

Chapter 7

1. Jean-Marie Sevrin, dealing with Sethian-Valentinian forms of baptism, still seems to judge repeated baptisms as decadent; see his *Le dossier baptismal Séthien*, Bibliothèque copte de Nag Hammadi, Section "Études" 2 (Quebec: Les Presses de l'Université Laval, 1986), 290–91. As noted, H. Jonas takes almost no interest in Gnostic rituals.

2. Max Weber, *The Sociology of Religion* (London: Methuen, 1965), 152.

3. Rudolph, "Antike Baptisten," 6.

4. An example of such a study is E. Segelberg, *Maṣbuta: Studies in the Ritual of Mandaean Baptism* (Uppsala: Almqvist and Wiksell, 1958).

5. Kurt Rudolph, *Die Mandäer*, vol. 2, *Der Kult* (Göttingen: Vandenhoeck and Ruprecht, 1961), 93.

6. Ibid., 95.

7. Fuller descriptions are found in Rudolph, *Der Kult*, 61–104, and in Drower, *Mandaeans*, 100–123.

8. See figure 7 in Drower, *Mandaeans*, between 134 and 135.

9. Two other, shorter, forms of ablutions, the *ṭamaša* and the *rišama*, do not require a priest, and a person may perform them virtually anytime, but especially after bodily or emotional pollutions, for instance, after sexual activity or after subsiding from anger at somebody.

10. During Panja (*parwaniia*), the intercalary period, the doors to the Lightworld are wide open, and it is a particularly auspicious occasion for baptism.

11. Rahmas (establishing prayers) are one among several types of prayer in Mandaeism. There are different rahmas for the seven days of the week (see Drower, *Prayerbook*, 106–70 for these prayers).

12. This is the loose-hanging end of the burzinqa. A priest ties it across the lower part of his face during rituals.

13. The baptism liturgy runs from nos. 1 to 31 in Drower, *Prayerbook*.

14. Ibid. no. 13, 9.

15. Ibid.

16. See Segelberg, *Maṣbuta*, 44, where he speaks of "coronation" instead of "wreathing." However, the term *coronation* should properly be reserved for acts concerning the priestly crown, the taga.

17. Laypeople, related to the female, earthly realm, do not acquire crowns, but priests have both crown and wreath. This is so because priests inhabit the male, Lightworld level, which nevertheless paradoxically always requires a balance between male and female elements. The complex Mandaean symbolism of male and female will be explored further in subsequent chapters, especially 8, 9, and 12.

18. Drower, *Mandaeans*, 100.

19. Drower, *Prayerbook*, 13. The original is not so clearly addressed to a male as Drower's translation indicates.

20. See Segelberg, *Maṣbuta*, 115–30.

21. Ibid., 128 and 122 n. 5. The text is *Masiqta Zihrun Raza Kasia*, no. 27 in the Drower Collection in the Bodleian Library, Oxford.

22. Segelberg, *Maṣbuta*, 122 n. 5.

23. Drower and Macuch, *Mandaic Dictionary*, 332 a and b.

24. Drower, *Prayerbook*, no. 18, 14 (adjusted to gender).

25. Segelberg, *Maṣbuta*, 148.

26. Drower, *Prayerbook*, no. 23, 19.

27. Segelberg, *Maṣbuta*, 75.

28. Drower, *Mandaeans*, 113.

29. Original 16mm copies of this film exist at the Peabody Museum, Harvard University, and at the Ashmolean Museum in Oxford, England. Video formats are now in the public domain.

30. Drower, *Prayerbook*, 60, n. 3.

31. Jean-Marie Sevrin, "Les rites de la gnose, d'après quelques textes gnostiques coptes," in *Gnosticisme et monde hellénistique*, ed. J. Ries, Publications de l'Institut Orientaliste de Louvain 27 (Louvain-la-Neuve: Université de Louvain, 1982), 450.

Chapter 8

1. Drower, *Haran Gawaita*, XI.

2. For the various forms of the ritual, see Drower, *Water into Wine* (London: Murray, 1956), 243–44.

3. Drower, *The Great "First World" and The Lesser "First World,"* XI.

4. Drower, *Coronation*, XI.

5. See Drower, *Mandaeans*, 201 f., and also her *Water into Wine*, 245–47.

6. See Drower, *1012*, 257–58 (206); Drower, *Water into Wine*, 242–43.

7. In light of the GL story (in chapter 3), one might have expected the first masiqta to be that of Šitil, but the masiqta named for him is a different matter, as noted in chapter 3.

8. Drower, *The Great "First World,"* 12–13. "In the name of Life and the name of Knowledge-of-Life" refers to a formula. Consult also Drower, "Sacraments during the Five-Day Feast of the Mandaeans," *Symbolon, Jahrbuch für Symbolforschung* 1 (1960): 25–26.

9. Drower, *Water into Wine*, 248; Drower, and *The Great "First World,"* 13 n. 3. Adam's ascent is the model for all rising souls.

10. Drower, *Water into Wine*, 248.

11. Ibid., 250 n. 1.

12. For a list and description of the various pieces of the priestly garb, see Drower, *Mandaeans*, 30–31.

13. It is not real wine, for Mandaeans use no fermented liquids in their rituals.
14. Drower, *Prayerbook*, no. 33, 33.
15. Ibid., no. 34, 33–34. Here Drower translates the name of Manda ḏ-Hiia, the supreme ʿutra, as "*Gnosis* of Life."
16. Drower, *1012*, 240–41 (143), with note 1, 241.
17. Drower, *Prayerbook*, no. 35, 36. The name is that of Yuzaṭaq-Manda ḏ-Hiia.
18. Ibid., no. 75, 74. Ruha's lament occurs in this prayer (see chapter 4).
19. Ibid., 76.
20. Drower, *1012*, 241 (144).
21. Ibid.
22. Ibid., 241 (146).
23. Ibid.
24. Ibid, 241 (147).
25. Drower, *Prayerbook*, 36.
26. Drower, *The Great "First World,"* 15.
27. Drower, *Water into Wine*, 251. See her *Mandaeans*, 35, for a description of how the priest makes the wreath.
28. Drower, *1012*, 242 (148). The pihta prayers are nos. 36-43, 36–40.
29. Drower, *The Great "First World,"* 15.
30. Drower, *Prayerbook*, no. 45, 41 no. 44 is the first mambuha prayer).
31. So says Drower, *1012*, 243 (152).
32. Ibid., 243 (153).
33. Drower, *Prayerbook*, 43.
34. Ibid., 44.
35. Ibid., 45.
36. Drower, *Water into Wine*, 251.
37. Drower, *Coronation*, 28, referring to Drower, *Prayerbook*, 44–46.
38. Drower, *1012*, 244 (154).
39. Drower, *Prayerbook*, 47. There is an omitted part of prayer 51, an error for which Drower apologizes in her later works. For the full, omitted text, see her *The Lesser "First World,"* 81 n. 3.
40. Years ago, I thought that the long prayer 170, called "Our Ancestors," was inserted at this point into prayer 49. But this is not the case, for it is the phrase, not the prayer, that now occurs (see my "The Mandaean Ṭabahata Masiqta," *Numen* 28, no. 2 (1981): 146).
41. Drower, *1012*, 246 (166).
42. Drower, *Water into Wine*, 252.
43. See Drower, *The Great "First World,"* 18 n. 5. This information comes from an unpublished scroll, *Šarḥ Ṭabahata* (no. 42 in the Drower Collection, Bodleian Library, Oxford). Drower, *Coronation*, 29–30, with note 8, has related material.
44. Drower *1012*, 246 (166).
45. Drower, *Water into Wine*, 253. See also her three other works: *The Secret Adam* (Oxford: Clarendon Press, 1960), 79–80; *1012*, 207 (95); and *The Great "First World,"* 36. The content of the bowl was fertilized earlier, too, by the dipping of the priestly ring into the liquid.
46. Drower, *Coronation*, XVII and 29.
47. Drower, *1012*, 246–47 (166–67). The "body" here is the Lightworld ʿuṣṭuna, not the corporeal body.
48. Drower, *Prayerbook*, 47.
49. Drower, *Water into Wine*, 253.
50. Drower, *The Great "First World,"* 21.
51. Drower, *Mandaeans*, 164.
52. Drower, *The Great "First World,"* 23.

53. Drower, *1012*, 155 (187).
54. Drower, *The Great "First World,"* 38.
55. Drower, *1012*, 239 (138).
56. Drower, *Water into Wine*, 255.
57. Drower, *Prayerbook*, 90. Drower says that a Mandaean who dies during Panja needs no masiqta at all.
58. Drower, *1012*, 249 (176); see also 239 (138).
59. Ibid., 258 (209).
60. Drower, *The Great "First World,"* 39.
61. Ibid., 40. See also her *Prayerbook*, prayer 9, 7–8.
62. Drower, *The Great "First World,"* 42.
63. Ibid., 42–43.
64. Drower, *The Secret Adam*, 32.
65. Drower, *1012*, 246 (166).
66. See Ethel S. Drower, "The Sacramental Bread (*Pihta*) of the Mandaeans," *Zeitschrift für die neutestamentliche Wissenschaft* 105, Neue Folge 30 (1955): 121–22.
67. Drower, *The Great "First World,"* 50, with notes.
68. My statements here reflect my ongoing historical research.

Chapter 9

1. Aside from Drower's description of the ganzibra initiation in *Mandaeans*, 169–77, I know of no analysis of this ritual. It would be an interesting project to compare the initiations of the two levels of priesthood.
2. In the main, I will correlate Drower's three texts *Coronation*, *Prayerbook*, and *Mandaeans*. Eric Segelberg's "Traṣa ḏ-taga ḏ-Šišlam Rabba: Studies in the Rite Called the Coronation of Šišlam Rabba," in *Zur Sprache und Literatur*, ed. R. Macuch, Studia Mandaica, vol. 1 (Berlin: de Gruyter, 1976), 171–244, deals mostly with comparative issues and is of little relevance to my objectives.
3. As noted, a woman may become one, too (see chapter 5, and also chapter 14).
4. See Drower, *Mandaeans*, 146–47.
5. No mental illness or any physical imperfection is permitted. There are stories about young men who wish to become priests but are ineligible because of a lost part of a finger or similar accidents. Certainly, a Mandaean who has been forcefully circumcised, a not uncommon form of torture in times of persecution, can never become a priest.
6. Compare this with the dove (ba) in the masiqta.
7. Drower, *Mandaeans*, 153.
8. Note that this hut is not the Mandaean mandi, the clay-and-reed sanctuary.
9. Drower, *Coronation*, 5. The prayer is number 323.
10. Or: prayers 1–103 (the baptism prayers, "The Book of Souls," are prayers 1–31 only). The texts differ on this point.
11. See Drower, *Prayerbook*, 228–29.
12. Drower, *Coronation*, 9. The prayer here is not number 44, as Drower indicates (with a question mark), but prayer 18.
13. Drower, *Prayerbook*, 59.
14. Ibid., 61.
15. Drower, *Coronation*, 11. See also Drower and Macuch, *Mandaic Dictionary*, 463b; Segelberg, *Maṣbuta*, 20–21, for the loosening prayers.
16. Drower, *Prayerbook*, 1 (this formula is given at the very beginning, before prayer 1).
17. The information in Drower, *Coronation*, 11, and in her *Mandaeans*, 148–49, differs slightly.

18. Drower, *Prayerbook*, nos. 233–56 (186–213).

19. "Your thought shall be filled with ours and your garment and our garment will be one" (Drower, *Prayerbook*, 211).

20. Ibid., 2. What Drower translates as "circlet" is *klila* in the facsimile of the text.

21. Ibid., 163–66. In the ganzibra initiation, a "real" marriage takes place, though not for the postulant.

22. The set for each consists of seven prayers, possibly correlating with the seven drafts of hamra.

23. Drower, *Prayerbook*, no. 105, 104–6 (Drower also gives it in her, *Mandaeans*, 245–47).

24. Drower, *Prayerbook*, 36. As noted earlier, prayer 35 is "good for all occasions."

25. Drower, *Coronation*, 21–22 (Drower's footnote 1, 22, is thus misguided).

26. For mana, see Drower and Macuch, *Mandaic Dictionary*, 246b-247a, mana 1 and 2. Translations range from "implement" and "vessel" to "garment," "soul," and "intelligence." The word merits a study of its own.

27. Drower, *Prayerbook*, 52.

28. See Drower, *Mandaeans*, 154–55.

29. At an earlier stage in the ritual, the rba was warned *not* to utter these prayers (see note 15).

30. Drower, *Coronation*, 23.

31. Consult the chapter on the masiqta. What seems to be missing from the current speculation is any attention to the second part of the masiqta, the first treatment of the six biscuits.

32. For the ṣa at a marriage ceremony, see Drower, *Mandaeans*, 67–68.

33. Drower, *Coronation*, 25.

34. Here these three prayers are called "rahmas," although, according to Drower, this is not strictly their correct appellation (see contents, *Prayerbook*).

35. Ibid.

36. Ibid.

37. Ibid., 4-5.

38. Ibid., 36.

39. Drower, *Mandaeans*, 215; Segelberg, *Maṣbuta*, 19–21. The roots are QUM, QRA, and TRṢ.

40. Again, only the second treatment of the six biscuits is called the "Father masiqta," while the combination of all three sections makes up the "masiqta of the Parents" performed exclusively at Panja.

41. Drower, *Coronation*, has actually started its prayer sequence before prayer 323.

42. Both texts add a prayer here that is not in the prayerbook.

43. Drower, *Coronation*, 9, seems to indicate that prayer 57 occurs here; I consider this an error.

44. End of novice's baptism. Note that the other text has been silent on the entire preceding segment, except for *one* sentence; Drower, *Coronation*, 9.

45. The second text leaves out any mention of prayer 191. While the coronation text emphasizes marriage, *Exalted Kingship* stresses the investiture.

46. These are not really in sequence, for *Exalted Kingship* here refers back to an earlier section, which is a technique characteristic of this text (as we shall see in chapter 12).

Chapter 10

1. This text, in Lidzbarski's *John*, 196–200, is a curious one. I had asked Mr. Sobbi to read this particular tractate because I was working on it at that time (see my "Professional Fatigue").

2. I did not know that I would travel to Iran a little more than a year later and that I would meet these three priests. Then, Sheikh Salah had become a ganzibra.

3. See Drower, *Mandaeans*, 30–31, for a description of the ritual dress.

4. See chapter 6 for Sheikh Choheili. This is the man who made possible R. Macuch's *Neumandäische Texte im Dialekt von Ahwaz*, one of the few books to contain a large number of stories, anecdotes, and events told in modern Mandaic (another one is Macuch's *Neumandäische Chrestomathie*).

5. In Ahwaz, Iran, I visited a walled-in Mandaean cemetery.

6. This comes from the Muslim custom of reading the first sura of the Qur'an at funerals. The sura is titled "Fateha" (beginning).

7. Lamea taught me that before food, the formula is "In the name of the Life and in the name of Manda d̲-Hiia!" After food, one says, "Thank you, O my Lord!"

8. Later I checked this with my friends at General Theological Seminary. We consulted the computer and looked at maps. The answer, though debated, is negative: "Zobah" seems to refer to a region near Damascus, not to a people.

9. See chapter 12.

10. A phrase from the initial formula of the *Prayerbook*.

11. Compare this with Lamea's explanation, chapter 2.

12. Drower, *Mandaeans*, 169–77.

Chapter 11

1. Like the other illustrations in the text, the figure appears only in the facsimile part of Drower, *The Great "First World"* and *The Lesser "First World."* The translation of the text on the figure is in *The Great "First World,"* 8–9.

2. Drower accidentally leaves out this third line.

3. Drower, *The Great "First World,"* 9 n. 2.

4. Drower, *Prayerbook*, 89.

5. Ibid., 122.

6. Ibid., 89.

7. This is my translation (Drower's is in her *Prayerbook*, 90). Instead of Drower's phrase "At the fountainhead I came forth," Macuch has very helpfully supplied the correction, "I went out to the waters," which is a Persian idiom (personal communication to me from Macuch).

8. Lidzbarski, *Ginza*, 142.

9. For Dinanukht, see chapter 4, on Ruha. Other scholars have recently taken an interest in Dinanukht, especially in his Persian roots; see Ezio Albrile, "L'estasi di Dinanukht," *Rivista del Teologia, Asprenas* 46 (1999): 195–224. One looks forward to Dan Shapira's so far unpublished essay "Anuš and Uthra" and current research by Sinaşi Gündüz (personal communications).

Chapter 12

1. As noted in chapter 9 , two of these, *The Great "First World"* and *Exalted Kingship*, must be present in the škinta during the tarmida initiation.

2. See my *Exalted Kingship*. Lines 1–7 give the set initial formula for most Mandaean texts—as found at the beginning of prayer 1—with the requisite petition for forgiveness of sins for the copyist and his family members.

3. Ibid., line 15, 2

4. Ibid., lines 16–17, 2.

5. Drower, *Prayerbook*, 1.

6. In another, longer section on mystical companionship, the text states that "there is an inner and an outer in all things" (*Exalted Kingship*, line 733, 42, with commentary, 91–92).

7. *Exalted Kingship*, lines 35–36, 3.

8. Ibid., line 54, 4.

9. Drower, *Prayerbook*, 11.

10. "And with the bonds of kušṭa" is left out in Drower's translation, *Prayerbook*, 23, but it is present in the facsimile section, ibid. 37.

11. *Exalted Kingship*, line 75, 6.

12. Drower, *Prayerbook*, 28.

13. *Exalted Kingship*, lines 83–84, 6.

14. Ibid., lines 87–88, 7.

15. Drower, *Prayerbook*, 33.

16. Ibid., 36.

17. Ibid., 44.

18. *Exalted Kingship*, line 107, 8.

19. As noted, this part is omitted from Drower, *Prayerbook*, 47 (see her, *The Lesser "First World,"* 81 n. 3).

20. *Exalted Kingship*, lines 112–13, 8.

21. Ibid., lines 118–19, 9.

22. Parts of Drower, *1012*, Book II, iiia (195–210) and V(a), (262–65)—which may be versions of the same text—deal with ritual mistakes and the effects of such (see chapter 13).

23. Drower, *Prayerbook*, 49.

24. *Exalted Kingship*, lines 128–29, 9.

25. Ibid. lines 171–72, 12.

26. Drower, *Prayerbook*, 72–78.

27. *Exalted Kingship*, lines 187–88, 13.

28. Drower, *Prayerbook*, 35 (this prayer was treated in chapters 4 and 9; recall the problem with Drower's translation of it).

29. *Exalted Kingship*, lines 194–95, 13.

30. Drower, *Prayerbook*, 90–91.

31. *Exalted Kingship*, line 199, 13.

32. Ibid., line 211, 14.

33. Ibid., lines 212–13.

34. Drower, *Prayerbook*, 99.

35. *Exalted Kingship*, lines 214–16, 14.

36. Ibid., line 225. 15.

37. In ecstasy and similar states of consciousness, others may enter the upper worlds, too. Examples may be found in the folk tales in the last part of Drower's *Mandaeans* and in *GR* 6's tale about Dinanukht.

38. For this issue, consult the discussion in Charles L. Briggs, *Competence in Performance: The Creativity of Tradition in Mexicano Verbal Art* (Philadelphia: University of Pennsylvania Press, 1988), 13–14.

39. Pierre Bourdieu, *Outline of a Theory of Practice*, Cambridge Studies in Social Anthropology (Cambridge: Cambridge University Press, 1977), 133, 119.

Chapter 13

1. See Drower, *Mandaeans*, 241–44.

2. Drower, *1012*, 266 (310).

3. This section, "Tafsir Pagra" (The Explanation of the Body), is a form of Mandaean kabbalism; it is found, ibid., 162–94.

4. Ibid., 180 (258).

5. Ibid.

6. Ibid., 181 (258).

7. The story is in Lidzbarski, *GR* 15,13, 348f.
8. Drower, *1012*, 181 (258).
9. Ibid.
10. *Exalted Kingship*, 59.
11. Drower, *1012*, 181 (260).
12. See Drower and Macuch, *Mandaic Dictionary*, 420 a and b.
13. Drower, *1012*, in the booklet containing the facsimile of the text, 23, on the right side of the page.
14. Ibid., 182 (261).
15. Ibid., 182 (262).
16. *Exalted Kingship*, lines 364-69, 23; see also my commentary section, 81–82.
17. Ibid., lines 1167–1330, 64–71, with commentary, 102–5. See also Drower, *1012*, Book, I, i , 119 (20)-158 (200) and Book II, iiia, 195 (2)-210 (43).
18. Drower, *1012*, 152 (175).
19. Ibid., 153 (178).
20. Ibid., 155 (187).
21. Ibid., 153 (178).
22. Ibid., 144 (134), with note 4.
23. *Exalted Kingship*, lines 1325–30, 71.
24. Drower, *1012*, 135 (90).
25. Ibid., 128 (63-65).
26. Drower, *Mandaeans*, 210–11.
27. Drower, *1012*, 131 (74), with note 3.
28. Drower, *Mandaeans*, 46.
29. Lidzbarski, *GR* 6, 207 (20–25).
30. Lidzbarski, *John*, 103–9.
31. Ibid., 242–44.
32. See ibid., Lidzbarski's 242 n. 4.
33. Drower and Macuch, *Mandaic Dictionary*, 35b.
34. Ibid., 481b.

Chapter 14

1. For example, a Jewish temple in Cleveland, Ohio, has a Mandaean inscribed bowl so far unstudied by scholars.
2. J. de Morgan, *Mission scientifique en Perse*, vol. 5, *Études linguistiques, 2. Textes mandaïtes* (Paris: Imprimerie Nationale, 1904). When I first saw this report in the musty stacks of the Widener Library at Harvard University, I noticed that no one had ever borrowed it from the library. For a report on two of de Morgan's acquired texts, see my "A Study of the Two Liturgical Collections."
3. See chapter 6.
4. This title is a misnomer in the context, as I have shown in "A Study of the Two Liturgical Collections."
5. Noting the unorthodox creation of priests right after the cholera, some scholars have tended to belittle the Mandaean religion as having become degraded and corrupt since the epidemic. This is, in my view, an unjust denigration.
6. In zharas, the person's baptismal (maṣbuta) name is used. The name designates the person in relationship to the person's mother, not to the father.
7. This is my translation of de Morgan, *Mission scientifique*, 18: see my "A Study of the Two Liturgical Collections," 195.

8. Ibid., 200 (de Morgan, 204). The text is corrupt and Yahia Yuhana does not return to prayer 5 after the interruption.

9. DC 12, in the Drower Collection in the Bodleian Library, unpublished.

10. Yahia Bihram was born ca. 1811. See my "Glimpses of a Life: Yahia Bihram, Mandaean Priest," *History of Religions* 39, no. 1 (1999): 32–49.

11. These two scrolls are DC 24 and 50, respectively, Neither has been published.

12. This is my translation from DC 50's tarik.

13. DC 47, 37, 28, and 43, respectively.

14. This information is in DC 43's tarik.

15. The king of the underworld (see chapter 4).

16. Mandaean texts often associate evil earthly rulers with the planets and the zodiac spirits.

17. Petermann, *Sidra Rabba*.

18. See my "The Colophons in H. Petermann's *Sidra Rabba*," *Journal of the Royal Asiatic Society*, 3d ser., 5, no. 1 (1995): 21–38. I have also correlated these colophons with those in seven other *Ginzas*, which makes nine sets of *Ginza* colophons in all, i.e., sixty-three colophons (this research is unpublished).

19. "The Colophons in H. Peterman's *Sidra Rabba*," 26.

20. I have had valuable help in deciphering the information about local Islamic rulers and history from Professor John E. Woods of the University of Chicago. Evidently, scholars of this time and region have not been aware that Mandaean tariks provide sources for Islamic history.

21. A similar photograph is in Drower, *Mandaeans*, plate 1b.

22. For an account of the letters between the two, see my "A Mandaean Correspondence."

23. See Rudolf Macuch, "Zur Grammatik und zum Wörterbuch des Mandäischen," in *Zur Sprache und Literatur der Mandäer*, Studia Mandaica I, ed. R. Macuch (Berlin: de Gruyter, 1976), 75.

24. Yahia Bihram married his cousin's sister, Bibia Mudalal, an illustrious woman copyist, book owner, and a priest herself. For women priests, see my "The Evidence for Women Priests."

25. Except for *one*, which is broken off (manuscript D, in Petermann).

26. See chapter 1.

27. See my "The Colophons in *The Canonical Prayerbook of the Mandaeans*."

28. See Petermann's *Sidra Rabba*, 137–38, and my "The Colophons of H. Petermann's *Sidra Rabba*," 36–38.

29. "Rbai," literally: "my teacher." From here on, "rbai" is simply indicated by "R."

30. Because of the time difference, this man cannot be identical with his namesake, who went in the mid-seventh century with a delegation as the head of the Mandaeans to ask the Muslims for protection.

31. The term is *kiniana*, which means "father's family line." In Drower and Macuch, *Mandaic Dictionary*, 214a, this is not clearly indicated.

32. The term is *laqab*. Here, too, ibid., 228a, simply says "tribal or family name."

33. This should probably be "he," i.e., Manṣur ʿUbadia (= Anuš, son of Zihrun).

34. Notice that the two brothers have the same initiator, Adam Bayan.

35. The two different "fathers" or initiators given for the two brothers seem garbled: Šadan is not the father of Bayan Hibil, but a fellow initiate of three other men: Bayan Hibil, Banan Bihram, and Bihram; see Petermann, *Sidra Rabba*, 232, for GL's MS. C, where the four appear as co-owners of the GL MS.

36. A woman.

37. A woman.

38. A woman.

39. I do not think that baptismal names, giving the mother's name, are used in the formula from here on. Consult my arguments in "The Evidence for Women Priests."

40. See chapter 1.

41. See "The Evidence for Women Priests."

42. Drower, *Prayerbook*, 151–54. I have been able to place, historically, many of the names of the priests in this prayer.

43. Ibid., 71–72. See also my "The Colophons in *The Canonical Prayerbook of the Mandaeans*," 38–39.

44. See *ARAM*, 11–12 (1999–2000). The Mandaeans (pp. 197–331): *ARAM* Thirteenth International Conference. The Mandaeans: 13–15 June 1999. Harvard University.

Frouzanda Mahrad

1. A suburb of Baghdad.

2. Libya, although an Arab country, supported Iran in the Iran-Iraq war of 1980–88.

Bibliography

Albrile, Ezio. "L'estasi di Dinanukht." *Rivista del Teologia, Asprenas* 46 (1999): 195-224.

ARAM, vols. 11-12 (1999-2000). The Mandaeans. (pp. 197-331): *ARAM* Thirteenth International Conference. The Mandaeans: 13-15 June 1999. Harvard University.

Bianchi,Ugo, ed., *Le Origini dello Gnosticismo: Colloquio di Messina 13-18 Aprile 1966, Testi e Discussioni*. Studies in the History of Religions, Supplement to *Numen* 12. Leiden: Brill, 1967.

Bourdieu, Pierre. *Outline of a Theory of Practice*, Cambridge Studies in Social Anthropology. Cambridge: Cambridge University Press, 1977.

Briggs, Charles L. *Competence in Performance: The Creativity of Tradition in Mexicano Verbal Art*. Philadelphia: University of Pennsylvania Press, 1988.

Buckley, Jorunn J. "Spirit Ruha in Mandaean Religion," Ph.D. diss., University of Chicago, 1978.

——. "The Mandaean Šitil as an Example of 'the Image Above and Below.'" *Numen* 26, no. 2 (1979): 185-91.

——. "Two Female Gnostic Revealers." *History of Religions* 19, no. 3 (1980): 259-69.

——. "The Mandaean Ṭabahata Masiqta." *Numen* 28, no. 2 (1981): 138-63.

——. "Mani's Opposition to the Elchasaites: A Question of Ritual." In *Traditions in Contact and Change: Selected Proceedings of the XIVth Congress of the International Association for the History of Religions*, edited by P. Slater and D. Wiebe, 323-36. Waterloo, Ontario: Wilfrid Laurier University Press, 1983.

——. "A Rehabilitation of Spirit Ruha in Mandaean Religion." *History of Religions* 22, no. 1 (1982): 60-84.

——. *Female Fault and Fulfilment in Gnosticism*. Chapel Hill: University of North Carolina Press, 1986.

——. "Tools and Tasks: Elchasaite and Manichaean Purification Rituals," *Journal of Religion* 66, no. 4 (1986): 399-411.

——. "Mandaean Religion." In *The Encyclopedia of Religion*, vol. 9, edited by M. Eliade, 150-53. New York: Macmillan, 1987.

——. "Conceptual Models and Polemical Issues in the Gospel of Philip." In *Aufstieg und Niedergang der römischen Welt*, pt. 2, 25, 5, edited by H. Temporini and W. Haase, 4167-94. Berlin: de Gruyter, 1988.

——. "A Study of the Two Liturgical Collections in J. de Morgan's *Textes Mandaïtes*." *Le Muséon* 104, vols. 1-2 (1991): 191-203.

——. "The Colophons in *The Canonical Prayerbook of the Mandaeans.*" *Journal of Near Eastern Studies* 51, no. 1 (1992): 33-50.

——. "The Mandaean Appropriation of Jesus' Mother, Miriai." *Novum Testamentum* 35, no. 2 (1993): 181-96.

——. *The Scroll of Exalted Kingship: Diwan malkuta ʿlaita.* American Oriental Society Translation Series 3. New Haven, Conn.: American Oriental Society, 1993.

——. "Libertines or Not: Fruit, Bread, Semen and Other Body Fluids in Gnosticism," *Journal of Early Christian Studies* 2, no. 1 (1994): 15-31.

——. "A Mandaean Correspondence." In *Gnosisforschung und Religionsgeschichte: Festschrift für Kurt Rudolph zum 65. Geburtstag*, edited by Holger Preissler and Hubert Seiwert, 55-60. Marburg: diagonal-Verlag, 1994.

——. " The Colophons in H. Petermann's *Sidra Rabba.*" *Journal of the Royal Asiatic Society*, 3d ser., 5, no. 1 (1995): 21-38.

——. "With the Mandaeans in Iran." *Religious Studies News* 11, no. 3 (1996): 8.

——. "Professional Fatigue: 'Hibil's Lament' in the Mandaean *Book of John.*" *Le Muséon* 110, fasc. 3-4 (1997): 367-81.

——. "Glimpses of a Life: Yahia Bihram, Mandaean Priest." *History of Religions* 39, no. 1 (1999), 32-49.

——. "The Evidence for Women Priests in Mandaeism." *Journal of Near Eastern Studies* 59, no. 2 (2000): 93-106.

Büchsel, Friedrich. "Mandäer und Johannesjünger." *Zeitschrift für die neutestamentliche Wissenschaft* (=*ZNW*) 26 (1927): 219-31.

Bultmann, Rudolf. "Die Bedeutung der neuerschlossenen mandäischen und manichäischen Quellen für das Verständnis des Johannesevangeliums." *ZNW* 24 (1925): 100-146.

Cartlidge, David R., and David L. Dungan. "The Gospel of Pseudo-Matthew." In *Documents for the Study of the Gospels*, edited by David R. Cartlidge and David L. Dugan, 98-103. Philadelphia: Fortress Press, 1980.

Colpe, Carsten. "Die Thomaspsalmen als chronologischer Fixpunkt in der Geschichte der orientalischen Gnosis." *Jahrbuch für Antike und Christentum* 7 (1964): 77-93.

Crehan, J. H. "The Mandaeans and Christian Infiltration." *Journal of Theological Studies* 19 (1968): 623-26.

De Morgan, J. *Mission scientifique en Perse.* Vol. 5, *Études linguistiques, 2. Textes mandaïtes.* Paris: Imprimerie Nationale, 1904.

Drower, Ethel S. *The Mandaeans of Iraq and Iran.* Leiden: Brill, 1937.

——. "A Phylactery for Rue." *Orientalia* 15 (1946): 324-46.

——. *The Book of the Zodiac: Sfar Malwašia.* London: Murray, 1949.

——. *Diwan Abatur or Progress through the Purgatories.* Studi e Testi 151. Vatican City: Biblioteca Apostolica Vaticana, 1950.

——. *Šarh̲ d̲-Qabin d̲-Šišlam Rba: Explanatory Commentary on the Marriage Ceremony of the Great Šišlam.* Rome: Pontificio Istituto Biblico, 1950.

——. *Haran Gawaita* and *The Baptism of Hibil Ziwa.* Studi e Testi 176. Vatican City: Biblioteca Apostolica Vaticana, 1953.

——. *Mandaean Ceremony* (film). 1954.

——. "The Sacramental Bread (*Pihta*) of the Mandaeans." *ZNW* 105, Neue Folge 30 (1955): 115-51.

——. *Water into Wine.* London: Murray, 1956.

——. *The Canonical Prayerbook of the Mandaeans.* Leiden: Brill, 1959.

——. "Sacraments during the Five-Day Feast of the Mandaeans." *Symbolon, Jahrbuch für Symbolforschung* 1 (1960): 17-26.

——. *The Secret Adam.* Oxford: Clarendon Press, 1960.
——. *The Thousand and Twelve Questions: A Mandaean Text (Alf Trisar Šuialia).* Berlin: Akademie Verlag, 1960.
——. *The Coronation of the Great Šišlam: Being a Description of the Rite of Coronation of a Mandaean Priest according to the Ancient Canon.* Leiden: Brill, 1962.
——. *A Pair of Naṣoraean Commentaries (Two Priesly Documents): The Great "First World." The Lesser "First World."* Leiden: Brill, 1963.
Drower, E. S., and Rudolf Macuch. *A Mandaic Dictionary.* Oxford: Clarendon Press, 1963.
Drower Collection (=DC), DC 12. *Pašar Haršia. (The Exorcism of Wizards).* Bodleian Library, Oxford University.
DC 24. *Šarh d-Parwanaia (The Scroll of the Panja [Ritual]).* Unpublished.
DC 27. *Masiqta Zihrun Raza Kasia ([The] Masiqta [of] Zihrun, the Hidden Mystery).* Unpublished.
DC 28. *Pišra d-Bit Mišqal Ainia (The Exorcism of "I Sought to Lift My Eyes").* Unpublished, though another copy, DC 26, was published by Drower in *Iraq* 5 (1938): 31–54.
DC 37. *Šapta d-Masihfan Rba (The Scroll of the Great Overthrower).* Unpublished.
DC 42. *Šarḥ Ṭabahata (The Scroll of Ṭabahata).* (unpublished).
DC 43. A collection of exorcisms, called *The Poor Priest's Treasury.* Unpublished.
DC 47. *Pišra d-Šambra (A Phylactery for Rue).* See Drower, "A Phylactery," 1946.
DC 50. *Šarh d-Masbuta Rabia (The Scroll of the Great Baptism).* Unpublished.
Foerster, Werner. *Gnosis: A Selection of Gnostic Texts.* Vol. 2, *Coptic and Mandaic Sources.* English edition by R. McL. Wilson, Oxford: Clarendon Press, 1974.
Green, Tamara M. *The City of the Moon God: Religious Traditions of Harran.* Religions in the Graeco-Roman World, vol. 114. Leiden: Brill, 1992.
Gündüz, Sinaşi. *The Knowledge of Life: The Origins and Early History of the Mandaeans and Their Relationship to the Sabeans of the Qur'an and to the Harranians.* Journal of Semitic Studies, Supplement 3. Oxford: Oxford University Press for the University of Manchester, 1994.
Heidegger, Martin. *Being and Time.* English translation by John Macquarrie and E. Robinson. London: SCM Press, 1962.
Hennecke, Edgar. "The Protevangelium of James." In *The New Testament Apocrypha,* vol. 1, edited by E. Hennecke and Wilhelm Schneemelcher, 378–80. Philadelphia: Westminster Press, 1959.
Hölscher, Gustav. *Urgemeinde und Spätjudentum.* Avhandlinger utgitt av det Norske Videnskaps-Akademi i Oslo, II, historisk-filosofisk klasse 4. Oslo: Dybvad, 1928.
Hunter, Erica C. D. "Two Mandaic Incantation Bowls from the 18th Nippur Season." *Baghdader Mitteilungen* 25 (1994): 605–18.
——. "Aramaic-Speaking Communities of Sasanid Mesopotamia." *ARAM* 7 (1995): 319–35.
Jonas, Hans. *Gnosis und spätantiker Geist. Vol. 1, part 1, Die mythologische Gnosis. Vol. 2, part 1, Von der Mythologie zur mythischen Philosophie.* Göttingen: Vandenhoeck and Ruprecht, 1934, 1954 (reprint editions, 1964 and 1966).
——. *The Gnostic Religion.* Boston: Beacon Press, 1963.
King, Karen, ed. *Images of the Feminine in Gnosticism.* Studies in Antiquity and Christianity. Philadelphia: Fortress Press, 1988.
Klijn, A. F. J. *Seth in Jewish, Christian, and Gnostic Literature.* Leiden: Brill, 1977.
Lidzbarski, Mark. *Das Johannesbuch der Mandäer.* Giessen: Töpelmann, 1915.
——. *Mandäische Liturgien.* Abhandlungen der Königlichen Gesellschaft der Wissenschaften zu Göttingen, phil.-hist. Klasse, NF, vol. 17, 1. Berlin, 1920; reprint Hildesheim: Olms, 1962.
——. *Ginza: Der Schatz oder das grosse Buch der Mandäer.* Göttingen: Vandenhoeck and Ruprecht, 1925.
——. *Auf Rauhen Wege, Jugenderinnerungen eines Deutschen Professors.* Giessen: Töpelmann, 1927.

Lupieri, Edmondo. *The Mandaeans: The Last Gnostics*. Grand Rapids, Mich.: Eerdmans, 2002.

Macuch, Rudolf. "Anfänge der Mandäer." *Die Araber in der alten Welt*, vol. 2, edited by Franz Altheim and Ruth Stiehl, 76-190. Berlin: de Gruyter, 1965.

——. *Handbook of Classical and Modern Mandaic*. Berlin: de Gruyter, 1965.

——. "Gnostische Ethik und die Anfänge der Mandäer." In *Christentum am Roten Meer*, vol. 2, edited by Franz Altheim and Ruth Stiehl, 254-73. Berlin: de Gruyter, 1973.

——. "Zur Grammatik und zum Wörterbuch des Mandäischen." In *Zur Sprache und Literatur der Mandäer*, Studia Mandaica I, edited by R. Macuch, 1-146. Berlin: de Gruyter, 1976.

——. *Neumandäische Chrestomatie mit grammatischer Skizze, kommentierter Übersetzung und Glossar* (with Klaus Boekels). Porta Linguarum Orientalium XVIII. Wiesbaden: Harrassowitz, 1989.

——. *Neumandäische Texte in Dialekt von Ahvaz* (with Guido Dankwart), Semitica Viva 12. Wiesbaden: Harrassowitz, 1993.

Morony, Michael G. *Iraq after the Muslim Conquest*. Princeton, N.J.: Princeton University Press, 1984.

Ms. Asiat. Misc. C12-13 (R). *Diwan d-qadaha rba šuma d-mara d-rabuta udmut kušṭa* (*The Scroll of the Great Prayer, the Name of the Lord of Greatness, the Image of Truth*). Bodleian Library. Unpublished.

Nöldeke, Theodor. *Mandäische Grammatik*. Halle: Verlag der Buchhandlung des Waisenhauses, 1875.

Norberg, Matthias. *Codex Nasaraeus*. Vols. 1-3. London, 1815-16.

Pallis, Svend Aage. *Mandaean Studies*. London: Milford, 1926.

Pearson, Birger. "The Figure of Seth in Gnostic Literature." In *The Rediscovery of Gnosticism. Vol. 2, Proceedings of the International Conference on Gnosticism at Yale, New Haven, Conn., March 28-31, 1978*, edited by B. Layton, 472-504. Leiden: Brill, 1981.

Petermann, Heinrich. *Reisen in Orient*. Vols. 1-2. Leipzig: Von Veit and Co., 1865.

——. *Sidra Rabba: Thesaurus sive Liber Magnus vulgo "Liber Adami" appellatus, opus Mandaeorum summi ponderis*. Vols. 1-2. Leipzig: Weigel, 1867.

Reitzenstein, Richard. *Das mandäische Buch des Herrn der Grosse und die Evangelienüberlieferung*. Heidelberg: Sitzungsberichte der Heidelberger Akademie der Wissenschaften, 1919.

Roberts, A., and J. Donaldson. "The Refutation of All Heresies." In *The Ante-Nicene Fathers*, vol. 5, book 5, chap. III, edited by A. Roberts and J. Donaldson. New York: Scribner's, 1926.

Robinson, James M., ed. *The Nag Hammadi Library in English*. Rev. ed. San Francisco: Harper and Row, 1988.

Rochberg, Francesca. "The Babylonian Origins of the Mandaean Book of the Zodiac." ARAM 11-12 (1999-2000): 237-47.

Rudolph, Kurt. *Die Mandäer*. Vol. 1, *Prolegomena: Das Mandäerproblem* and *Die Mandäer*. Vol. 2, *Der Kult*, Göttingen: Vandenhoeck and Ruprecht, 1960-61.

——. *Theogonie, Kosmogonie, und Anthropogonie in den mandäischen Schriften*, Göttingen: Vandenhoeck and Ruprecht, 1965.

——. "Coptica–Mandaica: Zu einigen Übereinstimmungen zwischen koptisch-gnostischen und mandäischen Texten." In *Essays on the Nag Hammadi Texts in Honor of Pahor Labib*, edited by M. Krause, 191-216. Leiden: Brill, 1975.

——. "Die mandäische Literatur." In *Zur Sprache und Literatur der Mandäer*, edited by Rudolf Macuch, 147-70. Studia Mandaica, vol. 1. Berlin: de Gruyter, 1976.

——. "Die Mandäismus in der neueren Gnosisforschung." In *Gnosis: Festschrift für Hans Jonas*, edited by B. Aland, 244-77. Göttingen: Vandenhoeck and Ruprecht, 1978.

——. "Antike Baptisten: Zu den Überlieferungen über frühjüdische und -christliche Taufsekten." In, *Sitzungsberichte der Sächsischen Akademie der Wissenschaften zu Leipzig*. philosophisch-historische Klasse, vol. 121, no. 4, 1-37. Berlin: Akademie, 1981.

——. *Der Mandäische 'Diwan der Flüsse.'* Berlin: Abhandlungen der Sächsischen Akademie der Wissenschaften zu Leipzig, philosophisch-historische Klasse, vol. 70, no. 1, 1982.

——. "Die Mandäer heute: Ein Zwischenbilanz ihrer Erforschung und ihres Wandels in der Gegenwart." *Zeitschrift für Religionsgeschichte* 94, no. 2 (1994): 161–84.

——. *Gnosis und spätantike Religionsgeschichte: Gesammelte Aufsätze.* Leiden: Brill, 1996.

Säve-Söderbergh, Torgny. *Studies in the Coptic-Manichaean Psalm-Book.* Uppsala: Almqvist and Wiksell, 1949.

Schou-Pedersen, Viggo. *Bidrag til en analyse af de mandaeiske skrifter.* Aarhus: Universitetsforlaget, 1940.

Segal, J. B., with a contribution by Erica C. D. Hunter. *A Catalogue of Aramaic and Mandaic Incantation Bowls in the British Museum.* London; British Museum Press, 2000.

Segelberg, Eric. *Maṣbuta: Studies in the Ritual of Mandaean Baptism.* Uppsala: Almqvist and Wiksell, 1958.

——. "Old and New Testament Figures in Mandaean Version." In *Syncretism*, edited by S. Hartman, 228–39. Scripti Instituti Donneriani Aboensis, vols. 3–4. Stockholm: Almqvist and Wiksell, 1969.

——. "Traṣa ḏ-taga ḏ-Šišlam Rabba: Studies in the Rite Called the Coronation of Šišlam Rabba." In *Zur Sprache und Literatur der Mandäer*, edited by R. Macuch, 171–244. Studia Mandaica, vol. 1. Berlin: de Gruyter, 1976.

Sevrin, Jean-Marie. "Les rites de la gnose, d'après quelques textes gnostiques coptes." In *Gnosticisme et monde hellénistique*, edited by J. Ries, 440–50, Publications de l'Institut Orientaliste de Louvain 27, Louvain-la-Neuve: Université de Louvain, 1982.

——. *Le dossier baptismal Séthien.* Bibliothèque copte de Nag Hammadi, Section "Études" 2. Quebec: Les Presses de l'Université Laval, 1986.

Siouffi, M. N. *Études sur la religion des Soubbas ou Sabéens, leurs dogmes, leur moeurs.* Paris: Imprimerie Nationale, 1880.

Weber, Max. *The Sociology of Religion.* London: Methuen, 1965.

Williams, Michael A. *Rethinking Gnosticism: An Argument for Dismantling a Dubious Category.* Princeton, N.J.: Princeton University Press, 1996.

Yamauchi, Edwin. *Gnostic Ethics and Mandaean Origins.* Harvard Theological Studies 26. Cambridge, Mass.: Harvard University Press, 1970.

Yaqut al-Hamawi al-Rumi. *Muʿajjam al-Buldan.* Vol. 6. Cairo, 1906.

Yeʿor, Bat. *The Dhimmi: Jews and Christians under Islam.* Rutherford, N.J.: Fairleigh Dickinson University Press, 1985.

Index

abagada. *See* Mandaic, alphabet
Abatur, 35, 38, 46, 95, 145
Abraham, 27
Adam, 5, 11, 36, 38–39, 42–43, 55, 64, 88
Adonai, 4, 40, 50
afterlife, 29–30, 35–36, 38
Aldulaimi, Mamoon, 114, 116–119, 122, 125–126, 128
Aldulaimi, Shafia, 114, 116, 120, 122
Amara, Lamea Abbas, 21, 23–25, 27–35
Amara, Shafia Abbas, 23–25, 28, 30, 32–33
Anuš, 5, 8, 13, 35, 38, 44–45, 53, 151
Artaban/Artabanus, 3
asceticism, 18, 148
astrology, 15, 125
Ašuriyah, 124
Ayar Dakia. *See* Pure Ether

Ba, 88, 96
Babylonian Talmud, 4
baptism. *See* maṣbuta
Baptism of Hibil Ziwa, 14
Bihram, Yahia, 6, 155, 157
Book of John, ix, 45–46, 114, 116; and creation myth, 37–38; description of, 13; and Jesus, 150–151; and Miriai, 50–54, 56
Book of the Zodiac, 15
Borges, Jorge Luis, 18
Brandt, Wilhelm, 17
Bultmann, Rudolf, 17

celibacy, 18
Choheili, Sheikh Salem, 59, 61, 63-64, 66-68, 71-72, 74-76, 78-79, 122
Christianity, 3, 7-8, 17, 19, 48-49, 55, 150-151
colophon, 4, 6, 12, 151-159
conversion, 32, 50, 55, 123-124
Coronation of the Great Šišlam, 14, 97, 101-105, 107, 134

Dead Sea Scrolls, 27
death, 36, 39, 43, 119-121
Dehwa Rabba, 28-29
Dinanukht, 11, 45-46, 133, 150
Diṣai, 45-46, 150
Diwan Abatur, 15, 46-47
Diwan Nahrawata, 15
dmuta, 10, 37-39, 47
Drower, Lady Ethel S., ix, xii, 16, 32, 42, 47, 72, 75, 102, 113-114, 118, 126, 129, 134, 159; collects documents, 154, 156-157; edits and translates works, 14-15; and *Great "First World,"* 130, 132; personal background, 17; on ritual, 87-88, 90, 92, 96-97, 149

Eve, 43
Ewat, 46
Exalted Kingship, 14, 33, 43, 97, 99, 107, 123, 126, 134-143, 145-146, 148, 150

faṭira, 88, 91-94, 96, 104-105, 107
female Lightbeings, 8, 9

Field, Henry, 120
First Life, 7-8, 89, 102

Gaf, 41, 46
ganzibra, 9, 81, 88, 98-99, 104, 126. *See also* priest
Ginza, 4-5, 16, 101, 155; description of, 10-11, 13
Gnosticism, 3-4, 7, 11, 17, 35, 55, 80, 86, 145
God, 30
Gordon, Cyrus H., 118
Great "First World," 14, 90, 93-94, 97, 99, 130, 132-134
Great Life, 36, 47, 55, 83, 92
Great Mother, 43-44
Gubran, 45

Hackforth-Jones, Margaret, 156, 159
Haiuna, 5
Haran Gawaita, 3-4, 15, 41, 49-50, 87
Hawa. *See* Eve
Heidegger, Martin, 18-19
Hesse, Hermann, 18
Hibil Ziwa, 8-9, 13, 35, 37-38, 88, 114, 122; depicted in *Great "First World,"* 132-133; and Miriai and the Jews, 51-53; and Ruha and creation myth, 40-47

Islam, 5-6, 10, 23, 60, 173n2

Jerusalem, 4, 8, 15, 44, 50, 52-53
Jesus, 4, 8, 13, 15, 35, 49, 55, 150-151; and John the Baptist, 24-25; as a Mandaean, 24-25
Jews, 4, 44, 51-53, 124, 151
John the Baptist, ix, 5, 11, 13, 32, 53-55, 75, 102, 116, 150; birth, 49; and Jesus, 24-25; as a Mandaean, 24-25
Jonas, Hans, 17-18, 48
Judaism, 8, 19, 48-56, 151
Jung, C. G., ix

Khamenei, Ayatollah, 60, 77
Khomeini, Ayatollah, 6
Klijn, A. F. J., 35
Krun, 9, 41
kušṭa, 3, 82-85, 100, 103, 105; as personification, 13, 36, 51

laufa, 9-10, 19, 104; definition of, 8; and maṣbuta, 83-86; and Ṭabahata masiqta, 89
Lidzbarski, Mark, 11-13, 17, 114, 116, 133, 155
Lightworld: and afterlife, 29, 35; in cosmology, 7-8; and Dehwa Rabba, 29; and dmuta, 37-39; and female Lightbeings, 8-9; and maṣbuta, 80-83, 85, 104; and masiqta, 87, 104; and Miriai, 53; and priests, 44, 135-136; and ritual and prayer, 19, 148, 150; and Ruha, 40-47; and souls, 4, 9-10, 43; and Ṭabahata masiqta, 89, 91, 93-94, 97; and tarmida initiation, 98-99, 102-103, 105-106; and ʿutras, 8, 38
lofani, 120-122
Lord of Greatness, 133, 146, 148

Macuch, Rudolf, ix, xii, 3-4, 16-17, 66, 75, 114, 157
Manda ḏ-Hiia, 8, 11, 45-46, 54-55, 84, 102, 122
Mandaean language. *See* Mandaic
Mandaeans: population worldwide, 6
Mandaee, 21
Mandaeism: and Christianity, 3, 8, 19, 48-49, 55, 150-151; cosmogony, 37-38, 41-46; cosmology, 7-8; and Gnosticism, 3-4, 7; and Islam, 5-6, 10, 23, 60, 173n2; and Judaism, 8, 19, 48-56, 151; and Manichaeism, 3; origins and history, 3-6, 165n7; overview, 7-10; and world epics, 38; and Zoroastrianism, 3-4
Mandaic, 4, 7, 17, 28, 114, 148, 150-151; alphabet, 144-146, 151
Mani, 4
Manichaeism, 3, 9, 17
marriage, 15, 67-68, 71-72, 98, 148
Mary. *See* Miriai
maṣbuta: description, 81-83, 85; interpretation, 84-86; and Lightworld, 80-81, 104; for marriage, 67-68; place in Mandaeism, 10, 80; as repeated ritual, 53
masiqta, 9-10, 39, 87, 103-104, 107, 148, 166n27. *See also* Ṭabahata masiqta
maṭarta, 8-9, 11, 15, 35, 46, 94, 97
menstruation, 29, 33
Miriai, 4, 13, 25, 48-56, 173n20
Mohi, Sheikh, 31

Morgan, J. de, 61, 154
Mšunia Kušṭa, 10, 37

Nabateans, 5
Nag Hammadi documents, 3, 17
Negm, Sheikh, 156-157
'Nisbai, 49, 53-55
Nišimta. *See* soul
Niṭufta, 46
Nöldeke, Theodor, 16
Norberg, M., 16
Nuraita, 46

People of the Book. *See* Mandaeism, and Islam
Petermann, Heinrich, 11, 16-17, 155
pihta, 81-82, 84, 90-91, 97, 99, 101, 103, 105
Plague of Šuštar, 6
Prayerbook, 12, 47, 54, 56, 82-85, 97, 99, 132, 137, 139
priest: eligibility for office, 98, 177n5; and Lightworld, 135-136; and maṣbuta, 81-83, 85; and Ṭabahata masiqta, 88-94, 96; and tarmida initiation, 98-99, 101-105; as 'utra, 56, 82, 99, 106, 142-143. *See also* ganzibra; tarmida
Ptahil, 19, 37-38, 42-43, 47, 88, 145
Pure Ether, 37, 44, 88, 97

Qin, 41, 46
Qur'an, 23, 60, 123

Ramuia, 5, 14
raṭna, 7
Reitzenstein, Richard, 17
Rosenthal, Franz, 17
Rudolph, Kurt, xii, 3, 15, 17, 80-81
Ruha, 11, 45, 53; and creation myth, 39, 41-44, 47; and Jesus, 150; and maṣbuta, 84; nature of, 9, 39-40, 44, 46-48, 55; and tarmida initiation, 98-99, 136-138, 140-143
ruha. *See* spirit

Sabeans, 5, 23, 27
Ṣauriel Qmamir Ziwa, 36, 91
Scroll of the Marriage of the Great Šišlam, 15
Segelberg, Eric, 83-84
Seth, 5, 35
Sevrin, Jean-Marie, 86
sexes, creation of, 43
Šihlaun, 37
Simat Hiia, 9, 47, 51, 101, 104
Siniawis, 46
Šitil, 8, 11, 35-39
Šitlan, Yuhana, 6
Šlama, 4
Sobbi, Nasser, 33, 66, 113-114, 116-118, 120-121, 123-126, 128
Socrates, 27
soul, 29-30, 35, 135-141, 143; and spirit, 42-43
spirit, 9, 135, 137-143; and soul, 42-43
Šum Yawar Ziwa, 83, 91, 102
Šuštar massacre, 6

Ṭabahata masiqta, 87-95; interpretation, 96-97
tarik. *See* colophon
tarmida: initiation, 98-107, 134-143, 147; and maṣbuta, 81; role of, 9. *See also* priest
Tawoosie, Sheikh Jabbar, 59, 61, 63, 116
Tawoosie, Sheikh Salah, 59, 61, 64, 66, 72, 116
Thecla, 50, 55
Thousand and Twelve Questions, 38, 97, 134; commentary on alphabet and use of language, 144-146, 148, 150; and creation myth, 41-46; description of, 13-14; and Ṭabahata masiqta, 89-90, 93-94, 96
Tibil, 7, 9, 35-36, 40
Torah, 51-53, 123

underworld. *See* world of darkness
'Ur, 9, 41-42, 47, 141
'uṣṭuna, 87, 94, 97
'utra, 9, 11, 13, 35; and colophons, 157; and cosmogony, 37-38; definition and role, 8, 122; and first masiqta, 88; nature of, 19, 37-38; priest as, 56, 82, 99, 106, 142-143; and Ruha, 45

Weber, Max, 80
world, age of, 11
world of darkness, 8-9, 40-41

Yahweh, 50, 145
Yamauchi, Edwin, 4
yardna, 3, 43, 82, 104, 140
Yawar Ziwa, 9, 47, 101, 104
Yušamin, 37-38
Zahriel, 41
Zatan, 51
Zazai of Gawazta, 4, 12, 157
Zhir, 137
Zoroastrianism, 3-4, 60

Printed in the United States
48675LVS00002B/12

9 780195 153859